This book reads like a modern book of Acts. It is not only a fascinating and inspiring chronicle, but one of the best inside views of the rise of the Third Reich. Barth provides an invaluable account of how a community of Christians negotiated the moral and spiritual challenges of that terrible time.

—Robert Ellsberg, author of *Modern Spiritual Classics*

Emmy Barth has expertly and lovingly woven together a seamless narrative that vividly chronicles the Bruderhof community's sacrifice, heroism, faith, determination, and courage. *An Embassy Besieged* is an inspiration to today's readers.

—Ari L. Goldman, author of *The Search for God at Harvard*

This moving story raises profound questions: Can we deny God's presence in any enemy? What does it mean to carry out Jesus' command to love the enemy in the context of a nation carrying out demonic policies? And how should the church act today in a national security state whose weapons and policies threaten the world? Barth's depiction of the Bruderhof's life and trials in Nazi Germany offers inspiration and hope for our own equally profound questions of Christian discipleship.

—Jim Douglass, author of *JFK and the Unspeakable*

Arnold once said: "To be an ambassador for God's kingdom is something tremendous. When we take this service upon us, we enter into mortal danger." In 1937 the Gestapo confiscated the Bruderhof's farm and dissolved their community. The few remaining members were expelled under guard, apart from three men detained in prison for alleged fraud. Their escape to freedom makes a fitting close to this lively, detailed account of one community's courageous witness to the gospel.

—John Conway, author of *The Nazi Persecution of the Churches*

An Embassy Besieged

An Embassy Besieged

The Story of a Christian Community in Nazi Germany

Emmy Barth

With a Foreword by Johann Christoph Arnold

CASCADE *Books* • Eugene, Oregon

PLOUGH PUBLISHING

AN EMBASSY BESIEGED
The Story of a Christian Community in Nazi Germany

Copyright © 2010 Emmy Barth. All rights reserved. Except for brief quotations in critical publications or reviews, no part of this book may be reproduced in any manner without prior written permission from the publisher. Write: Permissions, Wipf and Stock Publishers, 199 W. 8th Ave., Suite 3, Eugene, OR 97401.

Cascade Books
An Imprint of Wipf and Stock Publishers
199 W. 8th Ave., Suite 3
Eugene, OR 97401

Plough Publishing House of
Church Communities Foundation
Rifton, NY 12471 USA

www.wipfandstock.com

ISBN 13: 978-1-60899-879-1

Cataloging-in-Publication data:

Barth, Emmy, 1961–

    An embassy besieged : the story of a Christian community in Nazi Germany / Emmy Barth ; foreword by Johann Christoph Arnold.

    xvi + 306 p. ; cm. 23. — Includes bibliographical references and index.

    ISBN 13: 978-1-60899-879-1

    1. Arnold, Eberhard, 1883–1935. 2. Bruderhof Communities — History. I. Arnold, Johann Christoph. II. Title.

BX8 129. B68 B35 2010

Manufactured in the U.S.A.

We are ambassadors for Christ,
God making his appeal through us.
—2 Corinthians 5:20

The Apostle says that we are ambassadors of God, representing Christ, the messiah king, the regent of that last kingdom. When the British ambassador is in the British Embassy in Berlin, he is not subject to the laws of the German Reich. The grounds of the embassy are inviolable. In the residence of the ambassador, only the laws of the country he represents are valid.

We are ambassadors of the kingdom of God. This means that we do nothing at all except what the king of God's kingdom would himself do for his kingdom. When we take this service upon ourselves we enter into mortal danger.

—Eberhard Arnold

Contents

Foreword by Johann Christoph Arnold • xi

Acknowledgments • xv

Prologue • 1

1. Historical Background: The Path to Community • 3
2. Hitler's Rise to Power • 22
3. March to April 1933 • 37
4. May to June 1933 • 54
5. June to October 1933 • 64
6. October to November 1933 • 81
7. Plebiscite and Raid • 95
8. November to December 1933 • 108
9. January to February 1934 • 131
10. February to May 1934 • 157
11. June to July 1934 • 166
12. Romans 13 • 177
13. July to August 1934 • 183
14. September to December 1934 • 198
15. January to March 1935 • 209
16. March to October 1935 • 227
17. The Revelation of John • 236
18. November 1935 • 241
19. December 1935 to July 1936 • 245
20. August to December 1936 • 253
21. January to April 1937 • 269
22. May to July 1937 • 278

Notes • 283

Bibliography • 297

Index • 299

Foreword

HERE PUBLISHED FOR THE first time is the story of my grandfather's resistance to National Socialism. My parents were young adults when Hitler came to power, and I grew up hearing the story from them. They both experienced the Gestapo raid of the community my grandfather founded after refusing to vote for Hitler in the plebiscite of November 1933. My father was lined up against the wall with other young men and thought they would all be shot. My parents' wedding took place hurriedly two years later so that they could use their "honeymoon" to escape the military draft by fleeing to England.

The Gestapo would come again, and this time they told the community that they had only twenty-four hours to pack up and leave. Community members could take only what they could carry on their backs. It was April and the community lived in the Rhön mountains where it was terribly cold and windy. There were many little babies, mothers and children. Several young men, including my father-in-law, were put into a Nazi prison. He never expected to come out alive, but by the grace of God he did. In fact, all of us safely escaped Nazi Germany.

We eventually made our way to England and then several years later, right during the war, we were forced to emigrate to South America. I was six months old when my parents risked a voyage across the submarine-infested Atlantic to the jungles of Paraguay. It was in these conditions that I grew up, and it was clear to me from childhood on that radical discipleship would mean suffering for my faith.

I have lived for more than fifty years in the United States, where the Bruderhof Communities have been allowed to live in peace. For this I am very grateful. But I am also very worried about what is happening in our country today. We are living in a culture of death, where euthanasia, capital punishment, abortion, physician-assisted suicide, and on-going military action are a mainstay of everyday life. We don't know where it will end!

There have been dramatic political and economic shifts as well. The level of frustration, anger, and fear combined with an ever-increasing rhetoric of hate and blame remind me a lot of the 1920s and 30s in Germany. We hear rumors of war, and governments on both sides of the Atlantic encroach on religious liberties, making it more and more difficult to live as true disciples of Jesus.

This brings me back to my grandfather. Engraved on his tombstone is the following verse from Revelations: "Blessed are the dead who die in the Lord henceforth . . . They may rest from their labors, for their deeds follow them." This epitaph seems particularly fitting when viewed through the lens of history. He died seventy-five years ago. Yet, while Hitler's "Thousand Year Reich" crumbled in defeat after a mere twelve years, the Bruderhof movement continues to flourish. More than that, however, my grandfather's prophetic vision speaks right into our situation and the questions that face society today.

I am struck by his literal understanding of the words of Jesus in the Sermon on the Mount: "Love your enemy. Pray for those who persecute you." My grandfather rejected power politics on the one hand but also spiritual quietism on the other. He practiced the politics of love: "You can love a man only when you have understood what is living in him," he told his community. "We have to find an inner understanding with the Nazis, and then we have to represent to them the politics of the kingdom of Jesus Christ. After coming to a heart-to-heart exchange with them, when we confront them with the policy of the coming kingdom of God, we are going to collide sharply with them."

My grandfather died shortly before the Bruderhof was forced to leave Germany. He knew it was only a matter of time, yet he never gave up hope that even Hitler could be reached by God's love. In a personal letter to Adolf Hitler in November 1933, he addressed him as "Our beloved Reichskanzler Adolf Hitler." He expressed his respect for Hitler's "God-given task of government" and pleaded with him to spare the innocent. He ended his letter: "We ask God from our hearts that at God's hour [our beloved Reichskanzler] may become, instead of an historical instrument of supreme state authority, an ambassador of the humiliated Christ, to whom alone it was given to reveal the perfect love of God's heart."

The greatest enemy of our country today is the polarizing forces of hate and violence that feed off the apathetic indifference of self-satisfied people. As the vanguard and embassy of God's kingdom, the church is called to show that only radical love can overcome the bankruptcy of these two extremes. Here is a story that demonstrates in very concrete terms what this love entails, why it matters, and why it cannot be defeated. May it inspire us, especially those who confess Jesus as Lord, but more importantly, may it move us to act while there is still time.

Johann Christoph Arnold
June 2010

Acknowledgments

I WOULD LIKE TO offer special tribute to Hela Ehrlich, who was my mentor for many years and who provided many of the translations in this book. She and her parents fled Nazi Germany to South America, where she met the Bruderhof. My thanks go also to Hugo Brinkmann, who compiled the raw material for the book's framework and translated all of Eberhard Arnold's correspondence with the Nazi government. Hugo, a young German studying in England during World War II, was interned in Canada as an enemy alien. I am also deeply grateful to Doug Moody, Art and Mary Wiser, and Derek Wardle. Without the help of each of these individuals this book would never have come to fruition.

Prologue

Kassel, April 9, 1937
Office of the Secret State Police

Order of the Gestapo:

In accordance with paragraphs 1 and 4 of the Reich president's decree for the protection of the Volk and the state of February 28, 1933, (RGB 1 I.S. 83): the incorporated society Neuwerk-Bruderhof, Veitsteinbach, district of Fulda, is being dissolved for state police reasons, this to take effect immediately. The entire property of the association is confiscated.

Violations of this order, in particular any further activity in the sense of the dissolved society, are liable to punishment according to paragraph 4 of the above-mentioned decree.

There is no means of legal redress against this order, but a complaint can be addressed to the Gestapo office in Berlin.

(Signed) Herrmann[1]

AROUND 10:00 IN THE morning of April 14, 1937, about fifty SS and Gestapo surrounded the community of the Rhön Bruderhof, some emerging from the woods, others arriving by car or bicycle. Armed guards positioned themselves at the doors of every building.

The forty members of the community were herded into the dining hall, and the Gestapo commissar read out the announcement: The Bruderhof no longer existed. Its members were required to return to their former homes, and those German nationals of military age were to register for military service. They were questioned individually: name, date of birth, names of their parents and of their children. From where had they come to join the community? Had they ever belonged to a political party banned in 1933? Books and papers were carried from the office to the cars below. The three members of the executive committee—Hans Meier, Hannes Boller, and Karl Keiderling—were questioned at length and then taken away in a Gestapo car.

Eberhard Arnold, founder of the Bruderhof, had been dead for over a year. Now his life work was destroyed and his followers were to be scattered.

But the little group refused to return to their former homes; neither would they register with the military. They had pledged their lives—not to Eberhard Arnold, but to the kingdom of God—and they trusted that they were in God's hand, even if this meant their deaths.

Two days later they were trudging up the hill to the waiting buses—carrying their little children, a sick woman who was unable to walk, and whatever bags they could hold. Thirty-one of them would go to England via Holland and the remaining eleven to the principality of Liechtenstein. Hella Römer, a thirty-one-year-old single woman, was left to close out the accounts.

1

Historical Background
The Path to Community

THIS IS THE STORY of a small group who dared to confront Adolf Hitler and the entire Third Reich with the love of Jesus Christ. Even before Hitler seized power, they knew that the National Socialist ideology stood in direct opposition to the teachings of Jesus, and they refused to participate in any way. They never said, "Heil Hitler." They did not vote in the plebiscites in which all Germans were expected to express their support for Hitler's actions. Their young men did not join the armed forces. But neither did they stage public protests nor conspire to assassinate Hitler. They believed that living in unity and humility was the only way to oppose party politics and the Führer cult. Only love could overcome hatred—even love of Adolf Hitler himself. In their own words, they were "less than a gnat to an elephant," but that did not matter: the message of Jesus Christ needed to be proclaimed in Nazi Germany, even if that should mean death to the messengers.

World War I

Germany was in chaos after the First World War. Soldiers returned—beaten and humiliated—or failed to return. The country was starving. The Kaiser had abdicated and social conventions were crumbling. New world views were gaining momentum: pacifism, communism, anarchism, socialism. Adolf Hitler surrounded himself with disgruntled war veterans and began building up the National Socialist Party based on the anger and bitterness of a vanquished people.

At the same time, Eberhard and Emmy Arnold were struggling to find God's purpose in the confusion around them. They were in their mid-thirties and had five young children. Eberhard, born on July 26, 1883, was a popular Christian speaker and author. He was on the board of the Student Christian Movement and was literary advisor of its magazine *Die Furche*. In his leadership role Eberhard had formed strong friendships with members of Germany's upper class and academia: Karl Heim (who became a professor in Tübingen), Paul Zander (the surgeon who would perform the fatal operation on his leg), Georg Michaelis (who served as Germany's chancellor for a few months in 1917), plus military generals and others.

As a theology student in Halle in 1907, Eberhard and Dr. Karl Heim had organized lectures for charismatic speakers, which sparked a revival in the town. He met Emmy in the home of a wealthy woman where an "impressive mix of artists, doctors, and military officers' wives" had gathered to hear him speak.[1] The two young people felt drawn toward each other immediately, and within weeks he had asked her to marry him. Their engagement and marriage were born out of this Christian revival, and from the beginning of their relationship they were determined to allow God to guide their lives and to live by their convictions, regardless of the cost.

When World War I was declared in 1914, the German Student Christian Movement was swept up in nationalist fervor. *Die Furche* began printing a special leaflet for soldiers on the front. To quote from its pages:

> When war was declared, our circles were prepared, by the grace of God, and the call of our king and Kaiser was accepted and followed in a noteworthy way. God's hand had suddenly brought the time of the seed, the long time of peace, to an end. Now we had to prove that the two things that stood side by side in our name, "German" and "Christian," bound the hearts of our brothers to a higher unity.[2]

Eberhard himself wrote numerous patriotic articles. But when soldiers began to come home, wounded and tormented by the horrors they had witnessed, he began to question the Christian role in warfare. Years later he described his difficult years of questioning and seeking:

> Groups of people often gathered around me, and I tried by means of Bible studies and talks to lead them to Jesus. But after a while this was no longer enough ... I was deeply unhappy. I recognized more and more that a personal concern for the salvation of souls,

no matter how dedicated it might be, did not in itself meet the demands of the life Jesus calls us to . . . I began to recognize the needs of people in a deeper way: the need of their souls and bodies, their material and social wants, their humiliation, exploitation, and enslavement. I recognized the tremendous powers of mammon, discord, hate, and violence, and saw the hard boot of the oppressor upon the neck of the oppressed . . .

Then, from 1913 to 1917, I sought painfully for a deeper understanding of the truth . . . I felt that I was not fulfilling God's will by approaching people with a purely personal Christianity . . . During those years I went through hard struggles: I searched in the ancient writings, in Jesus' Sermon on the Mount and other scriptures, but I also wanted to acquaint myself with the realities of working-class life, and I sought to share in the lives of the oppressed as they struggled within the present social order. I wanted to find a way that corresponded to the way of Jesus and of Francis of Assisi, not to mention the way of the prophets.[3]

Radicals

In 1910, Eberhard discovered Swiss theologian Hermann Kutter, one of the founders of Christian Socialism. In his book *Sie Müssen* (They Must) Kutter spoke sharply against the established churches and how they had aligned themselves with mammon at the expense of the poor.

> The same God who works in the inmost hearts of men, shall He not also change the outward aspect of man's life? He who dries up the root of sin in the heart by the power of His word, shall He not also use His power where sin flourishes like the green bay tree in the industrial world? Does God distinguish between inner and outer? Does not His energy work in every nook and corner of His vast creation? . . . And ye would deny Him the power to burst the bonds of a society in which sin has bound men by a false tie, and to create a new humanity in which righteousness dwells? He must stand quietly by and see the soil, this inexhaustible earth which He has given men for their joyous occupation, become the monopoly of a class living in luxury, while their brothers beg bread from their hands![4]

> If the poor victim himself cannot declare this war against evil, why do *you* not rise up for him as did the prophets of old, as did Jesus and his Apostles?

> Why is one constantly hearing from your lips the one message and not the other? Why always the comfortable, the bourgeois deliverance, that every disturbance of our present social order is dangerous and unsound; and never the sharp, decisive summons that we cannot serve God and Mammon? Why is it that you always console the poor with the future coming of the Lord, but never terrify the rich with the same theme—as Jesus did? Why never a complaint against the rich for their avarice, while you warn the poor so solemnly against covetousness?
>
> I think that your Christianity is a Christianity of the rich, not of the poor. If so, it has no part with Jesus—for Jesus "preached the good news to the poor."[5]

As time went on, Eberhard began to use Kutter's ideas more and more in his discussions of radical Christianity and the Sermon on the Mount. His views began to raise some eyebrows in the Student Christian Movement.

To the end of his life, Eberhard sympathized with socialist ideals. He said in September 1935 to some newer Bruderhof members:

> Hermann Kutter proclaimed that the worker's heart and soul, the worker's concern, is the fight for God's justice. I stand with Hermann Kutter! Today as always! I appeal to true socialism. The root question of Religious Socialism is innermost, essential justice, which is not a moral justice but a divine justice.[6]

~

By 1917, Germany was tired of the war. Hunger protests were staged in Berlin, and munitions workers went on strike. Eberhard grappled with the changes that the world was undergoing.

> As a result of this war, the European civilization in which we live is going through a tremendous upheaval that brings what is lowest to the top and the uppermost to the bottom. It brings judgment and chastisement from God over everything that men thought they had so firmly under control. It is an upheaval that has cast the European down from the heights of his presumption and pride. We feel that the greatest changes are taking place in the economic area and that the expected peace treaty will only make these changes deeper and more fargoing. Now too a new wave of social upheaval has started in Russia, and we cannot foresee the consequences of these events. We have no idea what sweeping

> changes must still take place in the distribution of wealth between rich and poor, in trade and commerce, in buying and selling. We cannot yet foresee how far this revolution in outward things will affect everything else. But one thing is certain: the whole of humankind has recognized that we need an upheaval. What the Social Democrats, the anarchists, and related movements have always had on their banners has grown into a general conviction: humankind needs an upheaval.[7]

By now, he felt clearly that a Christian could not take part in violence. He became acquainted with pacifist English Quakers who provided daily meals to hungry children in Berlin. One of them, John Stephens, joined the discussion evenings in the Arnolds' home and became a lifelong friend.

Eberhard sympathized with movements that were dissatisfied with the status quo. Unafraid of labels, he looked for the heartfelt ideals in widely varying world views, focusing on the positive without being blind to inherent dangers. This was true for the left-wing movements and would be true later for the right-wing National Socialist movement.

By 1920, his views were causing tensions in the Student Christian Movement and its publishing house, and he was forced to resign. With a number of like-minded friends he then began a new magazine, *Das neue Werk* (The New Work), which became the nucleus of a *Neuwerk* (New Work) movement—aligning itself with the poor and the radical left, but centered on Jesus Christ. Here, among other things, he published select writings of anarchists and communists such as Rosa Luxemburg and Karl Liebknecht, founders of the Spartacist League, which was the forerunner of the German Communist Party. He planned to publish some of the writings of the anarchist Gustav Landauer as part of his *Innenschau* (Looking Inward) series. Not surprisingly, such publications drew criticism. Eberhard answered a man who criticized his publication of a letter by Rosa Luxemburg:

> You are completely right: it cannot be possible to construct an identity between a life in Christ lived from grace, and a party socialism. Yet we feel very strongly that many demands of conscience raised by socialists and pacifists indicate the same longing as that in the eschatological atmosphere at the time of John the Baptist and the early Christians. We are convinced that everything in socialism, communism, and pacifism which comes from a movement of conscience, everything directing itself purely from the

heart against the rule of mammon and bloodshed, against class distinctions and individual possessiveness, comes from God. At the same time that does not prevent us from seeing how strongly satanic and demonic powers are at work in those movements. What we need today, and what none of us yet has to the degree that our times demand, is a simple discipleship of Jesus, springing from the longing of the present day.[8]

Eberhard spoke similarly about Kurt Eisner, a member of the Social Democratic Party, who led a revolution at the end of 1918 to overthrow the monarchy in Bavaria. Eisner was shot at point-blank range in Munich on February 21, 1919. In 1924, Emmy Arnold included his song "Wir werben im Sterben um ferne Gestirne" in her songbook *Sonnenlieder*. The reference note reads: "Text by Kurt Eisner, murdered 1919, sung at the first Munich revolution."[9] Years later Eberhard said about it:

> We have just sung a song that was composed in Munich by people who were seeking a new life. The writer of the words of this song fell by a murderer's hand. The meaning of the song—to translate it from poetry into ordinary language—is this: humankind struggles to grow better; humankind fights for people to be more just and fair to one another. Humankind wants freedom from all servitude and slavery. The writer of the song says that true freedom arises in fellowship of action, and the world will not be free until people join hands in working fellowship.
>
> There was a time when this incisive call was heard throughout the land: "Arise to freedom, the freedom-alliance of workers!" Jesus Christ has shown us that we do not need money and goods to become human; rather, we need to work together. For this we must join forces and combine all our energies. Only then will people find justice.[10]

With his frank, open-minded approach, Eberhard was able to bring opposing factions together. At the time of the Spartacus Revolt in Berlin in 1919, the most varied assortment of people met in the Arnolds' home: members of the Student Christian Movement, anarchists, artists, officers, and Quakers. During the short-lived Kapp Putsch the following year, Eberhard was offered a position at the head of the new Department of Youth under the rebel government. He wrote: "My house became a kind of headquarters for influential people. As I was constantly in touch with both warring parties, I had the opportunity to use my influence to a certain degree—not strongly enough to make our spirit victorious, but not without a certain effect…We were able to come to an understanding with the communist party leaders that led to a significant reduction of the so-called black list—the list of officers to be killed."[11]

But although he sympathized with their ideals, Eberhard did not join any of these movements. Rather, he tried to direct them to God and his kingdom, where a complete answer to injustice and suffering could be found. As he wrote in 1921:

> It is of great importance that Christians discern the awakening for God, and that they witness to Christ in the midst of the socialist, pacifist, and communist movements of conscience. Since no party as such represents the pure idea of the kingdom of God, we do not belong as a whole movement to any party, neither democratic, socialist, nor communist. But we rejoice when individuals take up the fight within a party, also within the most radical revolutionary groups, against greed for possessions, against bloody force, against the increasing immorality in questions of sex, against lying in all forms. Whoever, as a Christian, places himself with the tax collectors and sinners, the social democrats and communists, feels solidarity with their need and guilt.[12]

Free German Youth

Although they were in their late thirties, Eberhard and Emmy felt increasingly close to a movement of young people, the Free German Youth. Men and women exchanged conventional mores in clothing and personal relationships for a more down-to-earth lifestyle. The girls put on simple dresses, braided their hair, and decked themselves with flowers; the young men cut off their pants and put on berets and Russian-style tunics. They set out into the fields and woods with violins and recorders, held long discussions around camp fires, ending with spirited folk dances. Eberhard and Emmy's son Heiner remembered the change in the family household:

> When Papa came actively into contact with the youth movement, I noticed a change in our house, although I was only five or six years old. Even we children noticed that he had definitely been middle class, but left wing. At that time most people on our street wore the colors of the German flag (black, white, and red) in their lapels, but my father wore a red ribbon; and we were called communists or anarchists by the other children. Papa was working

> for a publishing house, and he and Tata [Emmy's sister Else] left together for work punctually every morning, always in a certain hurry, afraid they might be late. And Papa was always very neatly dressed. One day, at the time my father was expected home, we were on a balcony on the second floor—Mama, Tata, and we children—and suddenly we saw Papa. And how Mama and Tata laughed! Papa had cut his trousers short and was barefoot in his shoes, and they just doubled up with laughter! From then on Papa never wore his good suit again.[13]

Fritz Berber, a law student in Munich and a member of the Neuwerk Movement, corroborates Heiner's memories:

> Arnold was a highly educated theologian who had concerned himself particularly with the problems of original Christianity and who was trying to realize Christian and Tolstoian ideals in a life of simplicity and possessionlessness in a center in the village of Sannerz in the Rhön . . . He was a man who overflowed with love, but ignored outward conventions. When I arranged a lecture for him in the Maximum Auditorium of the University of Munich in winter 1921, he put me in a difficult predicament by appearing in shorts, despite the cold weather, displaying his naked, hairy legs before an academic world that had not yet grown accustomed to such things through the Beatles and hippies.[14]

The Sermon on the Mount

At the open evenings in the Arnolds' home in Berlin, Jesus' Sermon on the Mount began taking on new significance. Emmy wrote about this time:

> Our most wonderful meetings were those in which we read and discussed the message of the Sermon on the Mount, which dawned on us in a wonderful new way at that time. We felt it was not Eberhard himself who spoke, but that the words he spoke came to us directly from Christ. The beginning of the Sermon on the Mount, with the so-called Beatitudes; the words about loving one's enemy; the Lord's Prayer as Jesus teaches it to us; the urgently pleading words, "Ask, and it shall be given you"; the almsgiving in which the right hand should not know what the left is doing; the search for the kingdom of God and his righteousness, and the promise that through this search "everything else will be given you"—all this struck us like lightning. So did the end of

the Sermon on the Mount: "Whoever hears these words and does them is like a wise man."

Yes, something new and overpowering came over us: we felt it was a new period in our history, a part of God's history we were experiencing, and we felt that the expectation of the coming kingdom of God must fill us. Finally we had found a place to satisfy our hunger and thirst for righteousness and justice. After the injustice of the war and the pre-war times, Jesus' words burst in upon us with the power of a thunderclap. We felt we could no longer live the upper middle-class life we were used to and still proclaim the word of God. Faith had to become action, and we had to go new ways.[15]

In the Sermon on the Mount, Eberhard saw an answer to the questions of social justice and the radical movements of the time. If men and women could live according to these commands of Jesus, the kingdom of God would be among them.

The Neuwerk Movement

Neuwerk with its magazine *Das neue Werk* became a movement of which Eberhard Arnold was a central figure. Antje Vollmer writes in her thesis:

The beginning of the *Neuwerk* movement is unthinkable without Eberhard Arnold. He managed alone, within a short time, to set so many young people all over Germany on fire for his cause that as many as two to three hundred of them answered his invitation to the first Whitsun conference at Schlüchtern in 1920—the *Neuwerk* movement's hour of birth.

All who knew Eberhard Arnold speak of the extraordinary strength his person radiated, of his enthusiastic faith, which was the faith of the Sermon on the Mount, and of his radical way of carrying out the task he knew himself called to. H. J. Schoeps conveys the following ecstatic impression of him: "I remember a very tall man of about forty-five in a corduroy suit, with radiant brown eyes, which gazed down at you in a friendly but also challenging way. He looked unusual in every respect. Once when he was standing in front of the National Library in Berlin, curious Berliners formed a proper circle around him and just stared at him." About the Sannerz community, Schoeps goes on: "I state without hesitation that powers from another world were at work here, and Eberhard Arnold was their chosen instrument. If he had lived a few centuries earlier and as a Catholic, he would now most likely have a place assigned to him in a saints' calendar."[16]

One *Neuwerk* member was Norman Körber, who spent many hours in the Arnolds' home in Berlin. He and Eberhard co-edited a book, *Junge Saat* (Young Seed), that contained articles bursting with the enthusiasm of the youth movement:

> The time is fulfilled. Throughout the youth movement we clearly sense a secret excitement, just as was felt in Israel when a man sent by God came to the Jordan and called, "Repent, the kingdom is at hand!" . . .
>
> The strongest spiritual yearning moves us to the core; it leads us most deeply to unity and whispers to us timidly of "community." We have been gripped by the infinite. The spirit of God stirred us; it worked in us and brought us a restlessness that caused both happiness and pain. Some secret wellspring within us broke open never to dry up; something came alive in us and will never wither. Like the boy Samuel, a voice called us by night, and we had no choice but to obey.
>
> A mighty experience empowered all of us when we each awoke to the fact: Now you are a member of a unique community of young people. We felt new strengths come alive when for the first time we tried to take control of our life, mystifying life, to take our progress into our own hands, and to form it according to our own will. We think back to that day when it overcame us like a holy wind, and we hardly knew what to do with our great exultation. We think back to that time when we explored our homeland for the first time, when on a long outing a new sense of life grew in us that made us one with the Almighty.[17]

But Körber also represented a certain nationalistic pride which would intensify in later years:

> I believe that the road to other nations and to a new Christian Europe runs through our Volk, that all work for a new humanity runs through the one Volk. We have been born to this destiny. God laid into our cradle the disposition and gift to grasp that nation's silent need and yearning, its wordless soul—and to express it. He has made us Germans—not just any kind of people! What ought to make us reflect deeply is the fact that all the unrelenting champions of international fraternization are either enthusiastic zealots or intellectuals totally out of touch with reality, or they are democratic business politicians, but in

any case not true interpreters of German destiny, of our nation's fettered will and bound soul.

When will our German Volk with all its depth and richness be given leaders again who are an expression of its better self, who will lead it back to its true self and will weld a confused mob once again into a Volk?"[18]

Church Community

After weeks of discussions and arguments, Eberhard and Emmy sold or gave away all they possessed and rented a large house in the village of Sannerz in Hesse. They were determined to put their words into practice and live in community with anyone who cared to join them. Although the house was not immediately available, they could wait no longer. In June 1920 they moved into the barn with their five children. Emmy's sister Else and a few others joined them. The house became the Neuwerk Community, Sannerz. Emmy, who was a true partner to Eberhard, wrote of the reactions of their former friends:

> There was no financial basis of any kind, either for starting this proposed business venture or for buying the villa at Sannerz and realizing our dream of a community house. But that made no difference. We decided it was time to turn our backs on the past and start afresh in full trust. Well-meaning friends shook their heads. What an act of rash irresponsibility for a father of five little children to go into the unknown just like that! Frau Michaelis, the wife of the former chancellor of the Reich, visited me and offered to help the children and me should my husband really take this "unusual" step. After talking with me, she reported to a mutual friend: "She is even more fanatical than he is! There is nothing we can do."[19]

Eberhard and Emmy had left the Lutheran Church years earlier. During the revival in Halle at the time of their engagement, they had come to the conclusion that infant baptism, as practiced by the Catholic and Lutheran Churches, was not true baptism. At that time Eberhard had written to Emmy:

> Today I prayed a long, long time, and this hour of dedication has brought me to a momentous decision, one which will give our life a clearly defined direction, laden with suffering . . . As of today, I have been convinced by God, with quiet and sober

> biblical certainty, that baptism of believers alone is justified. Taking Galatians 3:26–27 as a starting point, I persisted in reflecting on Jesus with simple, honest prayer, and have come to feel that scripture recognizes only one baptism: that of those who have become believers ... I therefore regard myself as unbaptized and hereby declare war on the existing church system.[20]
>
> On Tuesday I'll briefly inform our parents of my conviction, according to which I must a) be baptized as a believer, since infant baptism is in opposition to what is meant biblically and is therefore not baptism; b) withdraw from the established church, since I consider it dishonest through and through and contrary to the spirit of the Bible; c) embrace as my ideal church communities of believing, baptized Christians who use church discipline and celebrate the Lord's Supper ...
>
> I can't postpone leaving the established church any more than I can postpone the actual baptism, since I regard the church's deceitful system as Satan's most dangerous weapon and the most treacherous foe of apostolic Christianity. Of course, I don't fail to recognize the uprightness of many churchmen and the fact that they are serious Christians (used by the system to disguise its shamefulness).[21]

Now thirteen years later, in the budding community at Sannerz, Eberhard was developing a genuine alternative: a church community of believers. He, Emmy, Else, and the hundreds of visitors who passed through the house were overwhelmed by something beyond anything they had imagined possible, certainly not of their own making, which they could only define as the Holy Spirit. Eberhard described it in several letters.

> Our communal household takes shape more and more definitely. The faithful cell group of an early Christian house church is coming into being. Yesterday, for the first time, the Lord's Supper was held in the circle of those firmly committed. It was a glorious and festive hour of deep resolve and clearness.[22]
>
> I wish we could describe how wonderfully our life is woven together and how many glorious high moments we find in our joy in community and in our love to one another. If we think of last Sunday, for instance, when we held the Lord's Supper with the ten who are dedicated completely to life in community (had all been home we would have been twelve disciples), then the deep joy and unfathomable strength of this experience cannot be compared with anything we had before.[23]

Georg Barth, who came to Sannerz in 1925, remembered:

> I felt at home there at once and inhaled deeply the spirit-filled air of the house. So strongly did I feel the nearness of the kingdom of God that I could physically taste it and smell it . . . The Sannerz house was filled with the atmosphere of the kingdom of God. Anyone in this house breathed a completely different air. Although I did not yet know who Jesus really was and what it meant to follow him, still I sensed this air of the kingdom powerfully.[24]

In 1934 Eberhard said about this time:

> If in Berlin our activity was anchored more in literary things, in Sannerz it was anchored in something living. There was a wind that blew through our rooms. In every pore, through every wall, the lively spiritual movements penetrated. Fresh people came every day. We were prepared for this storm, and yet it was new because it brought something more alive than we had ever guessed at; it was plainer to see. Each day was lived at a high level of inner interest and suspense. Some of our meetings had no limits whatever. We met at seven o'clock in the evening, mostly until twelve, and often, too, from noon until two in the afternoon. This wasn't because we wanted it that way, but because it was necessary inwardly in the powerful stirring of the exchanges of thought, in the explosive outward movement. Not a single day went by without the greatest agitation and excitement.[25]

Confronting Anti-Semitism

Many of the radical thinkers whom Eberhard respected after the First World War were Jews: Gustav Landauer, Rosa Luxemburg, and Kurt Eisner. In 1917, he wrote an article on the ideas of the Jewish philosopher Martin Buber:

> There is a Jewish movement that is stirring the innermost heart of Judaism anew. It is made up of two currents—one religious, the other nationalistic—that are deeply united in Martin Buber, their outstanding exponent. In his essays on the Jewish movement Martin Buber puts great emphasis on the national significance of Judaism. Like the Zionists, he hopes for a gathering of the Jewish people on their own soil, for the renewal of their historical continuity, for a healthy national organism; but in his striving for this

> nationalistic goal Buber seeks a liberation of his people through which "the transformed Jewish spirit" can be resurrected ...
> The expectation of the future Messiah is the sphere where the deepest encounter [between Jew and Christian] takes place. In the infinitely distant, infinitely near kingdom of the future, the Jew expects the Absolute, the tabernacle of God, the house of true life for mankind, the salvation of the world, and the redemption of man's spirit. Martin Buber points out that early Christianity, too, in the expectation of its returning Lord, was filled with and given direction by this very idea of an absolute future. The early Christian belief in the return of Christ was not speculation or calculation; it was an inner attitude of faith, love, and hope; it was nothing less than the deep inner relationship of love to the Redeemer, through whom redemption must be consummated. In this belief we see the deepest means for a mutual understanding between Christianity and religious Judaism. For us too, preparing for his appearance means being prepared in unity and in the deed.[26]

After the war, Eberhard was concerned to counter the rising tide of anti-Semitism. Besides expressing in various ways his appreciation of the Jewish contribution to the Christian faith, he published books and articles by Jewish writers. One of these was the book *Rasse und Politik* (*Race and Politics*) by Julius Goldstein, published by the Neuwerk Publishing House.

> The book is born of the fullness of a wealth of knowledge, a passionate justice and a serious, though joyful, hope for the future. Seldom have I read a book in which I had to put so few question marks. The sensitive feeling for reality, which plainly marks the book a classic against anti-Semitism, is heart-warming and gives the lie to those who say renewal-Christianity moves only on unreal, abstract heights (a belief that might rightly apply to some forms of religious socialism). Politics and religion belong together in a much deeper sense than the opponents of this statement imagine. They should have their source in what is eternal and flow into the great common tasks and creative forms of a new brotherly mankind, rich in content and on the way to full maturity. Goldstein has pointed this out in an unsurpassed way on the basis of reality and without the use of religious phraseology.[27]

Max Wolf was the wealthy owner of a soap factory near Schlüchtern. A practicing Jew, he was the only non-Christian on the Neuwerk board of directors, and he promoted its publications among Jewish circles. He wrote to a friend:

> I asked Dr. Eberhard Arnold about his attitude to anti-Semitism, and he answered me literally: "There is no place in Germany from which the fight against anti-Semitism, with its irrational and anti-religious character, is waged so clearly as from the Neuwerk! Just because our fight for a reconciling, constructive spirit of the national and human community is tied to the championship of international reconciliation and for understanding between classes, the struggle against anti-Semitism will be all the more fruitful. For here it is not a matter of an isolated question but an all-encompassing outlook on life which is linked to a deep recognition of the religious spirit of Judaism." It seems very important to me that the fight against anti-Semitism is being fought from a decidedly Christian point of view.[28]

Much later, in August 1932, four young Zionists, training for life on a kibbutz in Palestine, visited the Rhön Bruderhof. In a meeting with them, Eberhard was interested to learn about their philosophical foundation and, as he did in every encounter, he urged them to appreciate more deeply their own heritage:

> *Eberhard:* Are the Pentateuch and the prophets authoritative for you? What is the spiritual foundation of your outward structure?
>
> *Zionist:* The old life no longer pleases us. We want something new. Only on the way of community have we found anything new.
>
> *Eberhard:* Will that be in the sense of the Jewish prophets?
>
> *Zionist:* There are two groups. One is loosely connected with communism, and the other is more inclined to socialism.
>
> *Eberhard:* You will remember that we recently exchanged thoughts about Zionism and the driving force behind it. We sensed a strong urge to put socialist ideas into practice, and in that we found a comradely relationship with our movement.
>
> *Zionist:* The majority stands on a socialist basis and is politically oriented. A smaller group takes its stand on the prophetic basis and emphasizes religion.
>
> *Eberhard:* How is it with struggles within the community?

Zionist: When we arrive in Palestine we are already trained. We know there is nothing but community and we must surrender everything for it.

Eberhard: During the twelve years we have lived in community we have learned that it is not possible to avoid struggle. Each of us has to fight egotism.[29]

Over the next twelve years, the community matured through struggles and crises. One thing became clear, particularly after a difficult time in the summer of 1922: in order to preserve love, joy, and unity it was essential to speak up if differences arose between people. At that time Eberhard formulated "the first law of Sannerz":

> There is no law but that of love. Love means having joy in others. Then what does being annoyed with them mean?
>
> Words of love convey the joy we have in the presence of brothers and sisters. By the same token it is out of the question to speak about a brotherhood member in a spirit of irritation or vexation. There must never be talk, either in open remarks or by insinuation, against a brother or a sister, against their individual characteristics—under no circumstances behind the person's back. Talking in one's own family is no exception.
>
> Without this rule of silence there can be no loyalty, no community. Direct address is the only way possible; it is the spontaneous brotherly service we owe anyone whose weaknesses cause a negative reaction in us. An open word spoken directly to the other person deepens friendship and is not resented. Only when two people do not come to agreement quickly in this direct manner is it necessary to talk it over with a third person who can be trusted to help solve the difficulty and bring about a uniting on the highest and deepest levels (Matt 18:15–16).[30]

The word "unity" became a watchword: the spirit of Jesus overcomes all differences and unites people. From a letter:

> Doubtless you are right that in such a community life as ours, the light coming from Christ alone must again and again bring the decisive rescue and help. Congeniality and sympathy, mutual understanding, professional association, or unity of purpose cannot hold community together. If it is true community, then it can only be from Jesus Christ and the direct working of his Holy

Spirit. As soon as this working is set aside, we can of course still come together, but true community will be impossible till once again the spirit of Jesus Christ clears away the hindrances and renews the unity.[31]

Personal salvation became secondary to a greater cause. Individuals looked beyond themselves to see the tremendous need of humankind and catch a vision of God's kingdom. Eberhard expressed this to a former alcoholic who spent several years in Sannerz:

> We are not a welfare or salvation institute. The saving of the individual soul is not our main concern. In this respect we differ from the Salvation Army. Certainly we too carry on good works, and certainly people are also saved, but that is not the first concern, not the most important thing. Our interest is in the great, holy cause, the kingdom of God, and mission to the world. Whoever comes into the brotherhood must be clear on this point: from now on I am no longer concerned with myself, but with the cause to which I have surrendered myself in self-forgetfulness . . . We must take a stand: "I will forget myself completely here. If only I could be a doorkeeper in the house of God, I would prefer that to sitting in the palaces of the rich." . . . My interest is not in my personality but in Christ and his kingdom, in God's glory, also among people.[32]

Unity with the Hutterites

Through his study of church history, Eberhard learned about the Hutterites, a branch of the Anabaptist movement that had begun in Zurich in 1525. He was moved by the witness of their martyrs: thousands had been executed because of their radical faith. They had begun living in community around 1530 and some communities were still in existence.

When the house in Sannerz became too small and a larger property had to be purchased, Eberhard decided to establish it on the pattern of sixteenth-century Hutterian communities. They bought the neglected Sparhof in 1926 and named it "Bruderhof," the word the Hutterites had used. It had a school, communal dining hall and kitchen, a print shop, and a farm, and eventually accommodated over 120 people.

Eberhard had seen enough communal attempts, both current and historical, to know the dangers such groups faced: some suffered shipwreck following false charismatic leaders while others became frozen in tradition. He did not wish his community to become merely another sect. It was to be and remain part of God's great church, and as such, unite with any other groups who desired the same. In 1930 he took a long journey to the United States and Canada to get to know the Hutterites firsthand. He was moved by what he found:

> When I compared their life with what we have experienced, and when I thought about our own attempt at community, I saw how the [Hutterites] were able to set us endless examples and give us invaluable help for our life and its organization . . . The Hutterian Bruderhofs convinced me most deeply that here the three articles of the Apostolic Confession of Faith had grown into a single unity: creative life, life redeemed by the full forgiveness of all sin and all error, and the good life of the Holy Spirit arising out of the powers from the future world. This was given among them in a wonderful unity such as I had never encountered at all in present-day Christian groups in Europe, a unity that does not depend on the spirit of the times.[33]

By uniting with this tried and established movement, Eberhard felt he was securing the future of his small flock beyond his own death. The Hutterite elders accepted him as a minister and commissioned him as a missionary in Germany. He felt strongly the responsibility of this spiritual authority. He wrote about the experience to Emmy:

> The confirmation, a deeply moving act . . . is of the very greatest significance. My service has been confirmed on the basis of my insight into the history, faith, and life of God's church during the last four centuries, on the basis of our own history in Sannerz and on the Rhön Bruderhof, but above all because our dearly beloved members of Sannerz and the Bruderhof have again and again born witness to faithfulness and unity. My confirmation gives me unlimited authority to establish a genuine Hutterian community life, both temporally and spiritually, to the best of my insight.
>
> It means, too, that the brothers in America will fully and forever support our Bruderhof both in its inner life of faith and in its outward economic life, also when the two of us and all our older fellow fighters are no longer alive. Actually, that unspoken longing was one of the main reasons urging me to make this extremely burdensome journey. Our fellow fighters and fellow workers have shown unexampled trust and self-forgetfulness. For their sake, in place of the will a rich man would make, I want to establish

our community life on as deep, strong, and firm a foundation as possible, to ensure its continuance beyond my death.

That applies, to begin with, to our own five children—our children in the flesh and in spirit, who justify such great hopes. It applies to the dear children of the other parents and mothers in the community... It applies equally and no less to the spiritual children of our children's community.[34]

Eberhard hoped that unity with the Hutterites could provide the Bruderhof with some spiritual and financial security for the community's uncertain future. At the same time, he saw quite clearly that the growth and development of radical Christian discipleship would bring irreconcilable conflict with the established political and economic order. Words he spoke in 1928 were to prove prophetic:

All the various movements of the past decades will one day converge in a radical awakening of the masses that leads the way to social justice and to God's unity—that is to say, to the church, to the kingdom of God, and to community in action...

What we need now is mission. Mission means reaching the millions who live in cities, the hundreds of thousands in industrial centers, the tens of thousands in medium-sized towns, the thousands in small towns, and the hundreds in villages—all these at once. Like a volcanic eruption, a spiritual revolution needs to spread through the country, to spur people to crucial decisions. People have to recognize the futility of splitting life up into politics, economics, the humanities, and religion. We must be awakened to a life in which all of these things are completely integrated...

When the movement has reached its peak, it will be so dangerous that capitalism will see itself imperiled by it. Wealthy landowners will see it as a threat to their position, and the state will see its existence endangered—for where shall the state get its income from if its members live in absolute propertylessness? It will foresee its own dissolution, and so it will have to call in the executioners...

Everything will depend on whether or not the last hour finds us a generation worthy of greatness. And the only thing worthy of God's greatness is our readiness to die for his cause...Whether the twentieth century is shattered for God's kingdom or simply passes by depends in part on us. We know what is at stake; we know the will of God. We have felt the power of the Holy Spirit and the powers of the future world. So let us get going; now is the time![35]

2

Hitler's Rise to Power

WHILE THE DISILLUSIONMENT FOLLOWING World War I had driven Eberhard and Emmy to find a positive alternative in a life of love and social justice, Adolf Hitler found scapegoats for Germany's troubles in Jews and communists. By 1920 he was a star speaker of the National Socialist Worker's Party, expressing the deepest fears and desires of his listeners and exuding confidence in his uncompromising, aggressive speeches. But his attempt to take over the government in November 1923 in the famed Beer-Hall Putsch came to an ignominious end, leaving him under arrest with a dislocated shoulder.

However, Hitler was released on parole a year later and immediately began building up his party again. Fiery speeches, marches, and staged street fights gained the attention of the press and won new adherents. Hitler encouraged ambitious, ruthless young men to take leadership positions. As Max Amman, the publisher of *Mein Kampf,* said: "Herr Hitler takes the view today more than ever that the most effective fighter in the National Socialist movement is the man who pushes his way through on the basis of his achievements as a leader." Ernst Röhm had built up the Nazi Party's paramilitary group, the *Sturmabteilung* (SA or storm troopers), before the 1923 putsch. Although it was declared illegal after the putsch, it continued to grow to thousands of members in the late 1920s and into the 1930s: street violence escalated.

Eberhard Arnold wrote of his impressions of the mood of the country in a letter:

> Once again heavy clouds hang over Germany. The general crisis in world capitalism has oppressive consequences for us. I don't mean the occupation of the Ruhr territory and the economic demands of France, etc., although this enslavement of a great

working people is among the most terrible things in the history of humankind. But still more terrible is the repugnant contrast between the new wealth which, without the least refinement, takes possession of everything, and the new poverty which is increasing, with poorer nutrition and freezing conditions. I have heard of families who have introduced two days of fasting each week, simply lying in bed so they can spare the heating fuel. But it will get worse when, as a result of the scarcity of coal and the decrease of foreign trade, unemployment increases. Already now many factories work only three days a week or only half day, with half activity and half pay. Nevertheless the young workers with full working strength have on the whole enough to eat and to live on. It is more difficult for the older family fathers, and worst of all for families without a strong, healthy breadwinner. As a result the children and the old people suffer the most.

In the heavy spiritual fight behind all these outward horrors that weigh us down, one can sense everywhere a deep disillusionment and a general depression, especially in socialist, communist, and pacifist circles and in the radical youth movement. There is a sharp increase of grim nationalism. The new bitterness over the world situation is expressed not only in helpless anger against fate, in a general apathy, or in anxiety over one's own personal life. Rather it is expressed primarily in ever wider circles of young people in hatred against the French and the Jews, in tough preparations of new militaristic formations, which of course would be unthinkable without a military conflict in the Entente itself. And yet it seems that these so-called nationalistic and swastika circles have no real content. It is again merely love to those nearest, and hatred against those further away, the common struggle for economic existence, a somewhat wider circle of empty egoism. Where are those people who, when the critical moment comes, will refuse to join in killing or harassing, who will rather be crucified and bear the sign of the crucified one? There is a great emptiness, a great vacuum. What will fill this void? Will it be the old filth again, the old consolation of degenerate nature, or a new fresh wind of purest air, the holy breath of God? Now is the moment to proclaim the truth everywhere, now more than ever! In speech, song, and speaking chorus, through pamphlets and books, above all in work and life, and through community of daily action, the one and only message must be spread abroad: Jesus. We believe in him, that his future will again become the present, that his power must be proved anew in following his life. This is the miracle that is always new.[1]

A cult developed around the person of Adolf Hitler; the "Heil Hitler" salute became compulsory in the movement in 1926. A rally in August 1929 was attended by forty thousand admirers. Nazi organizations were set up to cater to the needs of particular segments of society such as factory workers and artisans. Young people were targeted by the Hitler Youth (which began as a recruiting arm of the brownshirts), the League of German Maidens, and the National Socialist German Students' League under the leadership of Baldur von Schirach. The Students' League campaigned for limiting the number of Jewish students and dismissing pacifist professors.

President Hindenburg's seven-year term ended in 1932. He was eighty-four years old and ready to retire, but his supporters encouraged him to run again out of fear that otherwise Adolf Hitler would be elected. Reluctantly, he agreed. Hitler campaigned vigorously. He rented an airplane and flew from town to town across Germany, delivering forty-six speeches. Although Germany's major parties backed Hindenburg and he won easily, the Nazi propaganda paid off. Hitler won 37 percent of the votes and National Socialism was clearly a force to be reckoned with.

New Year's Eve 1933

Members of the Rhön Bruderhof anxiously observed the shifting mood of their country. Eberhard Arnold's youngest son Hans-Hermann wrote to his brother Hardy in June 1932:

> At the moment we live in a very difficult time that could spell disaster for us. I am thinking of the political situation and National Socialism . . . I have a feeling that the time of our expulsion and emigration is near.[2]

In January 1932, Emmy Arnold's sister Else von Hollander died of tuberculosis. Her death was a great loss to the community. She had been part of the family since the first years of Eberhard and Emmy's marriage and had worked faithfully as Eberhard's secretary for years: recording meetings in shorthand, typing letters, and assisting in his research and publishing work. At the same time, her Christ-centered experience of death and dying was a challenge and inspiration for the still-youthful Bruderhof.

The community had grown slowly and steadily over the years. Another of Emmy's sisters, Monika, had joined them. She was a nurse and had married Georg Barth; they had three young sons. Adolf Braun, a veteran of the last war with his wife Martha and their two daughters had been with them since 1924. Others had also experienced the first years in Sannerz like Karl Keiderling, a former anarchist, with his Irmgard, as well as the teacher Trudi. And there were newer faces: Hannes and Else Boller from Switzerland, Nils and Dora Wingard from Sweden, and some young single men and women.

Eberhard and Emmy's oldest daughter Emy-Margret had married Hans Zumpe; their first child was the hundredth member of the community. Hans had come from a family of civil servants and had shown considerable organizational skills. He helped with the accounting and bookselling and gradually assumed greater responsibility for the spiritual leadership of the community. The younger Arnold children were still in school: Hardy was studying in Tübingen, hoping to help his father in the publishing house. Heiner was taking a practical training in agriculture, and Hans-Hermann and Monika were still in high school.

Every New Year's Eve, the community met at midnight to remember the year that was ending and express hopes and wishes for the coming year. At the New Year's Eve meeting in 1932, Eberhard spoke at length about the worrying political and economic developments of the world around them.

> We stand at the end of the old year and before the new, as at a winter solstice. Will it become still darker? Still colder? Or will the New Year bring again more light of love, more warmth of righteousness, more joy of community among people? Will a new humanity come about again, or will men grow still more inhuman?
>
> The hour of the world in which we stand at this historic moment shows itself, even to the most superficial observer, as an hour of the greatest crisis and decision. But it is necessary to see things quite apart from the daily newspapers, which, in a mass of detail, give such an unclear survey of events that most readers do not notice what is really happening. We must attain a view of the present world situation which grasps the essential events without being clouded by unessential diversions.
>
> It is not by accident that we live here in Germany right between the eastern and western powers. On the one side is the liberalism of the French Revolution. On the other side the attempt has been made in Bolshevism to limit free trade and free enterprise to the absolute minimum.

Eberhard went on to explain how the prevailing domestic and global tensions must lead inexorably to the rise of dictatorship in Germany and ultimately to a catastrophic world war:

> This new nobility of the oppressed proletariat exercises an unrestrained dictatorship. Again and again they have to resort to deeds of violence and to bloodshed.
>
> And to the south? In Italy a renegade socialist has become a dictator wielding the weapons of militarism and mass-suggestion. Mussolini takes Caesar, the first of the Roman emperors, as the model of the modern statesman. He wishes to attain world rulership, making the state, the Roman Empire, into a god, just as it was at the time of the Roman Caesars.
>
> In Japan and China and on other parts of the earth, there is further unrest and war; thus we are living in a continual state of war, which brings with it uninterrupted, never-ending bloodshed. At the same time, between the opposing ideologies mentioned above, in spite of all peace treaties, the new and perhaps last world war is being prepared. It will necessarily be considerably more barbaric than the last world war, because poisonous gases and other techniques of war have become absolutely demonic in nature. A ruthless war will be led, not only against men and military bases, but just as much against women and children far from the front.
>
> The parliamentary form of government in Germany is finished. It has governed itself to death in these last ten years, and it can be assumed that we will soon be under a dictatorship. This state leadership stands between parliamentary democracy on the one hand and revolution on the other. The parliamentary, liberal power cannot prevail, and the revolutionary power has no prospect in the present distribution of power to win control through violence. Since both of them cannot rise up, the consequence is evident: the Reich president and the Reichskanzler will take over complete power.
>
> Man's confusion has reached its peak. The present hour is such that a political catastrophe must be approaching, because the present suspense is not tenable. In the spiritual outlook of the world there reigns an absolutely hopeless confusion. No one knows any more whom he can trust or upon what he can rely. That is the position at the present hour of the world.

In the midst of this mounting crisis, Eberhard believed that Christians had a responsibility to continue God's work.

We stand now confronting this—a most insignificant group of people, so small and so lacking in talent that we cannot even be thrown into the scales against present events. What can we do against these political and spiritual powers? We are less than a gnat on an elephant, less than a grain of sand on the seashore, less than a drop in a bucket of water. And yet our faith tells us that this does not matter. For it is not that *you* have something to say, that *you* have responsibilities, that *you* have something to bring into the world. Rather, that which is planted within you must be brought to the whole world. You need not worry to what extent you personally will be used. You must have the faith that what is said and given to you must be said and given to the whole world. Therefore you must be ready for the new hour, for the new day that will come over the world. You must be ready to do your utmost in our small, insignificant work. You must be very courageous; the hour demands it of you. In the face of these great events you must not be found too small. In the face of God's great plan you must not be found too petty.

How can this come about? We do not know. We have no money to build houses, to buy farms, to clothe people, to strengthen our economic basis so as to feed an additional forty people or more. And yet we are filled with the belief that there is only one possible answer: the unity of the church, the righteousness of God's kingdom, the spirit of God in Jesus Christ and his coming reign. Therefore we must be prepared now to risk everything. We must build. We must enlarge the farm. We must increase the publishing work, the printing and bookbinding work. Love demands that we throw ourselves in with all our strength for this need of the world.

Then we must go out. Through the publicly spoken word and through the publishing house and print shop, through letters to our friends, through messages to the governments of all states we must send out the good news. We must call everyone to the way of communal brotherliness and allow them to be released from strife and once more be united with the spirit of the future, which is the spirit of righteousness. This is only very little of all that should happen in the year 1933 if we have faith.

Therefore we come together to call upon God. In him we find an answer for what is to happen, for that which moves the whole world, and what has to be done in the face of this hour.

If this is our certainty, then—to work! All hands on deck! Let us dare it, whatever it costs![3]

Eberhard walked up to an unlit Christmas tree in the center of the circle and lit one of the candles. One by one, others expressed their hopes for the New Year and lit their candles. They spoke with courage and determination—even a solemn joy—of the witness they wished to give.

Midnight struck: 1933 began—a year that would bring greater changes and challenges than Eberhard could have imagined.

But the mood in the meeting room was hopeful and courageous. After the older people and parents of little children went to bed, the young people went outside. The light from the full moon reflecting on the snow was bright enough to read a newspaper by. Much too beautiful to go to bed! Someone started a folksong, and they joined hands and danced for a long time.[4]

~

"President Hindenburg has appointed Adolf Hitler as Reichskanzler." At the dinner table in Fulda all conversation ceased as everyone listened to the rest of the radio announcement. Knowing that the community had no radio, Heiner went to the telephone and called his father. At the other end of the line Eberhard was silent for a moment. He was not completely surprised; for the past three days the papers had been filled with speculation as to who would replace Schleicher, who had been forced to resign. "The president has no idea what demons he is conjuring up," Eberhard said to his son.

Most Germans trusted that their parliamentary system and the conservative members of the cabinet would contain Hitler's ambitions. Under the Weimar constitution, signed into law August 11, 1919, power was divided between the president, the cabinet, and the Reichstag (or parliament). The president was elected for a seven-year term; Paul von Hindenburg, elected in 1925 and reelected in 1932, served in this capacity until his death in 1934. The Reichskanzler was appointed by the president and accountable to parliament. Few could have imagined how quickly Hitler would seize complete power. That evening at the Rhön Bruderhof, Eberhard shared the news with the community. He encouraged everyone to trust that God still held his hand over the country. Later that night Emmy wrote to her three sons who were away at school: Hardy in Tübingen, Heiner in Fulda, and Hans-Hermann in Buchanau.

> The moment of crisis is here, and Hitler is Reichskanzler. We have to wait and see what will happen. Papa does not see it as too critical at the moment, since Hitler will be in the government together with Hugenberg and von Papen and others.* We ask you for now to behave quietly and cautiously. We will take communal action as soon as any laws are passed that we cannot reconcile with our conscience; that is, we will send a petition to the government. But it is also possible that for the present things will go on as before. By the time you come home the situation will have become more clear to us. In any case, we want to put ourselves completely under God's protection, and faithfully follow the way we began. The times are such that each has to do the best as he sees it. In our brotherhood everyone is calm and prepared to face what lies ahead. If anything extraordinary is imminent, you will come home before we do anything. May God protect you and us.[5]

That night all over Germany the Nazi Party took to the streets to celebrate their victory. Curious and naive, Heiner left the house and followed the crowds. Fulda was a small, conservative Catholic town. But young Nazis had come in from neighboring villages, and he saw them on every street.

> The Nazis in uniform marched through Fulda proclaiming, "Without bloodshed, we will not leave the village." . . . I was very young; I did not know how serious it was. I thought, that is Berlin; it will take a long time before that comes to the Rhön. But Hitler acted pretty fast. It was all organized. Everywhere there was someone already appointed—immediately, completely disciplined and organized for an attack. It simply was amazing. I walked through the streets and parks, and everywhere there were these uniformed Nazis, who were not allowed on the streets a few hours before.
> Near the center of the town there stood a uniformed Nazi with a terrific gift of speech. He spoke to the masses, and more and more people came. He said, "We are now in power. Tonight Hitler will still be merciful; if you join the party tonight, he will still be merciful." In Berlin the SA and the SS marched past the house where Hitler was, and he stood there with his arm raised

---

* Alfred Hugenberg was the head of the Nationalist Party, a rightwing party that initially supported the Nazi party but was ultimately taken over by it. Franz von Papen had been appointed *Reichskanzler* by Hindenburg in 1932 and believed Hitler could be controlled.

for several hours while thousands of troops marched by. I do not know how he managed it.

I was not afraid. A meeting was announced in the city hall, the biggest hall of the town. There was a podium with a microphone, and in front of it there were two or three rows of SS in black uniforms with a skull and crossbones. I went into that meeting without permission from my father. I did not know how dangerous it was. There were many in that room who were not Nazis yet, but they were nationalistic. There was a speaker who spoke like the man outside, that Hitler is still compassionate. Then they sang *"Deutschland, Deutschland über alles,"* that is, "Germany, Germany forever." That was not a Nazi song; it was sung under the Kaiser. Everyone had to stand up to sing that song, but I remained sitting. It was a big hall and very emotional. I thought they would beat me up, or worse, but I got away with it. When I told my father, he said, "What business did you have to go to that Nazi meeting?" That was the last time I went.[6]

~

Adolf Hitler was Reichskanzler and Germany had changed. To Eberhard, this presented a new missionary challenge. Earlier, he had appealed to that which was of God in the pacifist, socialist, communist, vegetarian, and back-to-nature movements. Now he sought to find something of God even in National Socialism:

> We feel as if we had been set down in another country; we live now in a different nation than we did a year ago. And we have a missionary task here in this new country. We can take on this task only if we recognize all that is positive in National Socialism. We must learn to understand the people, try to grasp the positive elements of what is moving among them. We must not face this phenomenal change cold-heartedly. In National Socialism there are the elements of family life, of the community of the nation, of the Old Covenant—shielding what is good and right from evil.
>
> If one encounters such a national movement by simply rejecting it, finding nothing ideal, nothing good and positive in it, one soon finds oneself completely outside it. This we must not do. In the same way as we recognized the good elements in the German youth movement, in the movements that expected and longed for a future of justice and fellowship, we must find the vision to recognize the positive values in the present-day national movement.[7]

The conflict between the National Socialist and Communist Parties was well known, and it would intensify over the next months. Eberhard had been openly sympathetic to the communists for years, because of their support for the oppressed poor. On February 10, an article about the Bruderhof appeared in the *Frankfurter Zeitung*, a large, liberal newspaper. Already in its headline it referred to the community as "Christian communists."

> The Bruderhof lies at the edge of a wood on the windy heights. No road leads to it, no cars or trains pass it. Completely isolated from the rest of the world, it consists of several houses. The work is hard. The swampy meadow is evidently to become a potato field . . .
>
> A girl of about fourteen with big blue eyes and blond hair that sticks out from her kerchief greets me with a simple, "Good morning." "Are guests welcome here?" I ask. Yes, but I should wait a moment as the men are at devotions. She leads me to a room with blue walls and simple heavy furniture. This is the communal meeting room. On the table is a blue cloth, on the wall a simple black cross. After a few minutes the men enter. All have beards. We greet each other.
>
> "Welcome! Come have lunch with us. You can tell us about Frankfurt and then we can chat." The man who is speaking shakes my hand and slaps me on the shoulder as if we had known each other for years. Everyone laughs—including me. In their unrestrained, honest manner these people know how to win the friendship of strangers within two minutes. There are no conventions here.
>
> Meals are eaten together. The community numbers 108 members including 54 children and youth. Eighteen families live on the Bruderhof, but only half of the children belong to these families. The others were taken in by the community. During lunch I am told: "The Bruderhof is a social, educational community of work, made up of men and women who live in voluntary poverty. They dedicate all their physical, spiritual, and emotional energy for a life of active love."
>
> At the Bruderhof there are no wages and no employers and employees as understood by capitalistic economy. Within the Bruderhof there is no exchange of money. The members lead a sharp inner battle against private property and against everything that can disturb the unity of their common life.
>
> We spoke little about religion. To summarize in one sentence: The Bruderhof believes that the solution to all the religious and

social questions of our time can be found in original Christianity. It is independent of any church but is considered by all denominations to be an example of early Christian community. All the people I met at the Bruderhof are good Christians, but also ideologically good "communists."[8]

The name of the Bruderhof was here associated with communism in black and white before all Germany. The danger was obvious.

Tübingen

Eberhard's oldest son Hardy was studying in Tübingen in southern Germany. One of his professors was Karl Heim, Eberhard's friend from their years together in the Student Christian Movement. Because of this friendship, he invited Hardy to lunch once a week and every month gave him some pocket money. Heim was a popular professor of Christian ethics, and his lectures in the university's largest hall were packed. Hardy recalled:

> Every student could present questions that he would answer. But so that there would be no chaos, the questions had to be presented in writing. He would read out the question and call the student up to the microphone to discuss the question with him.
>
> Professor Heim was talking about the Sermon on the Mount in this Christian ethics course. He represented that there were many different ways to interpret the Sermon on the Mount and that it was not valid for everyone. I was most surprised that what he said was absolutely different from what my father said. So I took a piece of paper and wrote down that I could not agree that the Sermon on the Mount was not for everyone. I believed that Jesus had taught the way of Christianity in the Sermon on the Mount, and that it was valid for us now. So he read this paper out and called me to the microphone, and we went into a discussion. He admitted that you could interpret the Sermon on the Mount the way my father did if you wanted to, but he said, "I have different interpretations."
>
> This episode, which happened at the beginning of my first semester, made me known among the students. They came to me and wanted to discuss the Sermon on the Mount with me.[9]

Another professor at Tübingen was Jakob Wilhelm Hauer who taught comparative religion. He had spent time in India and studied Sanskrit. He too knew Eberhard Arnold and was friendly to Hardy; in 1921, he had spoken at a Pentecost conference in Sannerz about "spirit and culture." In 1933 and 1934, Hauer developed a new "German Faith Movement," based on ancient eastern and Nordic religions, which became quite popular among young Nazis.[10]

Edith Boeker was one of Hauer's students, and she was deeply impressed: "I had never experienced anything like it. Everything was represented: anthroposophy, National Socialism, theology, and science."[11] She wrote in her diary:

> Last night Professor Hauer invited us to his house. He is the man of Indo-Germanic faith. One room has a whole corner consisting of windows without curtains, so one can see the trees. Many books, and a beautiful woman's bust with big eyes and long hair. On the walls are Indian and Persian symbols. He is actually a professor of Sanskrit and is similar to Nietzsche with a large forehead and a hanging red-blonde mustache. He is very likeable, peaceful, going into everything calmly and clearly. I love the educated, artistic atmosphere.[12]

Hardy shared several classes with Edith, and they talked about the world views presented by Heim and Hauer. As he wrote:

> There was a small group of students who met for lively discussions of essential questions of life, inspired by the points of view represented by the professors Karl Heim and Jakob Wilhelm Hauer. One represented a rational, pietistic, protestant theology and the other a mystic, mythological Indo-Germanic heathendom. Several of us were deeply impressed, because what Hauer had to say seemed more truthful and honest than Heim's theology. To me it seemed that what was important was to be genuine: honest paganism—that is, love to creation that is nourished by the primal, though unredeemed power of nature—was closer to God and to Christ than hypocritical Christianity that is marked by compromise and self-righteousness.
>
> On midsummer eve, 1932, we celebrated the summer solstice. Professor Hauer gave the fire speech. It was one of those occasions when the night seemed to breath and we humans felt closer to the source of nature than usual. After the celebration, some went to sleep next to the fire, and others talked until dawn ...
>
> After Hauer's classes, some of us would get together over cake and coffee and talk excitedly about the questions that concerned us. Why has Christianity failed? In what has it failed? We all recognized that Hauer's attack on Christianity was justified, but

> we also saw that he only criticized the hypocrisy of the churches without understanding the joyful news [of the gospel.] Into these questions, the testimony of original Christianity fell like a bomb. Here was something alive and all-embracing that transcended the confused teachings of Hauer in its power and universality.[13]

Edith Boeker and her friend Susi visited the Rhön Bruderhof in summer 1932, and early in 1933 they both decided to quit their studies and join the community. Edith wrote:

> It became clear to me that there are two powers, darkness and light, and that each person has to make a decision between them. At the Bruderhof light rules! Killing evil men will not decrease evil . . . I knew I had to stay. I went for one more semester to Tübingen. Hardy, Susi, and I met every day and spoke about the absoluteness of truth. It is impossible that there should be more than one truth, as Hauer says. It is impossible that there are two ways, as Heim says—one for the churches and another for the Bruderhof, for example, on the one hand to recognize that people can live together in love and on the other hand to say that it is impossible for the masses.[14]

∼

At the end of February, Eberhard took the train to Tübingen. Hardy had arranged for him to speak at the university. They met in the YMCA building where two to three hundred students and several professors were gathered. Eberhard did not wish to advertise the Bruderhof as such, but spoke of the need for a Christian witness. The lecture lasted an hour and a half and was followed by a discussion. Here Eberhard got a sense of what young people were thinking. One student, dressed in an SA paramilitary uniform, picked up on what Eberhard had said about nonviolence. "Have you ever spanked a child?" he asked. A young woman who was studying theology quoted Matt 10:34: "Jesus said, 'I have not come to bring peace but the sword.'" Another student asserted that the apostle Paul had claimed the right of Roman citizenship and thereby acknowledged the emperor's use of military force.

Clearly, the mood was already nationalistic and militaristic. Eberhard countered all the arguments. "The followers of Christ have a special task, namely to live according to love, according to the heart of God." Then he put forth an idea that would become a favorite theme of his:

> I must confess that I have a double set of ethics. For the followers of Jesus there is a different set of laws than for the world. Pharaoh was an instrument of God—not an instrument of his love, but of his wrath. Christians are not called upon to represent the wrath of God, but his love.

One young man said, "Your community is a pest to the German people. You are refusing to help the Fatherland that is bleeding to death."

Eberhard responded adamantly to these criticisms: "I want to point out to you that in a tense political situation you are accusing our Bruderhof of being detestable and dangerous. With this you are bringing an accusation against brothers who are earnestly concerned to live according to Christ. I ask you, as Jesus asked Judas, go at once to the authorities and inform on us. Though I myself am no longer of military age, yet I can be arrested for influencing others against military service. I am ready, but be clear that by doing this you are slandering my beloved Jesus Christ." Surprised at Eberhard's reaction, the young man and several others left the room.

For three evenings following Eberhard's lecture, thirty to forty people met with him for a two-hour discussion. They were able to speak on a deeper level about unity and the Lord's Supper, and also about the role of government.

> Certainly the government is from God and should be recognized with respect, in so far as it fights evil and protects the good. But the government is not only from God; it is also from men. It is conducted in a purely human manner and from this point of view must be treated with extreme caution. Thirdly, government is also from the devil, for it is the beast of prey out of the abyss that we read of in the Revelation of John. Unless we see these three facts together, as they are clearly shown in the New Testament, then we cannot do justice to the government.[15]

∼

Meanwhile, significant political events followed in quick succession. On the night of February 27, 1933, fire destroyed the Reichstag, the German parliament building. Hitler denounced this as a communist plot and used the opportunity to persuade President von Hindenburg to sign a decree "for the protection of the people and the state." This Enabling Act suspended freedom of the press, the right of assembly and association, security from house-search and interference with postal and telephone communication. Now the Nazi terror was backed by the government; truckloads of storm troopers roared over the country rounding up communists and other dissidents, torturing them in SA barracks.

At the Rhön Bruderhof, it was of crucial importance that men and women become decisive as to what attitude they would take. Eberhard spoke with some visitors, explaining the brotherhood's calling. One married couple decided to leave.

> Our calling is to represent the kingdom of God and the church of Jesus Christ, with all the consequences. This means that we feel our own love to Jesus, born of the personal experience of God's love in our hearts, very deeply and gratefully, but that is not the main thing. For us the main thing is that God and his kingdom, in his coming world rulership, in his coming world peace, shall prevail among us in such a way that we represent this one cause over against all other circumstances, conditions, and relationships. As a result we come to a powerful and decisive opposition to the world around us. This also means opposition to the state, which has to be maintained by violence and the military. It has to defend private property with violence and enforce the law to uphold its power.
>
> We do not withhold our respect from God-ordained government (Romans 13:1). Our calling, however, is a completely different one; it brings with it an order of society utterly different from anything that is possible in the state and the present social order. That is why we refuse to swear oaths before any court of law; we refuse to serve in any state as soldiers or policemen; we refuse to serve in any important government post—for all these are connected with law courts, the police, or the military.
>
> We oppose outright the present order of society. We represent a different order, that of the church as it was in Jerusalem after the Holy Spirit was poured out. The multitude of believers became one heart and one soul. On the social level, their oneness was visible in their perfect brotherliness. On the economic level it meant that they gave up all private property and lived in complete community of goods, free from any compulsion. And so we are called to represent the same in the world today, which quite naturally will bring us into conflicts. This was also the case with the early Christians and the Anabaptists. We cannot put this burden on anybody unless he or she prizes the greatness of God's kingdom above everything else and feels inwardly certain that there is no other way to go.[16]

3

March to April 1933

The Werkhof

AS THE POLITICAL SITUATION in Germany intensified, Eberhard tried to gain the support of likeminded people within the country and abroad. Early in 1933 he sent a message to a community in Switzerland, imploring them to work for unity as a "witness to the power of Jesus in the present world situation."

The Werkhof had started in November 1930. Its members came from the Swiss peace movement, inspired by Leonhard Ragaz who was, in turn, influenced by Hermann Kutter, whose book *They Must* had had such a profound effect on Eberhard in 1910. Ragaz and Eberhard Arnold had been corresponding and exchanging articles since 1920. Eberhard wrote about him in an article in the *Wegwarte* in 1928:

> It was given to Leonhard Ragaz to point the way to the kingdom of God. He did this by means of his books, lectures, conferences, and his periodical, *Neue Wege*, with their untiring challenge; but most of all by laying down his professorship in an attempt to immerse himself in the problems of the proletariat.
>
> We should remember that Leonhard Ragaz, at a time when those who largely accepted his views later were still tied to bourgeois conventionality, pointed out the radical difference between official Christianity, even that of genuine leading Christians, and what the kingdom of God truly is. Leonhard Ragaz is able to point us to that cause which consists purely in God's actual rulership. This means that God alone, and no human being, is supreme. And this very fact makes it possible for true social justice to break in, taking the form of brotherhood, where God's spirit of unity is all that counts because it is stronger than all other spirits.

> Our deep concern as a Bruderhof is to continue on the way that is pointed out and clearly marked for us, while remaining in strong and living contact with Leonhard Ragaz and his work. We owe him thanks for an important help in understanding God's will as it has appeared in Christ and as it seeks to take shape in his church, which already now lives and proclaims the kingdom of God, changing nothing of its character.[1]

A friendship developed between the Werkhof and the Bruderhof. But by fall 1932 the Werkhof was disintegrating, torn apart by strong opinions. As one of its members said later: "There were as many ideas as there were idealists. The diversity of opinions about leadership, the form of meetings, the education of the children, the attitude to politics resulted in frictions and tensions within the group."[2] Some of the members visited the Rhön Bruderhof to see what they could learn. Sensing a profound unity and an atmosphere of love, they decided to withdraw from the Werkhof and join the Bruderhof. Believing that God was leading the two groups together, they were eager to go back and tell those who remained that they had found a place where the love and unity the Werkhof wished for were reality. While still at the Bruderhof, Peter and Anni Mathis and Leo and Trautel Dreher discussed this idea at a meeting:

> *Peter Mathis:* We have to go to Leonhard Ragaz and simply testify to what has happened.
>
> *Leo Dreher:* We should challenge them to complete unity. They should allow themselves to be led by the Spirit of the church.
>
> *Trautel Dreher:* It is quite simple. Peter and Anni should go back and bring those who want to come.
>
> *Eberhard:* We want to appeal to the Werkhof to unite insofar as they know themselves to be one in faith and in the uniting Spirit. It can be granted to them because it is a matter of grace; we simply have to ask God for it. It is not ultimately to the Werkhof that we must turn but to God's Spirit and the complete gospel of Christ and of God's kingdom. The reason we should do this is that these dear people have put the greatest effort into struggling for community for years and years, although their motives were often mixed. We have to respect that. Perhaps the hour of their call has come; may God grant it. It is wonderful.
>
> For the sake of the public witness it is important that we form one big community. We went so far as to say to them: We ask this not only for your sakes but for ours, because our Bruderhof

is much too weak. We need your help. Has the hour come for us to stand together as one great witness? What concerned us was that the world is going to destruction and the kingdom of God is approaching, but this did not fall on good soil and hardly sank in ... We have heard from all sides that a real unity in the Spirit and a true spiritual community has been missing at the Werkhof for a long time. Therefore the Werkhof cannot be thought of as "church" in the sense of true community of the Spirit and a way of life. We are not asking the members of the Werkhof to come to the Bruderhof, but we are ready to unite with those among them who believe in the spirit of unity and are ready to unite with us in obedience to that spirit.

The question of where that shall take place—whether on our little hill or in a Swiss canton, on the American prairie or in the Canadian Rockies, or in some completely different place—all that we leave open. We declare ourselves ready for everything the Spirit says to the churches. We are certain, however, that the Spirit says the same to all the churches. And when it is a question of uniting in life community, we have to be completely one and we must not make any conditions.[3]

Eberhard respected Ragaz's calling as similar to that of John the Baptist, of "a voice calling in the wilderness."[4] But he believed that unity was the decisive mark of the church of God and the most important witness needed in the world.

The most necessary premise—the uniting spirit—is missing at the Werkhof, though we do have great respect for the reality of a life devoid of private property ... Our times are so tremendously serious that there is nothing more needful than the witness of a life based on the spirit of unity. Only a witness of deed and action can be of any help. Words are now being suppressed in Germany ... Their place has to be taken by the witness of deeds and by passing on the call from person to person.[5]

Unfortunately, those left at the Werkhof resented the Bruderhof's desire to join forces. Ragaz felt that his work was being criticized, and he accused the Bruderhof of presuming to be the only true church. As he wrote on February 22, 1933:

Dear friends, I agree with you regarding the evaluation of the church, both in itself and also in relation to the organized church, as well as to socialism. I also believe that the church is the ultimate word of holy sociology; I believe in the *promise* given to it,

> I believe in its *blessing* and in its *authority*, and I believe that you on the Bruderhof are a church of this kind and share in its promise. But at this point the problem arises, which amounts to a question to you, or rather to *the* question to you: Are you only *a* church or *the* church—excluding other forms of the church, which might also still be found elsewhere? . . . Several statements in letters and otherwise during the past few months make me unsure regarding this matter, and I am turning to you with the request now, to give me completely clear information regarding this.[6]

This question led to serious discussions in the Rhön brotherhood on the meaning of the term "church." On March 9, Eberhard answered Ragaz:

> We thank you warmly and respectfully for the brotherly service in your letter of February 22. It touched us deeply, and we took it as a service from one who calls like John the Baptist, one of the few who have pointed to and prepared the way that has led us into the charge of the church and of the kingdom.[7]

> If anyone asks us if we, a group of weak and needy people, are the church of God, then we must answer: No, we are not. We are the objects of the love of God like all other people. Like all other people, and still more than they, we are unworthy, unfit, and incapable for the working of the Holy Spirit, for the building of the church, and for the mission to the entire world. But if the question is asked: Is the church of God with you? Does the church of God come down where you are? Then we must answer: Yes, it is so. Wherever believers are gathered, having no longer any other will but the one, single will that the kingdom of God may come and that the church of Christ may be made manifest as the perfect unity of his spirit, there, in every such place, is the church, because the Holy Spirit is there.[8]

Unfortunately, however, stemming from this discussion Ragaz grew more critical of Eberhard and the Bruderhof. As the evil of Hitler's policies became more strongly evident—which should have brought together all who wished to serve God's kingdom—the rift between Leonhard Ragaz and Eberhard Arnold grew deeper.

~

A new election of the Reichstag had been scheduled for March 5. During the campaign, Hitler proclaimed repeatedly that Marxism was the archenemy of his party. "Our fight against Marxism will be relentless, and every movement which allies itself to Marxism will come to grief with it."⁹

Two days after the election, on March 7, a police officer appeared at the Rhön Bruderhof. He informed the community that complaints alleging that they were communists had reached the district administrator's office in Fulda, accusing them of printing inflammatory pamphlets and hiding weapons. Since the district administrator at the time was Baron von Gagern, a friend of the Bruderhof, it was easy to counter these accusations, and things seemed to settle down.

On March 23, the Reichstag convened in the Kroll Opera House (since the parliament building had burned down), and Hitler introduced the measure that would enable the Reichskanzler to prepare laws without the approval of the Reichstag and without reference to the president. As he stepped forward to stand beneath a swastika banner in his brownshirt paramilitary uniform, he was greeted with "Heil!" by his party.[10]

He started out by speaking of the "dethroning of the German monarchy" in the Revolution of 1918 and of the dangers of communism. This worldview, he said, had permeated society and threatened its basic principles of religion, morality, family, and economy.

> Starting with the liberalism of the past century, this development will end, as the laws of nature dictate, in Communist chaos... Beginning with pillaging, arson, raids on the railway, assassination attempts, and so on—all these things are morally sanctioned by Communist theory... The burning of the Reichstag, one unsuccessful attempt within a large-scale operation, is only a taste of what Europe would have to expect from a triumph of this demonical doctrine...
>
> The Government of the National Revolution basically regards it as its duty, in accordance with the spirit of the Volk's vote of confidence, to prevent the elements which consciously and intentionally negate the life of the nation from exercising influence on its formation. The theoretical concept of equality before the law shall not be used, under the guise of equality, to tolerate those who despise the laws as a matter of principle or, moreover, to surrender the freedom of the nation to them on the basis of democratic doctrines...
>
> The Reich Government intends to undertake a thorough moral purging of the German *Volkskörper*. The entire system of education, the theater, the cinema, literature, the press, and

radio—they all will be used as a means to this end and valued accordingly. They must all work to preserve the eternal values residing in the essential character of our Volk. Art will always remain the expression and mirror of the yearning and the reality of an era ... *Blut und Rasse* [blood and race] will once more become the source of artistic intuition ... Reverence for the Great Men must be instilled once more in German youth as a sacred inheritance. In being determined to undertake the political and moral purification of our public life, the government is creating and securing the requirements for a genuinely profound return to religious life ...

The National Government perceives in the two Christian confessions the most important factors for the preservation of our *Volkstum*. It will respect any contracts concluded between these Churches and the Länder [states].

Their rights are not to be infringed upon. But the Government expects and hopes that the task of working on the national and moral regeneration of our Volk taken on by the Government will, in turn, be treated with the same respect. It will face all of the other confessions with objective fairness. However, it cannot tolerate that membership in a certain confession or a certain race could mean being released from general statutory obligations or even constitute a license for committing or tolerating crimes which go unpunished. The Government's concern lies in an honest coexistence between Church and State; the fight against a materialist Weltanschauung and for a genuine Volksgemeinschaft equally serves both the interests of the German nation and the welfare of our Christian faith ...

For years Germany has been waiting in vain for the redemption of the promise to disarm given us by the others. It is the sincere desire of the National Government to be able to refrain from increasing the German Army and our weapons insofar as the rest of the world is also finally willing to fulfill its obligation of radically disarming. For Germany wants nothing except equal rights to live and equal freedom.

However, the National Government wishes to cultivate this spirit of a will for freedom in the German Volk. The honor of the nation, the honor of our Army, and the ideal of freedom—all must once more become sacred to the German Volk!

The German Volk wishes to live in peace with the world ...

The distress of the world can only come to an end if the appropriate foundation is created by means of stable political conditions and if the peoples regain confidence in one another.

> To deal with the economic catastrophe, the following is necessary:
>
> 1. an absolutely authoritarian leadership at home to create confidence in the stability of conditions;
>
> 2. safeguarding peace on the part of the major nations for a long time to come and thus restoring the confidence of the peoples in one another; and
>
> 3. the final triumph of the principles of common sense in the organization and leadership of the economy as well as a general release from reparations and impossible liabilities for debts and interest.[11]

Leaders of other parties spoke in response to Hitler's speech. Otto Wels, chairman of the Social Democrats countered forcefully: "No Enabling Law gives you the right to annihilate ideas that are eternal and indestructible."[12] But the resolution passed: Adolf Hitler now had complete power over Germany.

At the Rhön Bruderhof, the brotherhood met to discuss their position. Eberhard wished to go to Kassel, the regional government seat, and then to Berlin to speak openly with the officials in charge, even with Hitler himself. He read out parts of Hitler's speech and then asked each member to respond.

> *Emmy Arnold:* I believe that the journey to Kassel is urgent in order to sense exactly what is in the wind outside. We must know what is really happening, because nothing is written about it. A man in our neighboring village said one can't use the word "justice" anymore or one is immediately called a communist. The father-in-law of a woman in Heubach was beaten to death in Fulda. Now the Jews are persecuted, and Christians will be next.
>
> *Heiner Arnold:* After Hitler's speech I sense the necessity to stand together in the deepest unity and action of the heart.
>
> *Liesel Wegner:* We do not know how long we can still be together after this cutting, brutal speech.
>
> *Trudi Hüssy:* We must continue to build and not be held back by thoughts of what might happen. Sending Eberhard on our behalf to this present government is a very awesome thing to do, a historical act.

Annemarie Wächter: Listening to Hitler's speech, I felt as though we were an embassy in another country, with a completely different language and a completely different atmosphere. It is of the utmost importance that we represent within this embassy that other land—a land that is known to us—so powerfully that our testimony must be heard and cannot be ignored. We must all be filled from within by this living Spirit and be able to think of nothing else, so that we stand completely in the joy and power of the Spirit—and in unity.

Alfred Gneiting: The time has come when we will be forsaken and alone, forsaken by all who have till now stood close to us.

Adolf Braun: Historically, the times of freedom of spirit, of constitutional freedom, are very short, and the times of persecution are very long. Persecution is now coming, and we must call up all the strength we have in order not to be smashed to pieces right now. The state once more shows its claws like a beast of prey. The journeys to Kassel and Berlin are the most important next steps.

Arno Martin: When such a mass of people are ready to submit their whole will to a satanic power, how much more must we be enthusiastic, courageous, and on fire for God's cause, for the cause that really has a future.

Eberhard: We must ask Jesus to lay his hand on us so that we are free from inertia. We cannot free each other, but he must free us. We must be free from tiredness and worry, everything that robs us of the courage and energy to be active. We shall carry on mission without the slightest fear of men. We will not be allowed to publish a magazine now; we will go like the Anabaptists of the sixteenth century, from person to person.

He went on to lay out the path that he would follow. He felt clearly that the voice of the church needed to speak out, and for this reason they should remain in Germany to give witness. He mentioned several times over the next two years his desire to meet Adolf Hitler personally.

> We shall stay in this place where we have been led until God directs us to leave. We will go on building and working and must not give up praying for the means required.
>
> I look into the future without fear. I believe we can speak very clearly with this government, if from the first we take the initiative and openly express what we feel is positive and what we feel

is negative. I hope I can speak with Adolf Hitler. We must ask God for an opportunity for an open exchange with him.

In this hour it is not good to have such a large group of novices. During the passion week we should concentrate on accepting most of them as full members. We have to gather closely and firmly together in the brotherhood. Any visitors who are a disturbance need to leave. The brotherhood circle has to become an army, led by the Spirit.

Then we need to concern ourselves with people who are suffering or in prison. We should go to authentic sources and do as much as we can. We have to become very active.[13]

The following Sunday, Eberhard spoke to all members and guests:

Right now our society is unhealthy: present-day churches, the present-day economic system. We cannot go along and must seek a different way, even if it is very modest. For we reject political attempts to improve public conditions; we renounce playing any role in middle-class society today.

He then spoke of the efforts of well-meaning Christians to mitigate or correct various excesses of the Nazi movement. He made his point by referring to the symbol of the swastika, a hooked cross.

It would seem to be possible to reach larger numbers of people by compromising with evil. The danger is, however, that while you try to knock off the hooks which have grown on the cross, you are still unable to check the movement of the rolling wheel. For the swastika is not static; and it moves in a definite direction. The Reichkanzler's last speech makes very clear in which direction the swastika is going. The cause of the cross is completely different; it moves in absolutely the opposite direction.

Hitler spoke of the swastika as the sign of the sun, already used by Germanic ancestors. In the Far East it is seen as a symbol of the rotating movement of all things according to the law of cause and effect—the karma.

The rotating sun-wheel points to this stern sequence of cause and effect, sin and expiation, crime and retaliation. That is why the Nazi movement has a certain right to claim the swastika. First, there is the rotating movement (cause and effect) represented by this symbol; second, there is the idea of retaliation, of punishment, of judgment, of the karma—the concept that guilt calls inexorably for punishment. The state claims that it is justified in using the heaviest punishment against any act that threatens this government. National Socialism cannot be traced to the cross; it is a movement in absolute opposition to the cross.

We have to acknowledge the direction given by Paul, "Let every person be subject to the governing authorities," who have the power to punish evil and protect good, to demand retribution. That's what the governing authorities are there for, a weapon in the hands of the judging God of the Old Testament, in the hands of God who still must rule as judge over those not yet ready to follow his spirit.

I would feel authorized by the brotherhood to reach out to the president of our government, and if at all possible to Hitler personally. I would not only acknowledge his power as our governmental authority, but rather would bring more sharply to his mind—in the sense of God's justice—that he should only judge and punish evil with true justice, without excess. And not in such a way that good elements are also punished. They say, however, that the churches, the schools, the administration of justice—everything—should only serve the purposes of the nation. But that is not the final purpose of government: it must go further. The final purpose of governmental authority is to place the nation in the service of justice, for good against evil.

In all modesty, we have to represent to the government the prophetic spirit of the New Testament. We have to say to the government: we respect your task, your mandate; you are the government we must acknowledge. There is a higher law, however, which places the service of perfect love, the service of community and unity right into the midst of chaos. Accept this service for yourselves, let yourselves be reminded of the ultimate and final goal. This ultimate goal is the kingdom of peace and unity represented and lived already here and now by the church of Jesus Christ.

In this sense we appeal to you: allow us to live in this country—ruled by you—as a church with a quite different mandate. Over against governmental authority and the judgment you exercise, we represent God's ultimate and final purpose. And all nations, including the German nation, will find fulfillment when the kingdom of peace and joy descends on earth. Then there will indeed be a classless society, in which God alone rules and no human dictator.

You men of the government must receive that message, lest this ultimate goal vanish from your hearts. Therefore tolerate communities that live in this way, rejecting private property and armed violence. Allow them to live in this land; Germany will be the better for it.[14]

The county seat governing the Rhön Bruderhof was in the city of Fulda; at the regional level the Bruderhof was answerable to the office in Kassel. Both Eberhard and Emmy had acquaintances in government positions. He wanted to speak directly to those in the highest positions to explain the Bruderhof's position and try to establish a friendship. This, he believed, would be the best protection for the group as well as for its foreign and Jewish members.

The Bruderhof's private school was supported by the government. The building had been completed in 1928; the *Regierungspräsident* (regional governor) in Kassel, Dr. Friedensburg, had attended the opening ceremony. He had joined the community members on plain wooden benches and was moved when everyone stood up and sang a familiar hymn. When the cold winter weather set in, he phoned to ask how the children were doing and sent a truckload of coal for heating.[15] In mid March 1933, however, Dr. Friedensburg was relieved of his post as governor. On March 28, Eberhard took a trip to Kassel to meet his replacement.

The brotherhood gathered in the morning before he set off. "I would like a direction from the brotherhood for the charges that I will take with me from God and from the church," Eberhard said.

> We must be aware that this trip brings a decision as to whether we want to stay here or leave the country. We must consider the following: if part of the brotherhood is deported (the Swiss or Baltic members), we must see that as a good reason for us all to emigrate together. It will require a vital decision. We are not bound to any place. God will prepare the place for us, we do not know where. Perhaps that place is here—if we can carry on the work we are required to do and continue in our task of mission. Under no circumstance can we deviate from our one goal of the kingdom of God.[16]

They sat together in an intimate circle. Easter was approaching, and they remembered Jesus, who had died at the hand of the Roman government. They all knelt down and prayed for guidance and protection.

The new regional governor was Baron von Monbart. He showed little interest in what Eberhard had to say, and the trip was a disappointment.

On his way home Eberhard stopped in Fulda to see the District Administrator Baron von Gagern. Von Gagern had admired the Bruderhof ever since Eberhard had stopped in at his office years earlier to ask about purchasing the neglected Rhön farmstead—although he had not had the money to pay for it. The district administrator was a devout Catholic and had listened in amazement when Eberhard told him that he believed in miracles as his economic basis, and he had never been disappointed. Over the years von Gagern had watched the Bruderhof grow and flourish.[17] Now he too was feeling the noose tightening. "Herr Arnold," he said, "I have to tell you that I have received complaints against you. These will have to be investigated."

When Eberhard got home, he walked through the kitchen and asked the girls to bake a cake. "I think we will soon have a visit from the police," he explained. Two days later he asked if the cake was ready.

"Oh, Eberhard, I didn't think you were serious!" Sophie answered.

"Of course I'm serious," Eberhard said. "We need to be ready for our guests."[18]

They arrived on April 12: six rural police led by the district chief of police, five SS men, and a representative of the Nazi Party. They stayed for five hours, looking through the bedrooms, the library, and the office for anything that would "endanger the state." Then they went into the dining room where Sophie served them cake and coffee. Eberhard explained to them: "We respect the government in everything that does not conflict with our conscience as Christians. We must live for peace, for justice, for the joy of God's kingdom in full community, and we will not lift a finger for the armed services."

Although the men were quite friendly, the brothers and sisters were left with a sense of foreboding.

~

Communists, Social Democrats, and trade unionists were beaten and their offices trashed by storm troopers. On March 20, Himmler announced the opening of a concentration camp for political prisoners in Dachau, just outside Munich. Two days later, two hundred prisoners were transferred there from other jails. The Nazi's hatred was directed most intensely against the Jews. Storm troopers broke into synagogues, smashed the windows of Jewish shops, and beat and humiliated Jews on the streets. On April 1, a national boycott of Jewish shops was declared. Signs appeared: *Deutsche! Wehrt Euch! Kauft nicht bei Juden!* (Germans! Beware! Do not buy from Jews!) Laws excluded them from universities, from legal professions, and from any position of public service.

During this period, the Bruderhof print shop printed the chapter "Light and Fire" of Eberhard's book *Innerland*. This was a conscious testimony in the face of National Socialism, and later that year Eberhard sent a copy to Adolf Hitler personally. Here he explored in greater depth the confrontation between Christians and the state:

> Times of darkness call for faith in light from above. Before this light, all darkness will retreat, just as morning triumphs over every night. The ugliness and horror of darkness and its cold, murderous spirits must penetrate our consciousness. In utter helplessness, we must be on watch for the hour of redemption.[19]
>
> Christ stands in opposition to every worldly ruler. His kingdom is not of this world. Therefore he said: "The princes and powers of this world lord it over the people, but you should not." A Christian, therefore, is not a ruler, and a ruler is not a Christian. A ruler must exercise judgment with the sword. In the church of Christ there is an end of war and violence, lawsuits and legal action. Christ does not repay evil with evil. His followers show his nature in all their doings. They act as he did: they do not resist evil, and they give their back to the smiters and their cheek to those that pluck off the hair. Their task is to reveal the kingdom of love. Legal authorities are appointed to shed blood in judgment; the church of Christ, however, has the task of preserving life and soul. The law courts of the state must bring evil to account; the church of Jesus Christ must repay evil with good. The authorities that sit in judgment must hate and persecute the enemies of their order; the church of Christ must love them.
>
> With the instrument of governmental authority, God's wrath punishes the wicked. Through the authorities, he compels nations that are estranged from him to protect themselves from the worst harm so that the whole land does not become guilty of bloodshed, the whole earth does not have to be destroyed. Christ gives his church a completely different task. She must confront the forcible execution of justice in the world state with the peace of unity and the joy of love, with brotherly justice. She builds up and maintains her unity with no other tools than those of love and the spirit. In the faith of the church, death and the law come to an end. The freedom of the kingdom of God begins in the church.[20]

He wrote about the swastika, claiming it for all peoples, including the Jews:

> The swastika (symbolizing both a wheel of fire and the turning wheel of the sun) points to this kindling of flame, which from remotest times was held to be holy. The swastika is an ancient symbol of fire sticks laid at right angles. The hooks at the ends of the sticks suggest quick motion like a whirling wheel, showing the quick rotation that causes ignition. The spark is the result of the motion. Thus in the Far East the swastika, as the fire-cross denoting kindling in primitive times, became the symbol for cause and effect. Rotary friction was recognized as the cause and fire as the effect.
>
> The fact that we find this fire-cross of two hooked sticks as early as the new stone age proves that it had universal significance. As a symbol of life and community, the kindling of fire by the twirling of sticks is the common property of all peoples. As a symbol of fire-kindling and of the sun-wheel, the swastika belongs to primeval people. All descendents, without distinction of race and blood, have a right to it. So it is not surprising that all the Aryan tribes as well as the Phoenicians of Canaan preserved this sign of the life-giving power of sunlight and fire-kindling. Fire, the kindling of fire, and the community of fire belong also to the Jewish inhabitants of Canaan.[21]

He addressed the question of blood and race—an idea that would lead to the murder of millions of Jews:

> Without the fire of the Holy Spirit, community dies. It peters out in slavery to alien peoples where other flames burn—unholy fires of our own works and the emotional enthusiasm of blood, which is demonic.[22]

Innerland, and the chapter "Light and Fire" in particular, was a deliberate public statement Eberhard Arnold made at this decisive moment of Germany's history.

~

Everyone living at the Rhön Bruderhof recognized the need to be firmly grounded. On April 15, Eberhard baptized a group of twenty-one, including his two youngest children, Hans-Hermann and Monika. The next day, Easter Sunday, he spoke very seriously:

> There is so much suffering in the world. We hear rumors of a new European war. When a political and military alliance is formed between Italy and Germany, the war will be upon us. Right now Herr von Papen and Goering are in Italy negotiating with Mussolini. At the same time there is the war between China and Japan, and inside Russia the Soviet army is ready for war. A student told me that faculty circles in Marburg are definitely of the opinion that Germany will be at war in a very short time. And Marburg is a center for National Socialist university people.
>
> Christ was killed by the most disciplined army and the most thorough legal system: Rome. He was murdered by the most pious and religious people. He was crucified by the majority cry of the democratic masses. His execution was based on political and religious reasons, and we in our day can expect such executions once again—for political and religious motives ... In other words, in this year—1900 years after Jesus died on the cross—we find ourselves standing under the sign of the gallows, the cross. So with trembling hearts we hear that in the year 1933 Hitler has erected a gallows in Germany. The important thing now is to ask ourselves whether we are prepared in this year to be hanged on this gallows—in Fulda or Kassel or Berlin—to be hanged even this year.[23]

The brotherhood circle met every night after dinner. As they encouraged one another to trust in God, Eberhard repeatedly emphasized the seriousness of the hour.

> We gather for prayer in order to confess our nothingness and inadequacy, to declare before God that we cannot say the kingdom of God is here, but to plead that it come. We approach God with empty hands. We raise them and open them to him, and we kneel before him to express our smallness and emptiness. In this way we come to God in the absolute certainty that Jesus' words are true: The kingdom of God has drawn near! And when you ask God for the Holy Spirit, nothing will be impossible for you. Miracles will take place, mountains will be torn from their position, and the whole situation as it is on earth will be changed.
>
> This is true not only for you and the limited extent of your daily life, but if your prayer is genuine, if you really want nothing but the kingdom of God, then you will think of all the countries of the world. You will call upon God to intervene in the history of the nations, in the history of classes, in the history that has brought injustice to its climax; you will call upon him to come with his judgment and to let his righteousness and his peace break in like the dawn. That is the prayer of the church of God.

It is dangerous to call upon God in this way, for it means we are ready, not only to rise from our place, but to be hurled down from our place. Let us concentrate all our powers on Jesus' nearness, on the silent coming of the Holy Spirit, ready for everything to be changed by his intervention.[24]

∼

When the summer semester opened on April 1, Hardy transferred his studies from the University of Tübingen to Zurich. From the safety of Switzerland, he wrote a letter at his father's request to Elias Walter, a Hutterian elder in Alberta, Canada, informing Walter of the perilous situation confronting the Bruderhof.

April 27, 1933

Unfortunately, my dear father can no longer write in specifics about our Bruderhof because we are under constant police surveillance. Letters may be opened at any time without our knowledge. It is now forbidden in Germany, on pain of imprisonment, to write to anyone abroad about what the present authorities have done, will do, or allow to be done. Therefore we ask you not to write a single word about the German government in any letter you write to Germany. If you do, our servants of the Word will be put into prison.

Twice, armed police were on our property, the second time only a few days ago on the Wednesday before Easter. They surrounded our place with armed men as though we threatened them with war. Nineteen hundred years ago Jesus said, "You came out with swords and staves to take me, as though against a murderer" (Matt 26:55).

We will not leave Jesus Christ and his way. My father has notified the authorities . . . that we must live for peace, for justice, and for the joy of God's kingdom in full community, that we cannot lift a finger for the armed services of the German military but that we do respect and recognize the government wherever that does not conflict with our conscience as Christians and does not contradict the words of Jesus Christ.

They occupied our houses for five hours with armed power and searched everything. They examined our writings and books for anything against the government. It was clear that they would find nothing, because nothing evil or violent can ever be among us . . . A high government official warned us ahead of time that because unknown enemies had denounced us, armed police were coming. So my dear father … had asked for a cake to be baked, and when they came, he invited them to coffee and cake. The miracle happened: they came in a spirit of enmity, but all twelve men accepted our hospitality. They sat with my dear father at our communal table listening to the truth of the Gospel …

We expect the government to make it difficult for our school to continue. My father asks me to tell you that we will emigrate only if we simply have to shake the dust from our feet. We shall do it immediately if we are no longer allowed to proclaim the full gospel; if we may no longer go out on mission; if we are no longer permitted to instruct children and young people in the right way; and if no more people come to us seeking God and his kingdom, Christ and his church, who long for the life and movement of the Holy Spirit.

We do not know when things will come to that point in Germany. At present our church continues to gather and increase in inward strength and in mission. This was shown at our Easter celebration when more were baptized, and more were present at the Lord's Supper than we have ever had. Our dining room will soon be too small for all the brothers and sisters.

So our community asks you: please be on the lookout for a place for a hundred and twenty or more of us to come to you in America before long, should the time come for God to give us the great joy of being joined with you as neighbors.

All the brothers and sisters greet you, especially my dear father, in courageous faith and with joy and unity in the love of Christ. I have been entrusted to receive here in Switzerland all letters from you that deal with difficult questions concerning the German authorities and emigration.[25]

4

May to June 1933

"Honor the Worker!" Adolf Hitler proclaimed on May 1, 1933. For the past fifty years, the Labor Movement had made this day an International Workers' Day. Now Hitler announced that May Day would be celebrated throughout the coming centuries in Germany in honor of the German worker. In Berlin, thousands of people marched the streets led by brass bands of storm troopers playing patriotic songs. Over a million people gathered under a sea of Nazi flags in the evening to hear Hitler's voice booming over the radio.

The first of May was also an important day of celebration at the Rhon Bruderhof—a day to rejoice in the end of winter with singing, folk dancing, and often a maypole. The girls wound garlands of flowers for their hair, and little boys tied bunches of flowers to sticks: holding them high they walked around the buildings singing May songs.

The rising tide of nationalism cast an ominous shadow over this year's festivities, however. The day before, the police had come up to the Rhön Bruderhof to make sure its members would take part in the national festivities. How should they respond without participating in the nationalistic fervor?

The sun rose on a bright spring day. Apple trees were in full blossom, and the meadows were bright with dandelions. After breakfast the community gathered for worship. Eberhard opened the meeting:

> We need to meet this morning and remind ourselves of what the way of the church is. We want to let God speak to us in silent worship and to ask him to stand by us in all that confronts us.

After some minutes of silence, he spoke again.

> The First of May is kept everywhere as a day celebrating work. We too have every reason to think about it and to remind ourselves of what work means to us. What is the goal that we work for? What distinguishes our work from that done in the business world of capitalism? What is the ultimate meaning of our work? We have always rejected the bloody class struggle; we wage a spiritual fight to win all strata of society for the kingdom of God.
>
> In recent months the previous government was swept away. The red flags we used to see on the First of May have been suppressed, and if you walk through the streets of a town today, you will see the swastika displayed at every house.[1]

When the meeting closed, the young men and women prepared for their own parade. They had decided to make a maypole as they always did. On it they tied ribbons of black, white, and red, the colors of the German flag. Then they added blue and yellow for Sweden, white and red for Switzerland, and black and gold for Austria. When the delegation arrived from the neighboring village to invite them to join the parade starting at the firehouse, they apologized that they had already scheduled a procession and couldn't come. The whole community walked across their fields and over the knoll led by Hans and Margrit Meier on their violins, the children with their garlands and flower sticks.[2] Edith wrote about it to Hardy:

> The First of May was a fine day here, very festive. The maypole and the children with many flowers—like a painting by Richter. Everybody was very happy, and there was a unity that went right down into every smallest detail. We danced all day.[3]

That evening a few of the brothers went to the neighboring village of Eichenried to listen to Hitler on the radio. Hitler promised that compulsory labor service would reestablish manual labor as honorable work by the end of the year. But his words of honoring the worker were a clever piece of trickery. The next day brownshirts and SS men stormed the trade union offices throughout the country. Union officials were arrested. In Duisburg four were beaten to death.

~

After the war, many Germans were shocked at the atrocities that had taken place, of which they had been unaware. Eberhard was under no such illusion. He told the community:

> A hundred foreign newspapers have been banned. Max Wolf [a Jewish friend in Schlüchtern] is in protective custody, accused of being connected with communism. Marxist literature along with the classics and romantics will be confiscated. Many people have been put in concentration camps.[4]

Heiner later said:

> When Hitler came into power my father was extremely sad. Once when I was alone with him he told me quite a number of stories that did not appear in the papers. He told me that in the neighboring village of Sterbfritz the Nazis took a Jewish man, stripped him, and beat him, and left him in a ditch. He had to walk home without trousers, to his great humiliation and the joke of the Nazis. Papa told me some of the things that happened in the concentration camps. These things were completely unknown, and I asked him, "Where do you know that?" He said, "It is better you don't know in case you are once asked." He had some source where he got information, someone among the Nazis, I think, who was against it.[5]

National Socialism was attempting a cultural revolution "in which alien cultural influences—notably the Jews but also modernist culture more generally—were eliminated and the German spirit reborn. Germans were not merely to acquiesce in the Third Reich, they had to "support it with all their heart and soul."[6] As part of this revolution, German students organized the burning of "un-German" books on May 10. Huge bonfires were lit in Berlin and thousands of books were thrown into the flames—books by internationally respected authors such as Erich Maria Remarque, Friedrich Wilhelm Förster, Erich Kästner, Thomas Mann, Stefan Zweig, Albert Einstein, Jack London, and Helen Keller.

Annemarie Wächter followed with great interest and concern the developments at her beloved Keilhau. For decades, her family had run the boarding school founded by the renowned educator Friedrich Froebel. Now she learned that the school had been forced to hire a Nazi teacher. Eberhard answered:

> Teachers with a socialist view are being discharged everywhere. If my book *Innerland,* which I hope will be in book stores by October 1, were discovered as being in any way anti-Hitler, our school might also be assigned a National Socialist director, whom we would have to pay. If Hitler continues as he is now, not only the question of labor service but our whole attitude to life will

become critical. Let us ask God that we may hold on to freedom of conscience in these times of bondage; that we neither become silent and no longer speak up about our calling, nor become cowardly fugitives who leave the battlefield before their duty is done. Let us ask God that our conscience may be filled with the whole Christ, with the absoluteness of his truth, so that we in no point lag behind what he demands on the way of his discipleship.[7]

Love Your Enemy

Christians everywhere were clearly struggling to find a response to National Socialism. Leonhard Ragaz, the Swiss Religious Socialist, wrote a column on the world situation in his monthly periodical *Neue Wege* (New Paths). In recent issues, Germany dominated the scene. He wrote with justified indignation of the lies at the opening of the Reichstag in March, of suppression and mistrust, of the murder of dozens of people, the dismissal of Jewish professors, doctors, and lawyers, of the threat of war, and the fact that the churches were not lifting a finger in protest.[8] In the May issue he wrote about the concentration camps where 30,000 to 50,000 socialists, communists, and pacifists were being held.

> What is to be done? If anything is to be done, all those who recognize the danger need to stand together in a new, energetic politics of peace, to which Germany too needs to commit itself unconditionally ... The infamous Four Power Pact* was an attempt, but it has more or less died ... The danger is great and human help almost hopeless. But God sits on his throne and his path goes through deep waters. That is our only comfort.[9]

Ragaz's article was read and discussed at the dinner table one evening at the end of May. Eberhard did not deny Ragaz's allegations, but he was disappointed that he seemed to have lost sight of the kingdom of God. He explained his difference with Ragaz in a letter to their common friend, the Anabaptist historian in Vienna Robert Friedmann.

> You must know that, in many a service of truth, we perceive this Leonhard-John as a significant light kindled in the darkness of the present times.† And yet his work is not a light because it ap-

---

* The Four Power Pact between Britain, France, Italy, and Germany was called for by Mussolini on 19 March 1933 to ensure international security.

† Eberhard seems to be referring to Ragaz metaphorically as John the Baptist.

pears to be far too optimistic about the ability of the League of Nations to develop and assume government. Peace and justice of the kingdom of God? In this way? It should now finally be recognized that this evolutionism lies in ruins. It has been shattered by the judgment of God's anger. It is true that God's goodness is growing; but at the same time so is the evil of the devil.[10]

This led to discussions on different forms of government. "One thing that strikes me," Eberhard said, "is that for the future state Jesus is not proclaimed as president of the republic of God, but as the coming king."[11]

But one gets the impression that under the tyrannical despotism of the present government, one can no longer rely on any law. What Hannes says is right: the limits of the law have been overstepped by a monarch—not merely a monarch, but a tyrant, who can do as he wishes without any constitutional restraints.

If we look back to the time when we enjoyed the protection of the government (whereas now we can definitely expect persecution) I believe that in the Social Democrats [the previous government] there was a genuine respect for human rights. In this sense I am convinced that Social Democracy was better, more just, more devoted to freedom than the National Socialist Party. That is absolutely clear. It really is politics of the dirtiest kind that treads the law underfoot, a wickedness that cries to heaven, a revolting, lawless frivolity.

I can well imagine that a Swiss feels very deep pain on having to see and feel this around him. A religious feeling of reverence for life is injured. Consequently it comes to a point where he feels a kind of nostalgia about a democracy such as that in Switzerland. He also feels a certain obligation to protest now in the name of this relatively better thing against something that is much worse. It is good for us to be reminded of this.

However, we must see that even in the cruelest tyrants there is a certain amount of honest idealism. So too, in Hitler and Mussolini there is high idealism, a sacrificing of self so that the different classes can be leveled. Hitler has the idea he can set up a real community. We must realize that this is idealism, devotion to a high goal. But the means are evil, they are means of suppression, enslavement. It seems important to me that after we have recognized very clearly the relative differences between good and bad forms of government, we must also see that the wildest, most tyrannical violence by the state evidences to an intense degree something that is also evident in the best, noblest, most purified form of government: rapacious violence. We must not forget that in the Revelation of Jesus Christ the church that rules by wealth and might is designated as the harlot, and the state as the beast of prey from the abyss. (This includes the best form of government as well as the worst form.) And the connection is Babylon, which must be overthrown on the Last Day when God judges.[12]

Hannes Boller, a Swiss who had been inspired by Leonhard Ragaz, had trouble understanding what Eberhard said about finding something positive in National Socialism. He and Adolf Braun exchanged some sharp words. That night Hannes asked to be excused from the united prayer until he could honestly agree with everybody. Instead of excluding him, the brotherhood did not pray together.

The next morning, May 28, at 5:00, gunshots shattered the silence. Arno Martin, looked out the window—his baby daughter had woken from the noise. About sixty storm troopers were firing their rifles in the fields next to the community buildings. He called out to them to be quiet, that there were children sleeping. "No one should be sleeping at this time of day!" the storm troopers retorted. Some of them came into the yard and the barn and demanded to be shown the print shop. When they left, they trampled through the hayfield.

In the evening the brotherhood met again. Hannes felt terrible that at such a moment he had hindered the unity of the group. Eberhard encouraged him: "If in a moment you get worked up and cannot pull yourself together, it is right to do what Hannes has done. I do not know how you could have done better. For us it is better to wait for the prayer."[13]

Brothers and sisters continued discussing what attitude to take. Georg Barth spoke. "We reject Ragaz's one-sided view; our goal is a different one. We seek the way of love. We cannot put ourselves above those to whom we wish to speak. We are all children of one Father."

"There is a key to every human heart, and this key is the key to understanding. Only we have not yet found it," Eberhard said. Love, not politics, was the Christian response.

> We will not join a democratic party. We represent neither the politics of National Socialism and German patriotism, . . . nor those of the League of Nations whose negotiations demonstrate that politics and capitalism rule beneath the veneer of high ideals. Because of that we cannot say that the League of Nations has the same task that has been assigned to us.
>
> The ideals of National Socialism are neither great nor original, but that is no reason for us to look down on them. Everything

Hitler says today is familiar to us from its more idealistic form in the youth movement. What I read somewhere is true: there could be no Hitler without the youth movement. He is indebted to it for its wealth of ideas.

What are the National Socialist ideals? A national community of one blood, nation, and race. Within this people's community there should be no degrading inequalities based on status or class. All social levels are to enjoy equal rights ... The intellectuals should no longer look down on the uneducated. Employers should not treat their workers as though they were only figures on a balance sheet. The oppressed class, in particular the factory workers, should not feel hatred toward the upper class and call for a class war ... They call this concept socialism, which is, of course, a misnomer. Under true socialism the oppressed class is given material help; the Nazis do not give that help ...

Of course, in stark contrast to this lofty idea there are, exactly as with the Marxist communists, horrifying facts, which cry to heaven. That is quite clear to us. We want to be fair, however, and declare that in spite of these facts we do not reject the ideals. We want to appreciate the people holding them and show them that we love them just as much as we loved the petty communists in [our neighboring village]. They are the same people and have the same hearts. We will not let ourselves be deceived by the change in outer forms. They have not turned into another type of people. They are people with the same human feelings as before, they have only delivered themselves up to another leadership. But that is no reason for us to deny them our love or refuse our service ...

We must be given the attitude not to convert a man until we love him. But you can love a man only when you have understood what is living in him. I do not truly love my fellowman if I have not understood with my whole heart what is holiest and loftiest to him ...

We have to meet the Nazis and the now oppressed communists with exactly that same attitude. After we have found that inner understanding, we have to represent the politics of the kingdom of Jesus Christ. That is our stand, which contradicts that of Ragaz.

After coming to a heart-to-heart exchange with the Nazis, when we confront them with the policy of the coming kingdom of God, we are going to collide sharply with them ... The Nazi ideal is fragmentary; and their practice is utterly contrary to the goal of the kingdom of God.

> We represent the conquest of the earth for the peace of Jesus Christ ... We must challenge the Nazis as well as the communists to consider what true community really means and to ask themselves if they should not pursue that goal too. That's why it is so important that in our daily practical work ... we truly act as brothers and sisters. Above all, we must demonstrate in our whole life the perfect unanimity of true comradeship and community, so that despite the weaknesses of human inadequacy that are always with us, a little of this unity will shine through. We will not fight for the Third *Reich*. We shall fight for the final *Reich*, God's kingdom, and for nothing else![14]

When Eberhard went to call on the district administrator's office in Fulda to report the ugly early-morning incident, he was startled to find that his good friend Baron von Gagern had been moved to Melsungen near Kassel. There, higher Nazi officials could presumably keep a closer eye on him; he had been replaced as district administrator by Dr. Burkhardt, a former veterinary surgeon and now a fanatical Nazi.

∼

Norman Körber, a friend from the beginning of *Neuwerk*, developed a strong admiration for Hitler. In Sannerz he had tutored the older Arnold children. He was one of many who left after a dispute in 1922. However, he remained a friend and always respected Eberhard. He was a lawyer and had taken a position in Kassel as a youth councilor.

On June 8, 1933, Eberhard went to see him. "Believe me, Eberhard," he exclaimed, "if you would see and hear Hitler you would also be convinced!"[15] When Eberhard asked him if he thought compulsory labor service or military service would be introduced, he was reassuring. (The following year labor service was demanded of university students.)

Eberhard also visited von Gagern and several other acquaintances; he heard various points of view. When he came home he told about his trip at the dinner table:

> I have a strong, general impression that there are growing misgivings about the present form of government, especially among men who are conscious of their responsibility. Some of them feel that it is impossible for the present state of affairs to be maintained for many years. It seems as though we are heading toward a new collapse of the economy of the civilized world that can hardly be stopped. It is

so serious that this scourge of God, which has doubtless come over Germany through God's world rulership, may soon be dismantled and cast away. One of the leading men told me he felt people would be grateful to the National Socialists for revealing many evils, but that their task would then be fulfilled and they could step down. It amazed me to what extent people opened their hearts about all these things. Even people who were once National Socialists now have misgivings.

The whole thing seems to me like the labor pains of the last days. Whether it is the final end time we do not know. The end times of God move in circles; they return and begin again and again, until finally they break out altogether.

I spoke quite openly. I said that we do not want to hide, but that our intention is to take the offensive in decisive places. Our offensive will consist in an avalanche of petitions that will give us the opportunity to press forward and present the cause entrusted to us with seriousness yet still with love, recognizing their ideals. That is our task. No doubt we are facing difficult times, but I believe we have no reason for fear. We should look forward that it will be possible, and I hope very soon, to witness to God's innermost heart in front of these people.[16]

Several visitors were present in the dining room and heard what Eberhard said. Later that night, he worried that he had spoken too freely. The next day the brotherhood met and he apologized. "I should not have spoken as I did in such a large circle, particularly as I implicated several officials. I regret this from my heart. I want to submit to the judgment of the church and take on a discipline of silence for some days."

His son-in-law Hans Zumpe responded: "I'm sorry that we did not give you an opportunity to speak in a suitable circle after your trip. We were all eager to hear your very important report." Arno and Georg agreed.

Adolf Braun said, "I thought the bell would ring and the brotherhood be called together as soon as you returned. We are all to blame."

"How shall I continue?" Eberhard asked. "Should I lay down my service for a time and be silent?"

The members disagreed with this suggestion and expressed support for Eberhard's continued leadership.

"Good," he responded. "Then I will not speak about it any more. It is as dangerous as ever to talk freely in Germany. You should not think that anything has changed or that the power of National Socialism is over. What felt different was the mood among the intellectuals, including some very responsible officials."[17]

On June 25, Kurt and Marianne celebrated their wedding. This was an occasion the whole community took part in. The children sang and performed dances and Hans and Margrit Meier played a violin duet. Heiner did a skit by Hans Sachs, and Emy-Margret recited a poem. The bridal couple went to the state registry to make their marriage legal, but Eberhard Arnold would solemnize it.

> It is fitting for our couple to go to the registrar's office and register their marriage; this has to be done. Through this order of the state their marriage is made known to the material world. The real marriage or wedding, however, can be confirmed through the spiritual unity of the church alone. We are in a hard fight against a hostile government which would like to enslave our souls and spirits with false teachings, a government which again today would like to oppress our hearts and which has nothing in common with the way of Jesus Christ. We stand in the midst of this world as a fighting and persecuted group, persecuted for the sake of the cause of complete community of faith and unity of God's people. Let us always keep this persecution in mind and never forget that it is hard and heavy, but that it will yet lead to victory and to the final goal of peace. Many diverse and strange teachings are trying to gain ground in so-called Christianity. All these teachings seek coercion and suppression. They do not convey the pure teaching of Jesus Christ and his spirit of unity and justice, "Do not be led away by diverse and strange teachings; for it is well that the heart be strengthened by grace" (Heb 13:9).[18]

5

June to October 1933

The Churches

HITLER NEEDED THE SUPPORT of the Catholic and Lutheran Churches. In his speech to the Reichstag of March 23, 1933, he had promised to uphold religion. On July 20, a concordat was signed between Germany and Rome. The Vatican agreed to it, believing it would protect Germany's Catholics and grant them freedom of religion. But it effectively silenced Catholic criticism of Hitler's policies by excluding clergy from political parties, and it validated the National Socialist government before the world.[1]

German Protestantism was fragmented. Hitler proposed to unite Lutherans, Zwinglians, and Calvinists under the name "German Christians," which he hoped would eventually win the Catholics as well. The Evangelical church, with its twenty-eight autonomous regional churches, was to be replaced by a "Reich Church" under a "Reich bishop." The man Hitler had in mind for this role was Ludwig Müller, a military chaplain. But here Hitler met his first road block. Church leaders nominated Friedrich von Bodelschwingh, a humble pastor and director of a home for the disabled. Bodelschwingh did not desire the job. He wrote in a letter on May 23:

> No one who truly knows me and my work will believe that I could be considered for such a task. Here I am a pastor of the epileptics and of the brethren of the road, and I have attempted to carry on quietly the work of our Father ... I do not understand church politics ... I belong neither to the German Christians nor to the National Socialist Party.[2]

Bodelschwingh was elected, and he accepted this post with a call to repentance and humility:

> The German church confesses that it has been guilty of much and has neglected much. We Christians have not taken seriously enough the responsibility that God has given us in the gospel. We should have been more truthful, more humble, more active. We should have resisted more bravely the powers that make the human being the slave of money and put selfishness in the place of service.
>
> With its distress and guilt, the church comes into the light of the One who alone can cleanse us and make us alive. We place our trust completely in the God who has redeemed us from death through the dying and rising of our Lord Jesus Christ, so that we may be obedient to him from the bottom of our hearts.
>
> I have not coveted this episcopal office for myself: I am following the path of obedience. If those in authority in the church have entrusted me with a task, coming as I do from work among the poor and the sick, then that shows the way on which I have to continue. It is the way of the deaconate. If it were up to me, I would be rather called Reich Deacon than Reich Bishop. But the name does not matter. The ministry should receive its content from a will not to rule but rather to serve, in humble imitation of the one who "came not to be served but to serve and give his life a ransom for many."[3]

Unsurprisingly, Bodelschwingh was forced to resign under Nazi pressure, and a few weeks later Ludwig Müller became the Reich bishop.

On June 16, a census was taken throughout Germany. On the forms that every citizen filled out he had to include his religious affiliation.[4] This, of course, forced the Jews to identify themselves. At lunch that day, Eberhard took the opportunity to speak about the concept of the church of God and the brotherhood's relationship to the state church.

> On the occasion of the census we learned that there are thirty-two in our household who still belong to one of the large world churches. We must in all things live vitally, and all that is false must yield to that which is genuine. All that is not born of the living Spirit is false. The church is called the "ecclesia," that is, the gathering or group which has been called forth. If the world

church embraces all the falseness of present-day civilization, then there is nothing left from which it can be called out. Thus it can no longer be a true church. The nature of the true church is no different from that of the ultimate kingdom. The church shall be those called forth and gathered from all over the world during the time when the kingship of God's realm has not yet been established on earth.

The nations today, together with every aspect of the economic and social fabric, are utterly remote from justice, love, peace, joy, brotherhood, community, and unity. They do not live in and for each other as one communal, living entity. The world church is not an organism. There is no world society; there is no national community; there is no unity amid the conflicting beings. There is no justice, no peace, and no joy. Discord, misery, pain, the inflicting of mutual wrong and injury—this is the character of humankind's struggle for existence, both between nations and between families or individuals. It is a fact that people are more against each other than for each other.

The church of God is placed in this world as an embassy of the coming kingdom. This group which has been called out must again be sent back into the circles out of which they were called. In this way, the church which has been called out is at the same time sent out; it is commissioned to act according to the laws of the other state. Its policy is on a different basis from that of the worldly states; its policy is founded upon God and his will to love and righteousness. The task of the church is to be the embassy of a different kind of politics: to represent the kingdom of God.[5]

Just at this time, in early July, a Lutheran pastor was visiting the Bruderhof. In several meetings he was asked his opinion on the situation, and lively discussions took place. Eberhard said:

In the last two weeks churches face more and more difficulties. This Sunday, July 2, all pastors have to hoist the swastika flag at all churches and parsonages. Those who do not will be suspended immediately. Several have already been removed. Our dear Pastor Knote is an example of how the church lets itself be pushed around; he shows how soft the backbone of the church has become.

During recent weeks the state has taken other forceful measures with regard to the church. The army chaplain Pastor Müller has taken over the spiritual leadership. The Lutheran Evangelical church seems to be acquiescing in silence.[6]

As a result of these discussions, all brotherhood members who had not already done so resigned from the Catholic or Lutheran Churches. Edith wrote enthusiastically to Hardy:

> Today is an important day! Annemarie and I are sitting here in Neuhof and are tremendously happy. You see, we have taken an extremely important step: we have just declared our resignation from the church. Annemarie will confirm it.

Annemarie added a note:

> I can confirm with my own hand that this is true. It was a completely painless and friendly action.[7]

For the two twenty-three-year-olds this was a concrete move they could make—stepping out of the world church and confirming their commitment to a group that desired to embody the kingdom of God on earth.

Conviction: Are We Ready?

The seriousness of the Bruderhof's situation put every individual member as well as the community's friends at risk. There were lively, earnest discussions with guests. It was increasingly clear that the danger of persecution was real and present.

> God's righteousness and love do not rule. We see it in the fate of the hopeless, the millions upon millions of unemployed. We see it in the unjust distribution of goods, though the earth offers its endless fertility and abundance. Urgent work must be done to help humankind, but it is obstructed by the injustice of the present world systems. We are in the midst of a collapse of civilization. Civilization is simply man's orderly work on nature; but this work has turned into a disorder whose injustice cries out to heaven. Through God's grace we are able to experience—as on a small island—work, justice, love, and community.
>
> When we ask that God's kingdom come, we know that we are asking for judgment. When we ask God to intervene, it means baring our own breasts before him, so that his lightning can strike us, for we are all guilty; no one is without guilt in the injustice of the world as it is today.
>
> We must be prepared to be thrown into prison and killed. What Hitler said is true: "Where wood is being planed, the shavings will fly." As we watch the clouds of the approaching day of judgment mass in the sky, we must be prepared to go the way

of Jesus' cross with our minds completely at peace. Our willingness to accept the cross and death has to become still deeper; only when we are ready for this, can we ask God to intervene and make history.

To be ready is everything! Let us be ready! That means stretching out our hands to God in order to be crucified with him. It means going down on our knees, ready to be humbled by him. It means laying down all our power over ourselves so that he alone may have power over us.

In these days of wrath and judgment the heart of Christ is needed all the more to blaze up in the world and in history. The church is sent into the world for this purpose: in the midst of the mounting waves of panic, in the midst of the furious breakers of spilt blood, the church must fling itself against the waves and bring the banner of love to those who are drowning in loveless wrath.

For this we must be ready. Therefore, at the same moment that we plead for his day to dawn, we ask God to send us out. And not only to those few people whom we meet here on our hill, but to all, including the rich and the oppressed—especially the oppressed. But also as prophets to the wealthy, just as John the Baptist once went to Herod and sacrificed his head.

We cannot ask for God to come, for Christ's way to be followed, for the Holy Spirit to send down his stream, unless we for our part are ready for the utmost. And we all have to be completely agreed about this. Only if we are one in what we ask God for will he grant it, but then he surely will.[8]

Hans Zumpe met a man who had been a novice at the Bruderhof for four years. He wore a SA uniform and greeted Hans with "Heil Hitler." Eberhard spoke further of the way to face the days ahead:

> We will not deliberately have ourselves arrested through human heroism. But we do want to be ready to go to prison or to be dissolved and driven out of the country if this must be. In this sense, it is today a very real challenge when we ask ourselves: Are we ready? Worlds are colliding. If the present government is in conflict with the Catholic Church and the Protestant Church, it is in a much deeper conflict with the gospel of Jesus Christ and with the upper church of the Holy Spirit. We must fight this battle in love; we have no other weapon. And whether we are confronted with a mounted policeman or a labor camp official, a regional governor, a prince, a party leader, or even with the president of the Reich, it makes no difference. We must love them, and only

when we truly love them shall we be able to bring them the witness of truth. That is what we are here for.

This then is our mission: to proclaim the truth as being love, and love as being truth; to come before the mighty and the lowly; to say it because we live it, and to live it as we say it. We must realize that this is the way of death, for there was one who loved to the last, without going along with what was wrong. What was the consequence? The cross on which he was executed!

So it should be with us as well. It cannot be otherwise than that we are imprisoned and killed if we truly go the way of Jesus. If this has not yet happened, it shows we have not yet gone the way of Jesus to the end. And we must not be imprisoned or killed for the sake of any other cause!

In this prophetic spirit, Jesus proclaims the final future and his enmity to the spirit of the times. It is dangerous to declare war on the spirit of the times. Yet this is the prophet's task. The only way we can truly love those men who are tormented and crushed by this spirit is to wage war on the spirit that holds them in demonic bondage. It is the task of the church to be untimely, to be prophetic, to live in the future, and to die for that future.[9]

July 26 was Eberhard's fiftieth birthday. The community planned a big celebration. Some of the members had practiced a play based on the parable of the ten virgins, which they performed in the evening. The print shop had completed the first copies of the second volume of the community's song book *Sonnenlieder*. At lunch time the tables were set outside in the meadow, and they sang together for a long time.[10]

Eberhard was asked to tell about his life. He was quiet for a moment, and when he stood up he spoke humbly and seriously, surprising his listeners:

> On this day I have been especially conscious of my lack of ability, of how unsuited my own nature is to the work I have been given. I have remembered how God called me when I was only sixteen, and how I have stood in his way—with the result that so much of what he wanted to do has been left unfinished . . .
>
> I have had to think of Hermas, that early Christian writer who describes the building of the great temple—how he refers to the many stones that must be thrown away. The attempt is made to fit them into the building, but if they cannot be used, even

after their corners are chipped away by stern, sharp strokes of the chisel, then they must be thrown away—as far away as possible. But even the stones that are used must be chiseled very sharply before they fit and can be set into the wall.

When I look back on the years that Emmy and I have been seeking, then I become very serious, thinking of the many people who for years have been intending to seek this way. I have received a list of all the friends who felt they were called to join us. Many of these stones that seemed for a while to be possibilities have been thrown away again. That is very painful. It troubles me to think of all these stones that have been thrown away, and I wish the day might come when one or another of them would be taken up once more to be chiseled.

Another thing concerns me very much: the powerlessness of man, even of a man who has been entrusted with some task. Only God is mighty; we are completely powerless. We cannot fit even a single stone into the church community. We can provide no protection whatsoever for the community when it has been built up. But I believe that just this is the only reason why God has called us for this service: we know we are powerless. It is hard to describe how all our own power must be stripped off us, how our own power must be dropped, dismantled, torn down, and put away. But it must happen, and it will not happen easily, nor through any single heroic decision. Rather, it must be done by God.

This is the root of grace: the dismantling of our own power. Only to the degree that all our own power is dismantled can God work among us—not otherwise. If a little power of our own were to rise up among us, the spirit and authority of God would retreat in the same moment and to the corresponding degree. In my estimation that is the single most important insight with regard to the kingdom of God.

Let us use this day to give glory to God. Let us pledge to him that all our own power will remain dismantled and will keep on being dismantled. Let us pledge that the only thing that counts among us will be the power and authority of God in Jesus Christ through the Holy Spirit.[11]

Visitors continued to come and the community was growing. During the weeks of harvest there was much work to do. Eberhard and some of the other brothers traveled often, visiting friends in Fulda, Kassel, and other towns. They wanted to find others who felt as they did about the political climate, but they had to be careful what they said to whom. When Emmy wrote to her sons, she warned them in coded language to be careful. She wrote to Hardy, for example, "In every situation, remember the lovely song, *"Seiner Zunge Meister werden ist die schwerste Kunst auf Erden"* (To be master of one's tongue is the most difficult art on earth).[12] When Heiner went to visit Arnold relatives, she wrote to him: "We sang the song about Katharina, Camilla, and Sybilla. You must have thought of it too."[13] The words of this song were: When Katharina, Camilla, and Sybilla are together they gossip of this, that, and the other.

The community continued to meet often, grappling to fathom the dangers and to articulate their common response. As their spokesman, Eberhard wanted to be sure that he spoke for each of them:

> We do not believe that each nation and race has a special perception of God. We believe, rather, that divine truth is absolute, that it was perfectly fulfilled in Christ, is available to all people. Where the Holy Spirit is, there is the power of the future kingdom of peace, justice, love, and brotherliness.
>
> If anyone asks us, "What is your attitude to fatherland and nationhood?" we answer that we have a very high regard for the blood relationship and the common cultural history, the spiritual atmosphere of the nation, just as we have a high regard for the individual family. We believe this is part of the first creation and that we must hold it in high esteem and cherish it with faithful love.
>
> We do not believe, however, that these things should be placed higher than God's kingdom or that we can abandon the spirit of Jesus Christ because of the demands of the state. We believe we will serve our nation and our own family best if we follow most completely the spirit of Jesus Christ, his word and his way. The imitation of Christ is the best service we can render. And that is why we live in community.[14]

Hans and Margrit Meier had come in January. They were followed by Margrit's brother Emil Fischli with his wife; her sister Trautel had joined earlier. The Fischli parents came to visit. They had raised their children with an awareness of social injustice, and they understood the spirit that filled the Rhön Bruderhof. Eberhard spoke on the eve of their departure, urging them to accept God's call:

> The need grows increasingly monstrous. We stand before immense catastrophes that dwarf those of the last eighteen years. Do you want to hesitate until it is too late or will you in this eleventh hour submit your life to the only possible witness for God's kingdom so that true love, true brotherhood, and true justice of resolute courage may come upon the earth? Will you offer up your life for this unity of God's kingdom and brotherhood? It is not a call to a fine religious experience nor to a personal religious happiness, but it is to give everything in to the highest cause, the kingdom of God and its righteousness. To give up everything for this is the only goal worth living and dying for. If we have nothing to die for then we have nothing to live for.[15]

A letter arrived from Elias Walter, the Hutterian elder. Already when Eberhard visited the Hutterites in 1930 he begged for financial help which never materialized. Now once again Walter apologized that he could not collect the money from the other communities that Eberhard had asked for:

> I received your letter of July 22. It is difficult for me to answer because I cannot help you ... The harvest was poor; there was almost no rain. Joseph Stahl was here from South Dakota last week. They have nothing. The hail destroyed everything: geese, chickens, and pigs. A boy even died from hail. There is more misery than a sick heart can bear. The dear Lord will have a reason for it ... Even Arnold's nice letters cannot comfort me. Unwillingly I remember the advice I gave him before he returned home: to visit Rockyfeller [sic] in New York who gives away millions for pleasure. He is a Baptist, and Arnold could have convinced him. I would write to him myself, but don't have his address.[16]

~

In the midst of worry and tension, there were also times of joy. In August the community celebrated the raising of the roof of a new wing to the main house. It was a great encouragement that money had been available for the project, and that people continued to come for whom room must be found. Eberhard said at that occasion:

> The energy that builds this house is the gathering power that unceasingly brings to it those who belong to it. "How often would I have gathered you, but you would not." The desire of this house, and of those it sends out, is that people should be

gathered; its will is to bring together in complete unity all who belong together. This festival should be an occasion for honoring this house, which can be built up only through the activity of the Holy Spirit.[17]

August 18 was Hardy's twenty-first birthday. That day he and Edith Boeker were engaged to be married. Eberhard and Emmy loved the girl he had found, a sensitive, deeply thinking young woman. Everyone rejoiced with the new couple.

A few weeks later the community met to celebrate the completion of another building project: the enlarging of the dining hall. The enlargement of the dining room was the last construction at the Rhön Bruderhof. Many other hoped-for projects could not be realized, and even the dining room was never completely finished. The new dining hall was furnished with wood paneling and simple wood tables. A massive beam above the door to the dining room bore the hand-carved words: "He who is near to me is near to the fire; he who is far from me is far from the kingdom," words attributed to Jesus, quoted in Eberhard's book *The Early Christians*. Opposite the dining room another door opened into the smaller room used for members' meetings. Over this door another carved beam read: "That we from our hearts love one another, of one mind in peace remain together," a line from a hymn by Martin Luther. Georg Barth's artistic ability and sense of style contributed to the overall unity in design. Yet amidst the festivities, no one forgot the seriousness of the hour. Eberhard spoke:

> Often it has seemed as if all the forces of hell were let loose to put a stop to our modest growth. If we continue to meet together to receive the Holy Spirit in humility and lowliness, then this tiny work will have enduring historical significance, eternal significance. Assuming, that is, that no human importance or human piety or holiness is allowed to arise.
>
> We live in extremely dangerous times. I just had an amazing encounter in Kassel with a student pastor. Immediately after Hitler came to power he was given leave of absence. When I asked him about the fate of the state church in Germany, he said that financial support is well assured. And it is also true that the state church will have a political significance, since it will put its preaching at the service of the fascist state. But anyone who resists this state will disappear from the pulpit. The consequence is that the true gospel will be given up for the time being and will

flourish only in concealment. The age of catacomb Christianity will come again. Anyone who attempts to represent the gospel of Jesus Christ in public is immediately silenced. (These are the pastor's words, not mine.) He advises us to go on quietly working, holding firmly to truth in hidden, catacomb Christianity until times change.

He made the observation that a certain mania for martyrdom has started, particularly among students, who offer their breasts to the enemy and in a kind of panic try to be put into a concentration camp. He warned against this. He was convinced that it is not Christianity when martyrdom becomes a craze. Certainly, cowardice in the face of martyrdom is still worse; but a mania for martyrdom is not discipleship of Jesus.

In regard to *Innerland* he thought the book was not dangerous, for it is difficult to read, and in National Socialist circles only easy-to-read books get read. We want to take this book to Hitler, Goering, and Goebbels. He gave me the advance guarantee that they would not read it!

He also refuses to raise his hand in the Heil Hitler salute. He said he felt the demonism was so strong in the power of suggestion, carrying people rapidly back into paganism, that he would rather have an arm chopped off than use it. He saw what an enormous impression the Nazi rally in Nuremberg made: thousands of flags placed together, over four hundred thousand participants—all with arms raised in the air! *Ave Caesar imperator!* That was their mood: "Hail to the Emperor!"

The worst part is the deathblow to public justice. The persecution of the innocent cries to heaven. There is not one state church pastor who does not know of mistreatment in his village. And it is senseless to do anything against it, for it would only harm those concerned. Never before has a government simply abandoned all sense of justice. You cannot imagine a state not based on justice. This government asserts publicly that there are no human rights, only the administration of law in the interest of the fatherland—with no regard for what is just before a higher tribunal. The end result is a heap of ruins; this will kill any national feeling for justice!

We must draw attention to the kingdom of God and his justice, with no way of knowing what is in store for us in the present political situation. Anyone who cannot place the objectivity of the kingdom of God higher than his subjective need for peace and redemption will not be able to hold out here. No matter what we will go through in the great struggles that are coming, we must hold on to this one thing: that we strive first and last for the kingdom of God and his justice. Whatever happens, we ask God to help us keep to his way and direction, that we do nothing out of our own zeal or individual initiative but everything in God's light, following his leading, cost what it may.[18]

The threat of persecution was also a call to decisiveness on the part of members and guests. Quite a number of visitors came in spring 1933 but then left again as fall approached. Eberhard characteristically recognized the symbolic significance of these departures:

> It is a mistake to believe that such atrocities only happened centuries ago. We have to be reminded that Gustav Landauer was trampled to death by the boots of soldiers in our time [May 1, 1919, in a revolution in Bavaria] and in the news we read of similar instances every day. At this hour we remember with heavy hearts all those who left us this summer. All across the centuries there have been people who have wanted to follow the way in spring or summer but who have forsaken it with the setting in of winter and never found it again.[19]

In the last half of September, Eberhard tried to finish his book *Innerland*. In the last chapter he spoke of the "living Word" that God continues to speak into human hearts today as opposed to the "dead letter." When the community met in the evenings, he spoke of God's witnesses through history—giving the younger people a solid education in church history which he hoped would deepen their personal faith.

> I desire with all my heart that each one should be taught by God himself, that each one should learn to read the book of his own heart, that each one should hear the voice of the lamb within him, that each one should receive the living word in his heart and make it deed in his life. And I long, too, that as my book is read, so the books of all God's witnesses, and the Holy Scripture might be read as well—not as if they were God's word, but a testimony to God's word. Then God would remain our only teacher, and the Holy Scripture and all God's witnesses would remain nothing more and could be nothing more than what they are by their nature: that is, simply witnesses. They can and may witness only to that which they and their hearers and readers have been and will be taught within their hearts by God himself, and which they hear and practice in their deeds and in their lives. May God give us understanding of this.[20]

Edith wrote about these meetings to Hardy:

> In the meeting tonight Papa read from *Innerland* about the living word. It was a great experience for us all. It seems to me that something completely new has broken in, as if we are standing at the beginning of a new time. We have felt what a power this inner word of God is and we sense that if we are really open to the word, something immense will happen. If God's reality takes shape in us and gains full power in word and deed through the Spirit, a movement will come into being gripping thousands, as in former times. We have seen, however, how much we still need to be set free from ourselves in order to be able to take in this word, which alone is able to transform conditions and move mountains. I still feel as if I were half asleep. My eyes are just barely open, and the great light blinds me.[21]

When in late September 1933 a new baby was born into the community, Eberhard used the names chosen for the little girl—Katharina Sabina—to tell about the persecution and martyrdom of two historic bearers of those names:

> Katharina Hutter [wife of Jakob Hutter, executed in 1538] is an example to us. She surrendered her young life to Christ and his way, to the witness of his truth, and to the humble and simple doing of his will. The second name, Sabina, goes back to persecution in the Roman Empire. Sabina's determination as a martyr not to give homage to the state beyond the limits set in the New Testament means a lot to us right now, when we are under colossal pressure from the government to render divine homage to the regime and semi-divine reverence to its head. Martyrdom approaches, and only God's leading can protect us. There is no way we can evade it. We must meet the persecution with the right witness. We don't want to lash out with proud, scholarly irony at the Nazis' moral shortcomings. We want to approach them as brothers, with love that springs from our experiencing the same condemnation and the same redemption available through the saving power of Jesus Christ and the Holy Spirit. For we are not under the power of our ancestors' blood and their original sin, but under the authority of the Holy Spirit and the certainty of his coming kingdom.[22]

At the end of September, Eberhard's uncle died, and he traveled to Halle and Breslau to visit the family. While he was gone, an announcement was given in the news that October 1 was to be observed as a national harvest-thanksgiving day. Emmy wrote to him her anxieties:

> It looks like October 1 will be a difficult day for us. We have been warned several times, also by the chief of police of Fulda, to join the parade in Neuhof on Sunday. He said that there would be consequences if we didn't. Hans Zumpe is going to see what he can work out. We may have to submit a petition to the district administrator on Saturday, giving our religious position! We discussed it yesterday until late at night. Do you have any other advice? This could be the first of further difficulties. We would so much like to celebrate thanksgiving with a real religious celebration and a children's festival![23]

The social aspect of National Socialism was being strongly emphasized, and a general plea was made for contributions to the so-called Winter Aid, the government-run relief organization providing clothes, fuel, and food for the needy. The Bruderhof decided to "emphasize the positive" and to donate a load of potatoes and other vegetables to Winter Aid. Edith described the day in a letter to Hardy:

> Now the harvest festival is over, and we can be very thankful for how it went and that we were able to experience the day in the joy of unity. We had been told by the government to take part in the procession with a decorated farm wagon. We realized that through this wagon we could give a witness to peace and at the same time express our positive attitude to the government, to creation, and to the simplicity of peasant life, to our kinship with other people.
>
> It was not easy, and it took a long time to come through to unanimity. I learned a great deal. I saw quite clearly that we can't find unity on the basis of human opinions. It is a miracle of the Spirit that in spite of our weakness unity was given again. So God's will was really shown, and we were shown how to act in practice.
>
> You should have seen the wagon, fully loaded with vegetables, a true picture of peace. Mama and Arno Martin sat up on top of it. In the afternoon we had a proper children's festival with races for the little children, etc. In the late afternoon I heard Adolf Hitler's speech.[24]

In the neighborhood suspicion and antagonism towards the Bruderhof intensified. A field of cabbages ready for harvest was ravaged. Villagers resented the fact that the community's young men were not volunteering for the SS and SA, and because they would not say, "Heil Hitler." They were often called traitors and hypocrites.

Quakers

In spring, Hardy Arnold had transferred his studies from the university in Tübingen in southern Germany to Zurich to escape the oppressive Nazi mood. But he was unable to make friends in Zurich and in fall 1933 transferred again to Birmingham, England. Quaker John Stephens, a friend since the Arnolds had lived in Berlin, taught German at the university in Birmingham and agreed to take Hardy into his home and arrange for his classes. Before he left, Eberhard took several evenings to speak about the origins of the Quakers. He was particularly inspired by George Fox, founder of the Quakers, and how he had spoken boldly to England's ruler Oliver Cromwell.

In the seventeenth century Cromwell defeated the royalists, executed King Charles, and became Lord Protector of England, Ireland, and Scotland. In 1657 he was offered (and refused) the English crown. George Fox had written in his journal:

> I was moved of the Lord to write a paper to the Protector, Oliver Cromwell; wherein I did, in the presence of the Lord God, declare that I denied the wearing or drawing of a carnal sword, or any other outward weapon, against him or any man; and that I was sent of God to stand a witness against all violence, and against the works of darkness; and to turn people from darkness to light; and to bring them from the causes of war and fighting to the peaceable gospel ... After some time Captain Drury brought me before the Protector himself ... When I came in I was moved to say, "Peace be in this house"; and I exhorted him to keep in the fear of God, that he might receive wisdom from Him, that by it he might be directed, and order all things under his hand to God's glory.[25]
>
> After a little time Edward Pyot and I went to Whitehall to see Oliver Cromwell ... The power of the Lord God arose in me, and I was moved in it to bid him lay down his crown at the feet of Jesus.[26]

Eberhard spoke of this and then said:

> It must be given to us to say the same thing to today's dictators. But first we have to lay down all our own little wreaths at Christ's

throne, including our glittering self-will and all our personal wishes and presumptions.

Let us follow Jesus on the path of lowliness that he walked to his cross. Let us be united in our prayer that we may be protected in the spirit of complete unity, so that we can withstand the battle that has been laid on us, so that not one of us becomes unfaithful. For we know that the cause of unfaithfulness is the spirit of arrogance, of superiority and idolizing human works. May we be redeemed from the curse of this manifold idolatry and be led to a pure, holy worship of God, seeing nobody but Jesus on the mount of his transfiguration. Let us pray that this pure, childlike spirit, the spirit of the manger and the cross, rule among us and keep us united in complete love and complete joy to our last breath.[27]

The Quakers were known for their pacifism, and Hardy hoped to win support for the stand the Bruderhof was taking. In this he was disappointed. Coming from Germany, which was still suffering the effects of the Depression, he was also shocked at the wealth of the English Quakers.

I have encountered an unconsidered love of money in practically all the Quakers here. Recently, in a discussion after a lecture about the principles of the Quakers, when I asked why they do not take a stand against property, a general murmur of amazement went through the hall, accompanied by a shaking of heads, almost rhythmical. And I was told with a smile that the question of property had no connection with Christianity—it was a political matter; individual persons had to preserve the freedom of initiative, also in business . . .

I then asked how it came about that the Quakers had such clear principles in regard to war and swearing of oaths but were so unclear in regard to property, since property was after all the cause of most wars. I was told with a smile that the Quakers were much too individualistic and that they basically leave the question of war to the conscience of the individual and do not set up a standard rule. To be consistent, the Quakers must also recognize the Christian who is led by his "conscience" into war, for there are many such. The daily life of the Quakers, then, is tantamount to a slap in the face to all the suffering of our time. Whether they have cars or take trips to the Mediterranean, whether they own their own houses and eat food like I have never had in my life—all this speaks of a practically unheard-of, unsuspecting middle-class set of values and love of comfort. When will they be shaken out of that by God's judgment?

Never have I been so well off materially as I am here with John Stephens, but I do not feel good about it and can hardly imagine sticking it out for five months. In Tübingen we were more or less hungry all the time, never able to afford a really satisfying meal, and I experienced the same in Zurich; yet for us inwardly that was the only appropriate way, and the same with our plain food at the Bruderhof. But here, I am really afraid of getting fat.

They cannot agree on their attitude toward Russia or Germany, yet they haven't the least notion of what is lacking in their pacifism. They are fully saturated with the modern Western spirit of liberalism, capitalism, democracy, etc. Only by name do they differentiate themselves from nonchristian mysticism such as Plato and Gandhi, to whom they testify.[28]

I don't believe I have met a single Englishman who is not a "pacifist." What makes every Englishman a pacifist is his urge for quiet and "peace." They want security and safety. Therefore they have no thought of really disarming, no matter how much and how often they may talk about it.

The English people, even the best, do not understand that they get their comfortable and well-to-do life from the blood and oppression of other peoples. They do not know that they represent a ruling caste of 40 million people in an empire of almost 600 million, and that they live off the exploitation of the remaining 560 million Indians, Negroes, etc., apart from their own poor working-class people. They, even the best Quakers, have not recognized that. Hence the naïve, matter-of-fact way they conduct their business, live their lives in the comfortable affluence of their club chairs, and talk piously, while somewhere across the ocean maybe a couple of thousand workers in tea plantations languish in the sun, and even the most devout Quaker declares with joy that the tea dividends have gone up and that he, without even moving a finger, has gained a couple of thousand pounds. This is what is called "business" here; it continues to blossom and flourish almost the same as ever, in spite of economic crises. Only the unemployed working-class people have to suffer, in England too.[29]

Edith answered him, "The news about the inner attitude of the Quakers moved us very much. Papa said it is again obvious how much alone we are in our stand, though that is not what we want at all. Our longing is to find people spiritually akin to us."[30]

6

October to November 1933

IN MID OCTOBER a letter arrived from Ludwig Müller, the Reich bishop himself. Dated October 11, it said:

> To Herr Dr. Eberhard Arnold
>
> The Herr Reich bishop would be interested to learn from you what attitude you and your community take toward Christianity and the church. We would be grateful if you would let us have documents pertaining to this.

The brotherhood met to speak about how they should answer. This was the opportunity Eberhard had been waiting for to make a public witness. They would write respectfully, but they would make their position clear. Many wrote letters expressing their personal convictions. Eberhard wrote a cover letter and sent along several books and pamphlets.

> Bruderhof
> October 17, 1933
>
> To the Reich bishop
> of the Protestant churches of Germany
> Berlin
>
> Concerning the Reich bishop's inquiry of October 11, 1933
>
> Our brotherhood wishes to express its cordial thanks to the Reich bishop of the German Protestant churches (Lutheran, Zwinglian, and Calvinist) for taking an interest in our witness to Christ. Our Christian confession consists in the words of the prophets and apostles, grounded in the four Gospels. Repentance and faith in the kingdom of God are proclaimed daily among us. In the spirit of the Lord's Prayer and Jesus' high priestly prayer we intercede for the whole of Christendom and all nations, in particular for

> the German nation and the government God has set over it. We hold the Sermon on the Mount and the early church founded at Pentecost as described in the Acts of the Apostles, which are common ground for all believers, to be normative for the character of the church of Jesus Christ. Each member of our brotherhood acknowledges the Apostles' Creed as our common faith in the Father, the Son, and the Holy Spirit, as God's perfect unity in himself. The unalterable confession of faith for all the communities called Hutterian is to be found in Peter Riedemann's written exposition of the Apostolic Creed: *Confession of our Religion, Teaching, and Faith* of 1540.

Eberhard went on to describe the Bruderhof's connection with the Hutterian communities in the United States and Canada and their four-hundred-year history. Then he gave his own credentials:

> The twenty-volume *Quellen* series of Christian witnesses throughout the centuries, published by the undersigned, points to God, the universal reality.
>
> The undersigned, spokesman of the only Bruderhof in the German Reich, was appointed and confirmed in the service of the Word by the elders of the North American communities for the purpose of building up the Bruderhof in Germany according to their old church orders. The appointment was carried out by the unanimous decision of all Hutterian servants of the Word at the Stand Off Bruderhof in Alberta, Canada.
>
> Further brief information about the undersigned may be found under his name in the reference work, *Religion in Geschichte und Gegenwart*; the only correction to be made is to substitute "Hutterianism" for "Quakerism." His Christian conviction is set forth in his books, enclosed herewith, *The Early Christians After the Death of the Apostles* and *Innerland: A Guide Into the Heart and Soul of the Bible*. The first edition of the latter came out in 1914; . . . a new edition of two thousand is in preparation. We will be glad to send the other works on request, including the complete series of *Quellen* books already mentioned. Today we also enclose a few small publications telling about the building up and composition of our Bruderhof and its service of love.
>
> In the hope that this information will convey all the essentials without taking up too much valuable time, our whole brotherhood wishes the German Reich bishop of the Lutheran, Zwinglian, and Calvinist churches and his colleagues the grace of Jesus Christ and the enlightenment of the Holy Spirit in carrying out the will of God, who by the example of the disciples of Jesus wants to reveal his love and unity to all men.

with love and respect, on behalf of the brotherhood,
its spokesman

Eberhard Arnold

No evidence suggests that there was any further communication from the Reich bishop.

Injury

From the moment he became Reichskanzler, Hitler was deliberately driving Germany toward war. International disarmament agreements being negotiated in Geneva had reached a deadlock. On October 14, Germany pulled out of the negotiations and at the same time withdrew from the League of Nations, "in view of the unreasonable, humiliating and degrading demands of the other Powers."[1] The German people were expected to express their support of this action in a plebiscite or vote of confidence.

This announcement was of immediate concern to the Rhön brotherhood, as can be seen from the words Eberhard spoke a week later:

> In the extreme seriousness of the present political situation it is of the greatest importance that we are completely clear and united in the inner life of our brotherhood circle. Every day I am astonished that we are still allowed to be together, still in this place. I see this as a wonderful providence that one can hardly grasp. If our situation becomes worse through the reelection and the plebiscite on the present government's policy, it will be even more necessary to stand together in absolute clarity about the deepest things.[2]

> Two animals in nature show us the decisive contrast: the wolf shows us the sneaking predator, and the lamb shows us the gathered flock that is ready to be sacrificed. All works must be tested as to whether they have a predatory nature, that craves and tears and kills, or whether they have a lamblike nature, that is ready to be sacrificed, that draws together. This lamblike nature knows what serves the whole flock.

> Looking at the world around us, we see clearly how lonely our little community is—an isolation so deep as to be almost inconceivable. We cannot expect help from any human quarter! The professor of German in England [John Stephens] said that if we were thrown into prison, nobody in England would lift a finger

> on our behalf. We would just disappear, unnoticed, into a concentration camp. No one would rise up in our defense. In times like these, the church of Jesus Christ stands completely alone.
>
> Petitions from the American Bruderhofs would not alter that. Clearly, in this struggle we have to depend completely on the strength we are given as a community. And it is good so. In the coming weeks we will probably face very heavy political pressure. Unless God places a downright miraculous protection around our houses, we are going to be visited by the wild election propaganda of the Nazis; the roars of the beast of prey will penetrate our very rooms. We shall have to say *no* to their demands. We shall be called enemies of the people and of life. Persecution may soon start in earnest.
>
> If I look around the circle, I see that each one is burdened by the struggles of daily life. One feels oppressed by his lack of gifts, another has had a disagreement with someone and doesn't have the courage to clear it up. All of this dampens our joy and darkens our view. Let us not be anxious! Let us not be cowardly! We need to be brave.
>
> When the profound joy of our complete unity fills our hearts, we shall fear no man. Perfect love drives out fear.[3]

On Friday, October 27, 1933, Eberhard called on the district administrator's office in Fulda to ask for advice concerning the plebiscite scheduled for November 12. Every German citizen was required to vote. What would happen if they refused, or if they voted "No?"

"If you don't say yes, Dr. Arnold, there is only one thing left—concentration camp," he was told.

Eberhard came home discouraged and agitated. He felt responsible for the children, their mothers, the young people—for more than a hundred souls. His taxi dropped him off at the edge of the woods as usual, and he walked the last bit along a footpath down the hill. It had been raining and it was already dark. He slipped and fell.

Alfred Gneiting, a young gardener, had gone to meet him. Years later he recalled:

> I went out to meet him alone with a storm lantern, so he would be able to see the way better, as it was quite uneven. The grass was wet and Eberhard was wearing a lightweight pair of town shoes. They were not the kind fitted with nails, which could have given a good support at such a place. Suddenly he started slipping, and even though I supported his right arm, I was not able to hold him. I wanted to help him to get up, but he said: "It will not work. Go

inside and call for help." The meeting had already begun. Moni determined right away that the leg was fractured, as the bone was even protruding. So we carried Eberhard into his study.[4]

That night the brotherhood gathered around his bed. He was in great pain, but he spoke with firm faith and love. He suggested that everyone should go to the election booth and submit a statement of his or her beliefs. Knowing that the results of such an action were unpredictable, he asked that the brothers and sisters consider where they should meet if all should be scattered. They agreed on a farm belonging to Hannes Boller's family in Switzerland.[5]

The following morning Eberhard was taken to Fulda by ambulance, where the surgeon, Dr. Gunkel, wired the bone together in a three-hour operation. He was discharged from the hospital after six days (although the doctor would have liked to keep him longer) and given a non-weight-bearing cast and instructions for six weeks of strict bed rest. He was very pale, weak, in much pain, and had very little appetite.[6] From now on, Hans Zumpe took over much of the practical leadership of the community with the help of Georg Barth, Hans Meier, and Hannes Boller.

∼

At the beginning of November 1933, the following notice appeared in the villages of the parish of Veitsteinbach:

> Public Notice
>
> On Saturday, November 4, at eight o'clock in the evening in the hall of Mr. Leineweber's inn at Veitsteinbach, a meeting will take place to which all men fit for service in the SA between the ages of eighteen and forty-five are *urgently* invited. Those *failing* to attend will show by their absence that they have no interest in their nation and fatherland.
>
> Zeiher (Mayor)

When November 4 arrived, the brothers concerned sent Mayor Zeiher a list of their names along with this message:

> To: Mayor Zeiher, Veitsteinbach
>
> As we have a meeting for worship this evening, we shall not be able to attend the Veitsteinbach meeting. We are conveying our best wishes and hope the meeting will go well. We testify that

> we have the greatest interest in our nation and fatherland and that this evening, too, we shall intercede from our hearts for the government of Hindenburg and Adolf Hitler.
>
> The undersigned brothers of the Bruderhof

The national plebiscite was scheduled for November 12. Eberhard had been told that failure to participate would mean concentration camp. This was the moment, then, to make the witness he had been thinking about for the past nine months. Instead of checking the "yes" or "no" boxes on the ballot sheet, the Bruderhof members would write a statement giving their position in regard to the National Socialist government. At the same time he would send out the "avalanche of petitions" he had spoken of earlier, in the hope of pre-empting retribution. He dropped his work on *Innerland* (which he was never able to finish), and from his bedside dictated a series of letters to Nazi authorities. Six were mailed before the plebiscite on Sunday, November 12.

To begin with, on November 7, a letter was addressed to the adviser on church affairs in the Reich ministry of the interior, Ministerial Counselor Conrad. As in all his petitions, he boldly emphasized those ideals that the Bruderhof had in common with the Nazis and that might conceivably commend it to Nazi officials; by the same token he carefully distanced the Bruderhof from political parties, from Marxists and anarchists, to safeguard it from being lumped together with such groups anathema to the Nazis. He told of the close bond between the Bruderhof and the Hutterian colonies of ancient German stock in North America. He expressed his respect for the government of Hindenburg and Hitler, but stated clearly that the Bruderhof had a different calling and did not take part in politics.

> For our beloved country and nation, our great German fatherland, we do acknowledge the God-ordained necessity of that *other* calling—a calling not given to us—which by God's will and leading is now entrusted to the government of Hindenburg and Adolf Hitler. We pray earnestly every day for these beloved men and with all respect wish them the very best for all they have to do or leave undone, that they may carry out their great and heavy task in accordance with the will of God. We are able to offer no other or better help for this task of government than faithful intercession before God, and we ask that this be recognized ...

> In view of our task here, we are not inclined to contemplate the emigration of [one hundred ten] people unless the wish for the mass emigration of our whole group should come from our beloved German government itself. We love Germany and would not want to be absent, especially in the present hour of need. On the contrary, we want to place all our strength at the disposal of our country and nation by putting the full gospel into practice in a manner befitting that gospel; we want to bring all our love into action without getting involved in political, military, or legal affairs. That is why we request to be thoroughly investigated and to be given a basic direction as to whether we will be permitted to live and work in Germany in the Hutterian way by our conscience bound to Christ ...
>
> We ask the Reich minister of the interior to show kind understanding and grant us protection and help, also for the urgently needed building up of our farm settlement. This would enable us to continue the service of love to many a fellow countryman by allowing our branch of large Germanic families to increase for the benefit of the fatherland. Then the truly Christian life of early Hutterianism with its faithfully maintained customs would keep its roots among the people of Germany today and make its influence felt. By the grace of God its influence might be a greater blessing for the government's best intentions than one would expect of a cause so small and so absorbed in one goal.
>
> In that trust at this decisive hour we send copies of this letter to the Reich president, the Reichskanzler, our *Oberpräsident*, our regional governor, and our district administrator. At the same time, we respect the fact that the Reich minister of the interior is the authority in our German Reich from whom our free church group living in community must expect the investigation and decision we have requested regarding all our concerns. Therefore, we wish to close by requesting that as soon as possible a representative of the Reich minister of the interior visit our Bruderhof, Neuhof, District of Fulda.
>
> We sincerely and respectfully wish to be accommodating and submissive; our best wishes to Adolf Hitler; all salvation (*Heil*) through Christ!

As Eberhard had pointed out earlier, the salute "Heil Hitler" was related to the Roman imperial oath, "Hail Caesar." But the German word "Heil" could also mean "salvation." Therefore Bruderhof members, in refusing to use the "Heil Hitler" greeting, liked to say "Best wishes to Adolf Hitler, but *Heil* only through Jesus Christ."

A similar letter was addressed to Baron von Monbart, governor of the Kassel region, in which the Rhön Bruderhof was situated. Copies of the letters to Reich Bishop Müller and to Ministerial Counselor Conrad were enclosed.

By Thursday, November 9, 1933, the letter to "our beloved Reichskanzler Adolf Hitler" was ready to send. Eberhard deliberated over the wording of this letter: how to speak out against blatant injustice without provoking retribution on the community.

Bruderhof
November 9, 1933

To Adolf Hitler
Chancellor of the German Reich
Berlin
PERSONAL and CONFIDENTIAL

Concerning the Bruderhof called Hutterian, of Germanic and early Christian roots, and its loyalty to the government:

We greet our beloved Reichskanzler Adolf Hitler for November 12, expressing our loyalty to him in his God-given task of government and representation of the German Reich. We believe that our Reichskanzler and our Reich president alone have been entrusted by God with all political matters pertaining to the German state, since it is the purpose of God in his wrath, and as ruler of the world, to strike down all the ruling powers of recent decades insofar as they have violated morality and family life, justice and the common good, truth and loyalty. May God protect the innocent from suffering unduly under this judgment. We faithfully intercede with God and before men for our rulers Hindenburg and Adolf Hitler, that they be given grace to preserve their high principles in the face of all evil powers and to establish peace, justice, and a people's community to an extent hardly ever achieved before in world history.

For four hundred years we brethren known as Hutterian have, for the sake of Christ, renounced this calling of statesmanship, even in the humblest station. Our only calling in life is to love God in loving our Führer and deliverer Jesus Christ, whose discipleship we are called to put into practice in a communal life, fully united in faith and in all decisions.

Granted that enormous tasks face our beloved Reichskanzler on behalf of the millions of German people, nevertheless the following facts about our Germanic and early-Christian brotherhood (which gathered four centuries ago on Moravian soil) will be of great interest to him. Even though living among Slavs,

Hungarians, and Americans, our Hutterian brotherhood, constituting a people's community that practices positive Christianity, has to the present day kept its pure German customs and dress, its traditional Tirolean language, and its peasant culture so intact that in its selfless dedication to the common good it has allowed no alien influence to creep in. The Hutterian Brethren numbered at times twenty thousand souls and at present about four thousand. Over the years their heroism, their preparedness for the cross, has led to the martyr's death of more than two thousand. The last two died in the United States during the World War.

In view of these facts, our Bruderhof in Germany pleads with our beloved Reichskanzler to grant the Hutterian Brethren in Germany today the same freedom of conscience that Prussian kings once granted to the Mennonites, who have similar beliefs. We brethren, as ministers of Jesus Christ, cannot participate in military service or in government or judicial actions because we believe that love is the highest good. From this love springs the uninterrupted labor-service given in our life of full community that serves our whole nation and the aims of its government in the best possible way. Because we love our German fatherland, nation, and government, we ask that our Bruderhof be allowed to remain in Germany under the protection of the Reichskanzler and to live and work in accordance with our early Christian principles. We address this request to our beloved Chancellor also in the name of our fellow brethren of German descent who live in thirty-eight Bruderhofs in America. These German communities abroad ordained and confirmed the undersigned for the task of building up and maintaining in Germany a monastic Protestant community in line with their centuries-old faith and life. This community in Germany has existed for many years and today comprises twenty families, in all 120 souls.

For further information we enclose copies of our letters to the Reich bishop of the German Protestant Church and to the Reich minister of the interior, as well as a copy of the first part of the essay "Light and Fire," just off the press. We entrust these documents to our beloved Reichskanzler and ask God from our hearts that at God's hour he may become, instead of a historical instrument of supreme state authority, an ambassador of the humiliated Christ, to whom alone it was given to reveal the perfect love of God's heart.

With loyal respect,
the brotherhood,

[signed] Eberhard Arnold

Additional letters were sent to Dr. Burkhardt, the district administrator in Fulda, and to Prince Philip of Hesse, governor of the province of Hessen-Nassau, as well as a shorter one to Reich president, Field Marshal von Hindenburg:

> The undersigned minister and spokesman of the Bruderhof (Neuhof, District of Fulda), who from childhood on was known to Georg Michaelis, Reichskanzler in 1917, asks the Reich president for help to enable our brotherhood to remain in Germany without acting against their early Christian convictions. As is evident from the enclosed copies of letters to the Reichskanzler, the Reich minister of the interior, and the Reich bishop of the German Protestant Church, we loyally acknowledge that the Hindenburg-Hitler government has been given to our nation by God. We pray daily with gratitude and respect for our beloved Reich president and our beloved Reichskanzler.
>
> Our brotherhood requests that it may serve the German Reich and its government in works of love as a traditional German Christian community in the way that the Hutterian Brethren have done faithfully for four hundred years, without taking part in military, political, or judicial actions. We believe that by putting into practice the love of Jesus Christ we can best serve the national community and public interest.
>
> We ask that our petitions and letters may receive kind and thoughtful attention in view of the seriousness of our situation.

After the letters had been drafted, the brotherhood met to read them out. Because it was vital that everyone stand behind them, they met several times over the next two days until everyone was in agreement. Years later Hans Meier said:

> I had to overcome my hatred against Hitler. He was a murderer, and I felt I hated him. But Eberhard Arnold represented very strongly that we could only write to Hitler and Hindenburg—or anyone else—if we loved him. Out of love we have to tell him the truth. But love is not an emotional thing; loving the enemy means to challenge him, to tell him the truth. I had to fight against these feelings of hatred before I could write to Hitler in peace and become an instrument of God's love instead of hatred.[7]

Edith wrote to Hardy:

> Last night there was a *Rundrede** about this, including the novices, and we were completely unanimous and recognized more fully

---

* *Rundrede*: A meeting in which every individual present was asked to speak.

the historic hour. Love your enemies, see and affirm everything in them that is good. No "appeasement" can help them, however, but only a clear witness to absolute truth. We were able to give a witness in the letters and are infinitely thankful that we could.[8]

Transcripts of the meetings, partially reproduced below, show how the entire circle agreed with the witness they wished to make and were willing to overcome their personal prejudices for the sake of this witness.

> *Moni Barth*: Having just returned from Fulda, it was brought home to me how mighty is the power opposing us. There is a swastika hanging from every floor of every house. It is a gigantic movement that confronts us. One can only rejoice that we dare to go on the offensive, even though the powers ranged against us are so much stronger. I completely support these letters.
>
> *Sekunda Kleiner*: I am glad that a completely different, powerful world speaks through these letters and confronts the other one.
>
> *Anni Mathis*: Great clarity and love come through these letters and prove to us again that the Spirit does come down to the church community to give the right word at the right hour.
>
> *Karl Keiderling*: It is very important that we have read the letters once more. Yesterday I felt so overwhelmed I was not able to take it all in. What moves me is the straight line shown us as the direction to take, neither affirming the state too positively nor negating it altogether. These petitions have given me inner quiet and firmness.
>
> *Hannes Boller*: I am happy that Eberhard, in spite of his severe pain, was given strength to put them together. It seems to me that these letters can only be rightly understood as an expression of, and pure witness to, the forgiving and creative love of Christ.
>
> *Adolf Braun*: What Hannes has said is very important to me: the forgiving love expressing itself in fervent words as beloved Reichskanzler, the fact that we can address all these people as people we love, is only possible if we are ready to forgive. Later generations perhaps will write volumes about this letter to the Reichskanzler; it contains many thoughts that are only hinted at. Hearing these letters again today makes me even more happy that Eberhard has put into words what we all felt.
>
> *Georg Barth*: Without doubt, the hour we live in is a momentous one. We were waiting for it, yet it did not occur to us that it would come so soon. These letters represent an advance along the whole

front, a proclamation of the will to live for peace, against the threats coming from the opposing side.

Trudi Hüssy: I would like to take this further to say how overwhelming it is that in opposition to that power now in demonic revolt, Eberhard was inspired to give true expression to the highest command of love: "Love your enemies!" The fact that this hour has come upon us and has been taken hold of in this way has a downright freeing effect.

Edith Boeker: I am very grateful that the letters could be written the way they are. We all feel they have been written with the full authority of the Spirit. Recognizing that, we can look forward in firm faith to whatever response we may meet.

Annemarie Wächter: What I find to be a great gift is that in this case where two utterly conflicting worlds face each other, the testimonies pick out what is positive in the other side, so that these two opposing worlds can actually be brought together.

Arno Martin: I feel overwhelmed by the love they express: love precisely to people most closely involved in the use of force. They are being faced by the love and peace of God's kingdom. We must be especially grateful to Eberhard for composing these letters in the midst of his terrific physical suffering. Even in such suffering he has heard the Spirit's voice and has found the way to communicate it to the world.

Fritz Kleiner: Some of us who have come from socialist and peace circles do not consider being German terribly important. But what matters is that we deliver a clear message of Christian community to the government. At the same time we state the Christians' positive attitude to the state and say it so the government people can understand, what both they and we want.

Margrit Meier: These testimonies truly come from God. To be able to understand them I feel it is necessary to understand the love behind them. I can imagine they may make old friends think we are trying to accommodate the government; it may not be understood by them.

Hans Meier: Once more it has been made clear to me that this way can only be walked in complete love; never with the aid of a rational balancing pole. I want to stand completely behind these letters.

Peter Mathis: The great thing is the all-embracing love to the enemy, something I did not understand right away, coming as I do from Religious Socialism. I too stand behind everything the letters say.

Alfred Gneiting: What makes me especially happy is that the two tasks have been differentiated so clearly: the task of the church and the task of the state. It is a powerful witness.

Josef Stängl: I am amazed at the way we have been led. There was always the danger that the demonic powers might open a real gulf between the church and the nation. But the Spirit has guided us again and stressed the positive things the church can do.

Heiner Arnold: What makes me especially happy is the great love that at the end challenges Adolf Hitler to become a Christian. That is the greatest sign of love.

Monika Arnold: I find it so wonderful that in these letters the possibility of a new way comes out much more strongly than criticism of the old one. I am very thankful.

Emmy Arnold: I find it very disturbing for two worlds to clash the way these do. That is quite a collision—a more violent one than we may have experienced so far. That is an aspect we must bear in mind. I rejoice that the letters are being mailed and hope they will reach their destination.

Hans Zumpe: It's a great joy to find that we have once more come through to a unanimous feeling. We stand completely behind these testimonies. We are grateful we still have this opportunity to give such a witness, grateful that the church of the Hutterian Brethren in Germany has not simply been swept away without further ado.

Of course, this may be a turning point; in fact, we can definitely count on that. We do not know what will happen. It is in God's hands, but it will be a turning point. If Adolf Hitler thinks and acts in line with his earlier pronouncements, there will be no special privileges for us. He made particular reference to pacifist circles and to persons not taking part in actions organized by the state.[9]

Christian Löber and Arno Martin were sent on bicycles to mail these important documents on Saturday night; the plebiscite was scheduled for the next day. They skirted the villages on their way because of the unrest everywhere.

Except for a short acknowledgment from Hindenburg's office, the Bruderhof never heard whether their letters had been received. But Hans Meier related the following anecdote:

> Near the Rhön Bruderhof, there was once a big military maneuver. The control of the military maneuver was in the castle of Ramholz [just a few miles from the Bruderhof]. To the Stumm family, who owned that castle, belonged the big forest along the Weinstrasse. We bought our wood from that forest. The forester from whom we bought the wood told us that Adolf Hitler was in Ramholz and that he asked, "Do the Bruderhof people live up there?" So he must have had some idea about the Bruderhof, and he must have known what it is.[10]

7

Plebiscite and Raid

NOVEMBER 11 WAS ARMISTICE Day for most of the world, celebrated every year since 1918 with a period of silence at 11 o'clock on the 11th day of the 11th month—a day dedicated to peace. But most Germans remembered it bitterly as a day of infamy. Sunday, November 12, 1933, therefore, would be a proud affirmation of the new Germany, the Thousand Year Third Reich and its Führer. Every German was to stand up and pledge his or her support of Hitler's program. Out of the ashes of military defeat and the malaise of the Weimar years would arise the phoenix of a renewed Volk, an awakened and unassailable people.

The brotherhood considered whether they should simply stay away from this plebiscite; but Eberhard had been warned that such abstention would mean concentration camp. They felt they could not evade the direct question.

> Do you, as a German man, and do you, as a German woman, approve the policy of your Reich government, and are you ready to affirm and solemnly to pledge yourself to this policy as the expression of your own conviction and your own will?

Instead of answering yes or no, the members of the Bruderhof decided that they would write out a statement that Eberhard had drawn up:

> My conviction and my will bid me stand by the gospel and for the discipleship of Jesus Christ, the coming kingdom of God, and the love and unity of his church. That is *the one and only* calling God has given me as *mine*. In this faith I intercede before God and all men for my people and their fatherland and in particular for their Reich government with its different calling, given by God, not to me but to my beloved rulers Hindenburg and Adolf Hitler. [Emphasis in the original statement.]

Each brotherhood member copied the statement onto a piece of paper and signed it. That Sunday afternoon they all walked together down to Veitsteinbach, their designated polling place. Each pasted his slip of paper onto the ballot sheet and—"with a feeling of determination and even a measure of exhilaration," as one brother recalled—dropped it into the ballot box. Since his broken leg prevented Eberhard's going to Veitsteinbach, two election officials brought a ballot box to his bedside. No one was to be left out.

Edith described the day of the plebiscite in a letter to Hardy:

> In the morning we had a brotherhood meeting in which we considered our stand. After lunch we met for prayer. We closed with the song, "A mighty fortress is our God," and were all full of joy about our mission. Then we went to Veitsteinbach to vote and give witness that we recognize and esteem the calling of Hindenburg and Hitler as given to them by God. Of course we also testified to our calling.
>
> At about 5:30 or 6:00 p.m. we had another worship meeting with Papa. He was carried into the dining room. For me this was one of the most wonderful meetings. Our beloved Papa was given the word as only the Spirit himself can express it. I can't really describe it; it was as if the door to that other world that is our true home were being opened a bit wider. One more veil has fallen. That is such an immense joy, and the hope for the true fulfillment of life is growing.[1]

Eberhard's words lifted those gathered anxiously around him out of their worry. They caught a glimpse of the spiritual aspect of the step they had taken and how important it was that someone, there in Germany, was willing to take an unpopular position against the mood of their entire nation:

> It is a great thing when individual people are moved to stand firm in unity with Christ. It is greater still when a church is so firm that it can demonstrate to the whole world by its daily life and work the character of the kingdom of God.
>
> It is a great thing when people are found worthy to be thrown into prison or killed for the sake of the gospel. It is greater still when a church is found worthy to be called to abandon the place it has built up so laboriously and to venture into the unknown, when on the threshold between having and not having, it can grasp anew perfect unity, peace, justice, and brotherhood in the unity of Jesus Christ and the kingdom of God.

It is greatest of all if it is given in such an hour to love one's enemies in the spirit of Jesus Christ, to embrace those who intend to drive out the members of the church into misery and oblivion. It is useless to crawl on one's knees, to sing hymns and fold our hands, to babble about the cross, if we are not ready—ready as Jesus was to take the cross upon himself—to tread that way to the very last step, to the last breath. That alone is true discipleship of Jesus Christ; all else is lying and deception.

So we are joyful. Even though we do not yet know if we will be found worthy of experiencing that ultimate reality, this day's act brings that reality before our eyes as a real historical possibility. That makes us indescribably happy, for Jesus said: "Leap for joy when they denounce and curse you and lie about you. That is how their ancestors treated the prophets, and how they are bound to treat all apostles of the embassy, for that is the world's way. As they hated me, they are bound to hate you; as they persecuted me, they are bound to persecute you. But whoever listens to you, listens to me; whoever rejects you, rejects me." In the reality of the cross and of Jesus' utter surrender apostolic mission begins. Only in that way can the world be reached.

It is a great gift when we approach one individual or several people to tell them about the kingdom of God, when at a meal with others we can speak about the great cause, if we can send out our books, or if occasionally we can send out brothers on mission.

But it is a much greater thing if the world is confronted with a historical reality—a happening unforgettably branded into the records of history—as a witness to the truth of the gospel. It means far more to be called to participate in making history by representing the way of love and peace and justice in the midst of a hostile, untruthful, unjust world, a world bristling with weapons. We are called to live out this witness, unperturbed and unswayed, while a tempest of historical events rages fiercely all around us.

That is the church's true calling: to carry out a final, quiet, united action in the face of the horrors of the demon-gripped doomsday events of this time—an action expressing complete unity and faithfulness, complete love and forgiveness, complete goodness and truth, complete surrender and trust, united action that cries out: Repent and believe in the gospel, for the kingdom of God is at hand. It is alive in the church of Jesus Christ. For it does not consist in eating and drinking but in righteousness and peace and joy in the Holy Spirit![2]

All the next day the brothers and sisters trembled as they waited for the votes to be counted. On Tuesday, the Fulda newspaper reported the election results for Veitsteinbach:

> Plebiscite: votes cast 272
> Yes: 270; No: 1; Not valid: 1
>
> Parliamentary election: votes cast 262
> National Socialist Party: 221; Not valid: 41

The Bruderhof's statements had been counted as "yes" for the plebiscite, and "not valid" for the parliamentary election. The *Fuldaer Zeitung* reported:

> Election Day, like the campaign preceding it, was fundamentally different from previous elections. Gone were the effects produced by overheated electoral contests. Previously the police were present everywhere, but this time very few policemen were to be seen. In Berlin the array of flags is particularly impressive. From all houses—indeed, from almost every window—the black, white, and red flags of the old, victorious Germany and the symbol of the national revolution, the swastika flag, flutter in the breeze. Innumerable banners, with captions that point to the significance of election day, are strung across the streets or along the fronts of houses. Many cars with election posters cruise through the city, and at every street corner the advertising pillars with their giant placards remind the citizens of their electoral duty. Immediately after the opening of the polling centers the people turned up in crowds such as were never seen before. Before long, the streets were full of people all proudly wearing a voting pin reading "yes." Particularly impressive was the parade of disabled war veterans, who were pushed along the streets in their wheelchairs. They carried posters saying: "German citizen, have you voted yet? If not, our sacrifice is in vain."[3]

Raid

Tuesday and Wednesday, the days after the plebiscite, passed quietly. Perhaps nothing would happen. Thursday, November 16, dawned dull and gray. Families woke up as usual, ate breakfast together, and sent their children off to school. The adults went to their assigned work places.

But around 8:00 in the morning, the Bruderhof was stormed by 140–160 uniformed men: armed SS, rural policemen, and Gestapo, led by Inspector Dr. Hütteroth of the Gestapo office in Kassel. Later the members told what had happened to each of them.[4]

Kurt Zimmermann was on his way to the carpentry shop. His wife Marianne had gone to the school where she was teaching. Suddenly he heard voices and saw a whole crowd of uniformed SS men streaming down the hill. He ran back to the school and knocked on the window of the classroom where Marianne was teaching. "I want to say good-bye quickly; it might not be possible later," he said to her, fearing that all was over and they would be scattered or worse.

Heiner was in the barn hitching the horses to the wagon. Suddenly Alfred came running in: "Do you see those two SS men? I am afraid they are going to your father." Heiner looked out the door and saw them marching toward his father's room. He called to Josef and ran out. The whole place was swarming with SS and police. They had surrounded the property and now appeared from all sides, almost as if out of the ground. Some were armed. As he tried to run to his father's room they shouted at him, "Stop! Stop!" An SS man drew his revolver and shouted, "Stand against the wall! All of you!" Two of them took hold of Heiner and lined him and the others against the wall of the print shop. He was afraid they would be shot. There were Josef Stängl, Peter Mathis, Alfred Gneiting, Arno Martin, Kurt Zimmermann, Adolf Braun, Ludwig Kleine, and Friedel Sondheimer.

Friedel was Jewish and mentally handicapped; he simply refused to stand against the wall. Heiner pleaded with him, but he said, "No! I was told to bring firewood to the kitchen." The men were searched for weapons; every pocket had to be turned out. When no weapons were found, the Nazis shouted and herded them into the carpentry shop, guarding the doors. Armed men with revolvers drawn stood at the doors and windows. They kept asking where the weapons had been buried. "We are Christians. We have no weapons," Heiner replied. At this they laughed.

Heiner wondered what they were doing to his father and the women who worked in the school, kitchen, laundry, or nursery, where there were no men. Many hours passed. The sun rose higher.

On the second floor of the children's house Annemarie was tidying the bedrooms of the foster children she was caring for. When she looked out of the window she was shocked to see the SS men coming from all sides. Within minutes they were in the building at every door, and nobody could leave the room in which she happened to be. Annemarie was trapped. She was not allowed to go to the dining room and had no way of knowing what was happening.

Trudi Hüssy was teaching. Among the police she recognized Police Officer Weigand, who whispered a comforting word to her. The younger children were more curious than frightened; the older ones were aware of the danger. From the classroom they heard the tramping of heavy boots in the private living quarters above.

Emmy was helping Eberhard who was still confined to his bed. Suddenly her sister Moni (who was a nurse) appeared at the bedroom door to tell them that the whole place was crawling with SS and police. Two SS men were standing outside the living room, but Police Officer Weigand would not let them enter the room until "the doctor and his wife" were up. Two SS men were in Eberhard's study, and in the living room two policemen started to look through everything: writing desk, boxes, chest, cupboard.

Moni had her wits about her. She closed the door to Eberhard's room and told the intruders she must first treat the sick man. There was a little wood-burning stove in the room, and into it she threw potentially incriminating documents—meeting transcripts, notes, and letters containing Eberhard's sharpest criticisms of the Nazis.

From where they were held, the community members were called one by one to the dining hall, where the Gestapo from Kassel, a few SS men, and the district administrator were seated. The place no longer looked like their dining room. The Gestapo had taken over. The men and women were questioned individually, and everything they said was typed up.

Susi Gravenhorst was asked whether she had been persuaded by Eberhard Arnold to join the community. "No," she answered, "I came of my own free decision." Later she remarked, "In that moment, all my fear left me."

The chief Gestapo officer went to the carpentry shop where the young men were being held. Heiner asked him if he could go to his father. "Who are you?" the officer asked.

"Heinrich Arnold."

He was taken under guard to the dining room. As he walked past the room where his father lay, he heard shouting and scolding. "You are a communist, an enemy of the Fatherland, an agitator!" Heiner heard his father answer calmly and clearly, with no anxiety in his voice.

Chapter 7—Plebiscite and Raid

As a school boy Heiner had founded a club, the Sun Troop, with the mission of telling other children about Jesus. He and his friends had made a flag, red with a yellow sun, which still hung in the dining room. Now the soldiers pounced on this—red was a sign of communism. They had heard that Heiner had designed it, and now they questioned him about it.

To their amazement, the police got the same answer from everyone they questioned, and as the day wore on they became quiet. "There is a peculiar unity here," one of them said. "Nobody is afraid."

The raiders had probably expected resistance. They looked in, under, and on top of beds and cupboards, and underneath floorboards. Walls were torn open and all chests and boxes emptied. Hans Meier had to unscrew one of his electrical tools to show that it wasn't a time bomb. Books and letters, including personal letters of engaged and married couples, were scrutinized and sometimes ridiculed. Particular attention was paid to letters from abroad, in search for what was called "horror propaganda" against Germany which was punishable as treason. Artwork that the publishing house had collected was taken as "pornographic." Anything the raiders found offensive was carried to the dining room where pictures, books, and writings were heaped up.

The men searched longest in Eberhard's study and in the archives and library, for anything "hostile to the state." Eberhard lay on a sofa in the Arnold living room with his painful leg raised on a cushion. He asked repeatedly to speak with the men in charge. Finally they came to his bedside. He greeted them and thanked them for coming as he had been waiting for an open, heart-to-heart exchange with them. He told the Gestapo leader that out of love he would have to tell them the truth, and respectfully but very clearly he presented the Bruderhof's position. They questioned him sharply, however, and called him a dangerous, bloodthirsty agitator. One of the SS asserted he could swear that he had seen Eberhard agitate against Adolf Hitler at a communist mass meeting. Eberhard protested, "That is a lie! I challenge you to tell me that to my face! I never did that!" His accuser was silent.

The house search lasted almost all day. Gradually, though, the tension eased; there were conversations between the brothers in the carpentry shop and their guards. It turned out that the SS had been called together from a wide area; some were from the Kinzig valley ten or fifteen miles away and some from Gelnhausen twenty-five miles distant. When asked why they had come, some said they had been called out of bed at midnight "to eradicate a communist nest." Some of the guards said the Bruderhof way of life was actually also *their* ideal; they, too, wanted true community, where the common interest would supersede self-interest, but because people would not do it of their own free will, they had to be compelled to do it.

One of the Gestapo officers said: "If some crackpots want to live together and preach to one another, that is their business. But there is to be no propaganda. And the children are not to be brought up this way."

While looking about in the Arnolds' living room, Inspector Hütteroth noticed the von Hollander family's coat of arms on a piece of furniture. "Is there someone here by the name of von Hollander?" he asked.

Emmy Arnold answered: "Yes, that was my name. My father was Johann Heinrich von Hollander, professor of law in Halle."

"Then I helped carry your father to his grave," the Gestapo chief replied. He bowed and clicked his heels. He had been one of Heinrich von Hollander's students.

At 5:00, when it was already getting dark, the intruders left at last, marching off four abreast. A small crowd of peasants had gathered from the neighborhood to see how many from the Bruderhof would be arrested and were perhaps disappointed that no one was. The top officials drove off in a big car carrying several laundry baskets full of books, writings, and records of meetings. They took away all the books with red covers, assuming them to be communist. They also seized minutes of brotherhood meetings to see whether Eberhard or others had used subversive language against Hitler and his government. They left with the recommendation that the Bruderhof leave Germany.

Hans-Hermann wrote a rather dry account of this day to his brother Hardy:

> You asked me for a detailed report of that fateful day, the sixteenth. I must confess that I feel little talent for this. Actually it was pretty uneventful. In the morning one hundred SS men and twenty-two "protective" police came onto our land and confiscated everything. We were all sent into the dining room under guard while they searched the house from top to bottom for weapons and writings. Unfortunately they discovered brotherhood minutes which they confiscated and took to Kassel. They also found

a few suspicious books (Hans Volker). Then they left saying it would probably be good if we emigrated. That was all.[5]

After the Raid

The community breathed a sigh of relief. In the evening the brotherhood gathered at Eberhard's bedside and offered a heartfelt prayer of thanks. Danger had passed them by for the moment. Eberhard was in tremendous pain; he looked pale and worn. He fully expected to be arrested. "If you ever read in the papers that I committed suicide," he said, "do not believe it."

Leave the country, the SS had said. But where could they go? They were over a hundred people, many of them young children. Switzerland? England? The United States or Canada? They had invested so much in their beloved Rhön Bruderhof. But more than that, Eberhard believed the community still had a mission task, of witnessing to a life of brotherhood. They would not leave until they were forced to or God showed them clearly that they should emigrate.

The Bruderhof was now being watched even more closely. It was surrounded by enemies. One of the duties of the night watchman was to walk around the building during meetings to make sure no one was listening at the windows. The previous owners of the farmstead, an old peasant couple by the name of Valentin and Maria Schäfer with their twelve-year-old daughter Josephine, had a legal right to continue living in three rooms on the second floor of the main house. The relationship to the Schäfers was a friendly one, and Valentin was helpful in answering questions about the farm. But they had no wish to be identified politically with the community, on special occasions the Schäfers flew the swastika flag from their window.

Their living room happened to be directly below the Arnolds' living room, a little attic room with sloping ceiling that served often as a meeting room, especially while Eberhard was laid up with his broken leg. One evening the watchman caught sight of someone in the Schäfers' living room standing on a chair. Whoever it was could almost put his ear to the ceiling! The community had always been surprised how much the district administrator knew about details of their life. Now they discovered that Josephine Schäfer was asked every morning by her teacher in Eichenried what she could tell about the Bruderhof. The teacher herself admitted after the war that she had passed along to the Nazis all that she learned. As soon as Eberhard could bear the strain of going up and down the stairs, the community moved its meetings to the dining room on the first floor and on the other side of the house.

Following the raid and house search, Eberhard asked Fritz Kleiner's help to protect what was already printed of *Innerland* from being seized and destroyed. Fritz made special metal boxes to protect the signatures from moisture, and these were buried on the hill behind the Bruderhof. Only the two men who actually did the digging knew about it. Later, when the Alm Bruderhof was established, the signatures were secretly dug up and taken, over a period of months, to Liechtenstein. They survived remarkably well. In spite of the secrecy, prying eyes must have noticed the faint glow of the kerosene lamps used by the diggers; certainly rumors spread that the Bruderhof had a cache of weapons up on the hill.

Four days after the raid, on November 20, Eberhard wrote to the man who had led it, Inspector Hütteroth in Kassel. In this letter he did his best to defuse the explosive nature of some of the material the Gestapo had confiscated:

> The undersigned wishes once more to express to the director of the secret state police in Kassel his sincere thanks for their visit and thoroughgoing investigation of November 16. We are happy that the governments of both the Reich and the State of Prussia are now in a position to ascertain the real facts and true state of affairs with respect to all the complaints made against our brotherhood, which up to now we have had no opportunity to respond to. We had urgently requested and expected that visit. As you could see, we had left everything, important or unimportant, just as it would have been had we not expected such a visit from the government.
>
> We had not even gone through the important and strictly confidential minutes of our brotherhood meetings. They have to be understood as unchecked shorthand notes, which, though surely free of gross errors, give only a very imperfect and incomplete picture of our discussions and decisions. You will know how to safeguard everything of a personal nature as well as various letters—these being confidential family matters within our monastic order—from the irresponsible foolishness of persons with no active part in the management of the state and Reich, for in all that material you will find nothing that would warrant public exposure...

I would have liked so much to convey [our beliefs] to your youngest and most tempestuous companion, but it was hard to find a listening ear that would enter a heart-to-heart talk that alone can lead to clarity. After so many of you visited, the one point that grieves me deeply is that in proportion to the rest of your investigation you all took so little time to inquire about my and our inmost thoughts and feelings ... Perhaps your political duties will require you to engage in a more thorough exchange about these matters at some future time. I and my helpers and all brotherhood members will gladly be at your disposal.

I would especially have welcomed an opportunity to speak in greater detail about your repeated insistence that true Christianity requires nationwide mission. I would have told you how, just as all of us have done in our various ways, my wife and I, though our background was exclusively academic, went right out among the people to whom we belong. For the sake of Christ, and Christ only, we sought close contact with, and a deeper understanding of, all Christian movements, especially also, the German youth movements before and immediately after the war, and the various workers' movements—always with the one goal of helping as many people as possible to turn from their wrong ways and half-truths to the one and only truth of the gospel.

We ask you to understand in this light all the books and writings to which you took exception. In proportion to our total library of nearly eight thousand volumes and many thousand pages of writings they represent but a small fraction of what we need for our research work ... I inherited for our brotherhood quantities of books from the libraries of my father, my father-in-law, and my mother's last brother—all of them, like my grandfather and great-grandfather and other relatives, professors at German universities. Their libraries contained books and writings of the kind you object to. The owners in no way shared the world views and ideologies in question, but all the more they felt it their duty to be reasonably well informed about such contemporary trends.

True, in comparison with those ideologies, the floodtide of National Socialism has caught us quite unprepared, and even now we know much too little about its philosophy. But as you can gather from the *Confession of Our Religion* of 1540, the very sternness and severity of the National Socialist government could not but prove to us that it has been instituted by God, that is, by God's wrath, whereas we brethren are called to the love of Christ, to love alone. That explains on the one hand our misgivings, and on the other hand our declarations of respect for the present national government; we can therefore perceive no contradiction in our attitude. We love our German land and people and want to belong to them all our life. As you will gather from my writings, especially from my book *Innerland*, my German background and outlook were formed by the old folk songs, by German mysticism, by Fichte and Schelling, but above all by our Christian brotherhood movement, now 400 years old, which is so characteristically German in all its ways.

For just that reason I had hoped we would be enabled to honor the present government more and more and, vice versa, that we would be granted the privilege of living in the midst of the new Germany unmolested, following our conscience as Germans and Christians, learning ever better to render to the present government with respect and love whatever is due to it, since God has given it authority over us.

With sincere respect and love,
the spokesman of the Bruderhof,
a branch of the communal church known as Hutterian,

[signed] Eberhard Arnold

Two brothers were sent to Kassel to deliver the letter to Inspector Hütteroth personally—Hans Zumpe and Hannes Boller. They also called on the regional governor, Baron von Monbart. In reply to their request for his advice, he told them it was no concern of his; the matter lay in the hands of the Gestapo.[6]

As a safety precaution, a German brother traveled whenever possible with a brother from Switzerland or Sweden when visiting government officials. Eberhard often carried letters from abroad when he traveled, since at this time Germany was still trying to preserve an image of legality abroad.

Hardy asked Professor Karl Heim in Tübingen to write a letter of support for the Bruderhof. Heim consented, a brave step knowing that the Bruderhof was in disfavor with the government. Eberhard enclosed a copy of this letter in several of his petitions:

Tübingen, November 26, 1933

I have been in contact with the leader of the Bruderhof, Dr. Eberhard Arnold, ever since his student years. He is the son of the late church historian in Breslau. I have been in a position to observe the personal sacrifices and the hard work of the growing Bruderhof community in its agricultural development. They have built up this farm in the heart of Germany, and they have maintained it with tenacity and diligence through extremely hard times.

The early Christian pattern of community of goods practiced on the Bruderhof follows the example of the Hutterian Brethren of the Reformation period. It is much older than any political communism and has nothing whatever to do with it. On the contrary, the brotherly love practiced at the Bruderhof has contributed more—in an spiritual way—toward overcoming political communism than many a present measure designed to overcome Marxism. Year after year the Bruderhof has taken in hundreds of fellow Germans who are in economic and emotional need and given them a chance to share in the communal work for shorter or longer periods of time.

I understand the intention is to dissolve the Bruderhof. The reason given is that its members share everything in accordance with the Franciscan ideal and also because, in line with the Hutterian tradition, they reject any use of violence, including military service. Such dissolution would make a considerable number of farm families homeless and destitute and compel them to emigrate. They have no private property. With a religious vow, they have bound themselves to a lifelong observation of the rules that govern their life; they cannot turn away from those vows. For reasons of foreign policy alone I would consider a forced dissolution unwise. If present-day Germany were to drive these selfless people into exile, her reputation abroad would suffer seriously. Besides, I can see no legal grounds for such a measure. Consider:

1) The early Christian community of goods practiced at the Bruderhof has as little to do with political communism as the cooperative structure of the Moravian church. It is merely the expression of religious togetherness.

2) The refusal of military service, as practiced at the Bruderhof, is a purely individual decision. They clearly recognize the necessity for the state to use force. Thus such an attitude has nothing to do with pacifism. If, for example, members of Catholic monastic orders are allowed to abstain from active military service because they have bound themselves by a religious vow, it is hard to see why a similar exception cannot be made also in this case.

(signed) Karl Heim, Tübingen

8

November to December 1933

School Inspection

CHILDREN WERE AN INTEGRAL part of the community. In 1933 there were forty-eight children eighteen years old or younger, fifteen of whom were foster children. The community had taken in foster children from its beginning; most of them had an outside sponsor who sent a monthly sum for their upkeep, and the government gave some assistance as well. Some were teenagers now, having spent their entire childhood with the community; indeed some would remain with the community their whole lives.

As yet there had been no official word that the school should close, but Hitler was clearly targeting the young with his indoctrination. How long would they be allowed to retain their private school privileges?

On November 22, 1933—maybe in order to buy time, since they clearly had no intention of entrusting their children to the care of a Nazi teacher—the community wrote to the school authorities of the regional government seat in Kassel:

> Because of the stand we took on the November 12 plebiscite (see the enclosed copy of our ballot statement), the Gestapo in Kassel has objected to our children being taught by our own teachers. We are afraid our children will be exposed to harassment if they have to attend the nearest village school in Eichenried, and we turn to you with the following request: As soon as possible, please be so kind as to assign to our school a young, certified elementary school teacher who supports National Socialism. The Bruderhof would be responsible for free board and lodging and would pay the customary salary.

As they had feared, the foster children were the first to be taken away. Trudi Hüssy, who had been the community's teacher since 1921, described some of them.

> In 1927 Adolf Braun and his wife Martha took Karl Erhard, a neglected Gypsy child, into their home. Martha cared for the boy, who was plagued by scabies and lice. He was a toddler of a year and a half or so and completely helpless. He grew to be a healthy schoolboy, quite bright and very much loved. He was with us for six years. Then suddenly one evening in November 1933, there was a knock at the door. Karl Erhard's father came in, dressed in a storm trooper's uniform. He greeted us with, "Heil Hitler!" and produced an official document to the effect that he was to take the boy with him. There was nothing we could do.
>
> Another Gypsy child was with us even longer: Ulala. He was brought to us by his parents when he was four months old. He had been fed only cabbage soup and crusts of bread. Moni nursed him to health, and he grew to be a bonnie little fellow; he stayed with us from 1925 to 1933. His father, too, turned up in a smart uniform.
>
> With the four Helwig brothers it was similar. Their parents had brought them to us and gone to Canada. But they were dissatisfied there, and when Hitler came to power they thought they would have a new chance in Germany. They showed up on January 8, 1934, for their children.[1]

Beginning in mid-November, the community took steps to protect other children and young people from being removed by the authorities. Younger children were sent temporarily for safety to their guardians while the community tried to find a solution. Thirteen-year-old Rudi went to his guardian in Nuremberg. Helmut and Edgar, two thirteen-year-olds, went back to their parents. Apprenticeships were found for some of the teenagers. Wolfgang Loewenthal was of special concern because he was Jewish. He was placed in a nearby village until he could be spirited out of the country.

Hans-Hermann went to Switzerland for a few weeks because of illness; he stayed with relatives of the Bollers. From there he could write more freely than was possible from Germany, and he wrote to his brother Hardy in England:

> Under pressure from the government we had to send Luise, Liesel, Erna, Helmut, Edgar, Karl-Heinz, Albert, and Rudi away,

otherwise the SS or SA would have removed them and we would have lost all contact with them. For those among them who want to stand with the church, we found work as maids or domestic helpers. Some started a training. We are in close contact with all of them. Marie Eckhardt might adopt Rudi. We are still on the offensive, and the authorities will be surprised when they come to take the children and young people away and none of them are there.[2]

On December 5, 1933, Dr. Hammacher, the school inspector of the Fulda District, suddenly showed up to examine all the classes. He had come before and appeared then to be favorably impressed by the Bruderhof's education. On this visit, the children in Lene Schulz's class answered his questions well in math, geography, and history. But when he asked them to sing one of the Nazi songs, they didn't know it. Neither could they answer where Hitler was born or what he had done for the German people. "They were no longer so brilliant," Lene remembered. "Their intelligence appeared to have dried up!" In another classroom Trudi had a similar experience:

> To test my group on German poetry, he asked if they knew the Horst Wessel song, the Nazi anthem. They did not. He asked me if I knew it. I said yes. "Why then were the children not taught it, as ordered?"
>
> "We don't teach our children street battle songs," I answered.
>
> He then went on to other subjects. The last one was English, and the children had to read from their exercise book. Quite by chance I opened the book to a short account of the Mayflower, the ship that carried the Pilgrim fathers to North America in 1620. These people had left England and emigrated for conscience's sake. It was strange—we had the feeling we were confronted by something revolutionary, something beyond our grasp. I felt that this school inspector was moved too.
>
> At the end of this last test the inspector shook hands with every child and drew some small object out of his pocket for each of them: an interesting pencil, a little notebook, a little ruler, an unusually shaped eraser, a pencil sharpener in the shape of a globe. He then left us quietly, without any Heil Hitler.
>
> We continued our classes until the Christmas holidays. Each day began with the mute question, "Will this be the last day of school?"[3]

Toward the end of November, the brotherhood sent Hans Meier, a Swiss national, to look for possible places of refuge. He took with him two large knapsacks of documents—shorthand notes and minutes of meetings. At a railway station a suspicious policeman demanded to know what was in his bags. Fortunately he had covered the important contents with pamphlets advertising the Bruderhof's books. That worked; the policeman dug no deeper.

He boarded a train toward Switzerland. He had to change trains several times, and he soon realized he was being shadowed by another man. He reported:

> I went up to him and entered into conversation with him. I asked him where he came from and where he was going, seeing that we were fellow travelers. He asked me where I came from, and I answered truthfully that I came from a community in the Rhön hills. Thereupon he told me that he was a policeman in Worms and had spent his holiday in the Rhön. He had in fact become suspicious of me and had hoped for a good catch, which would have helped him on in his career. But now, he said, he was convinced that I was innocent.[4]

Hans got across the border into Switzerland without further adventure. He stored the precious records in his mother's house in Zurich and then began his search for a home for the Bruderhof's children. He went first to the Essertines sur Rolle on the Lake of Geneva. This was a community that believed the kingdom of God to be imminent. Hans knew that they had a large house that was standing empty and that they took in orphan children.

The Essertine community welcomed him warmly, and he sat with them until after midnight. They consented to taking the children, but not without the explicit agreement of the Swiss government. So Hans went to the education office in Bern. Here he was told that Switzerland was not prepared to add to its tensions with Germany by taking the children. The Bruderhof would have to look further. (The Essertine group did help with regular donations of vegetables.)

From Switzerland, Hans wrote a letter to the Hutterian elders to tell them what the Bruderhof was experiencing. He also sent out a letter to friends of the community:

The Neuwerk community of the Bruderhof sends you this letter in a serious hour.

You are familiar with the Bruderhof's basis of faith: to follow Jesus in complete community in spiritual and temporal matters, in the unity of the Spirit as did the Christians of the first church where nobody owned anything, but they shared all things in common . . . This witness cannot be given through human strength but only through the strength of the living spirit of Christ, and it also brings his cross.

However, today the German Volk stands under the leadership of the swastika, the hooked cross, not the cross of Christ. The deep, often unconscious, longing of humankind—and also of the German Volk—for redemption from conflict and injustice could not be fulfilled by democracy with its many unproductive party quarrels, and it has been derailed by the Antichrist . . .

The brotherhood of the Bruderhof stands in daily prayer to God for the German people and for all peoples, that he might give the government the true fulfillment of its task and give those whom it is persecuting the love of Jesus. We want to meet the need of the time with deeds that witness to the spirit of Christ: an example of life in unity and social justice, work for children, and practical help for the unemployed.

On the other hand, the brotherhood avoids those things that oppose this witness. It will not use the sword of violence; it will only educate the children and youth entrusted to it in the spirit of peace and justice toward all people, regardless of race; it expects salvation (*Heil*) from Christ alone and not from Adolf Hitler or any other person . . .

With this, the brotherhood has placed itself in opposition to the demands of National Socialism which rules Germany. This conflict broke out physically in response to the plebiscite of November 12, 1933, when, in response to the question whether we stood completely behind its policies, we pointed out the difference between worldly authority and the discipleship of Christ. We also expressed the hope that it might be given to those with the task of government to become an instrument of God's love rather than his wrath. As a result of this statement, the Bruderhof was thoroughly searched, though, of course, no weapons or political material were found. But because the conflict between National Socialism and the faith in Christ and his Holy Spirit is very sharp, since National Socialism strives for a unity of blood and race and wants no other witness, it was recommended that we emigrate. The education of our children will also no longer be supported . . . We are prepared, for the sake of Christ, to leave Germany—our home, all earthly goods, and even our lives. We do this not of our own will, but if God allows it to happen, we will bear this cross gladly.[5]

Hans planned to go on to Czechoslovakia to see if this country would be a possible refuge for the Bruderhof as it had been for the Anabaptists of the sixteenth century. Knowing that Leonhard Ragaz was a personal friend of Thomas Masaryk, the president of Czechoslovakia, he asked him for a letter of introduction. Despite the differences between them, Ragaz wrote a strong endorsement. He pointed out that the Bruderhof could not possibly continue in National Socialist Germany. He ended:

> From my observations over a decade and from my close spiritual contact with the founders and leading members of the Bruderhof, I can add that this work is born of the loftiest intentions and has been carried on in a spirit of heroism in the face of tremendous difficulties. An abundance of faith, love, hope, sacrifice, dedication, and admirable perseverance has been put into this work. The Bruderhof will certainly be a blessing for any country in which it settles. It is not of a political nature but rather inspired by early Christianity. It is interested not in political propaganda but in loving, brotherly service and in the expectation of God's kingdom.
>
> These are the facts that have led me to plead with you, dear Mr. President, to use your influence so that the Bruderhof may be allowed to settle in your country, to buy or rent real estate, and to carry on its work of faith and love. Thanking you warmly in advance for a kind consideration of this request.[6]

President Masaryk was seriously ill, and Hans only got as far as his secretary. It was soon evident that Czechoslovakia was not willing to take the community.

Hans returned home on December 13. In spite of his efforts, there was still no solution to the question of the Bruderhof's school children.

Additional Letters

Parents of some of the young adults who had joined the Bruderhof were unhappy about the decision their children had made. Baron von Monbart, governor of the Kassel region, warned the community that allegations against the Bruderhof from relatives would carry considerable weight in deciding its future. He informed the community that there would be a meeting on December 11, 1933, between himself, the Gestapo, and the district administrator, Burkhardt. If the Bruderhof wished to submit material to that meeting, they could.

In response, Eberhard drew up a statement entitled: "Material for the meeting about the Bruderhof," and mailed copies of it on December 6, 1933, to: the Prussian Gestapo, Berlin; the Gestapo, Kassel; the regional governor in Kassel; the district administrator of Fulda; and School Superintendent Dr. Kellner, Kassel.

This was the most comprehensive statement in writing by the Bruderhof to make clear its position to the National Socialist government. Eberhard wrote it, both as a spokesman of the Bruderhof, and as a senior minister in the Hutterian church. Extracts of the main points follow:

> In worship meetings and members' meetings we have continually acknowledged and stressed the God-ordained necessity of the present state and its military might. Over the last months we have said over and over that we are facing divine wrath, inevitable historic judgment over the widespread political, social, and moral disintegration rampant for many years. In opposition to all that, God's wrath wants the natural order rooted in God's creation—the nation with its culture and customs—to be reestablished under the strict discipline of the state and on the basis of its ideology. For months we have again and again acknowledged wholeheartedly that the state needs a government that leads toward national unity by sternly opposing everything that destroys and separates. In our daily church prayers we have interceded faithfully for all men in positions of authority.
>
> Over many months too we have expressed in numerous meetings our special love and respect for the present government and its Führer and chancellor regarding these specific points of their program:
>
> 1) The demand that the common good must everywhere come before self-interest, a demand we respond to completely.
>
> 2) The goal of bringing about a people's community in Germany—a centuries-old goal also for our Hutterian Brethren—and the avowed will to work for a more just and peaceful relationship between that people's community and other similar national units.
>
> 3) Ridding the public atmosphere of the spirit of bolshevism, of mammonistic corruption, sexual impurity, and marital unfaithfulness—a cleansing also strongly demanded and represented as part of our church's task.

4) The extremely successful fight against corruptive unemployment—an endeavor that on a small scale our Bruderhof, too, has been actively engaged in for many years at great sacrifice.

We acknowledge these positive points. We believe and teach, however, the fundamental distinction between Christ's original mission and the state's—whatever form the state might take, including the present government. An inevitable part of the state's nature is the use of force. The Christian church, as our Bruderhofs witness to on both sides of the Atlantic, cannot take any active part in that force, not even in military training or education. The discipleship of Jesus Christ, as the Hutterian Brethren seek to live it, means practicing the healing love of God, not the judgment of his wrath. For our consciences, therefore, the natural order of family and nation, though we hold it sacred, is clearly subordinate to the new creation of the Spirit, the church of Christ, and the kingdom of God. In such a church the enlightening discipline of the Holy Spirit of Jesus Christ, who cleanses and unites, takes the place of military, political, and legal severity.

It is on the basis of that faith and in that positive sense that we gather in our brotherhood meetings. In these members' meetings—strictly confidential and closed as befits a religious order—we have repeatedly expressed misgivings that spring from a deep inner Christian conviction with respect to the following points. We ask that our difference of opinion on these points not be mistaken for animosity; our faith demands us to sincerely love and honor all men in governmental positions.

1) The present government insists more strongly than ever before on the primacy of the state, which claims absolute authority and dominates the nation with its ideology. For a church bound to Christ, obedience to God and dedication to his kingdom take precedence over everything without exception and must remain paramount. We are profoundly disturbed that in the present situation anyone pledged to that obedience and commitment inevitably comes into a severe conflict of conscience.

2) The way of life required by the church's faith seems therefore to be threatened because its freedom of conscience is in jeopardy. In jeopardy is the freedom of conviction that asks nothing more than to follow and live the utter goodness and purity of Jesus Christ, the one Führer, master, and liberator of his disciples.

3) A particular concern is the freedom of speech and of education that the apostolic mission of Jesus Christ requires and without which we cannot live. For the sake of that freedom, all convinced Christians must obey the call of God, looking neither to the right nor to the left. We would appreciate a clear statement

about the extent to which that freedom will still be granted in Germany.

4) Our consciences are therefore under severe tension. Does the prevailing national movement place man and his importance, the state and its commands, above God and his word, above Christ and his spirit? Clearly, all who are called to be Christians must honor God above everything and obey him rather than men.

5) In particular, the seemingly absolute belief in Aryan—especially Nordic—blood causes a Christian to fear that the divine measure of equitable justice toward peoples of other blood will suffer.

6) Finally, we are warned by the history of all centuries that in spite of the responsible leaders' best intentions, whenever a state executes judgment with extreme harshness, the wrath of punishment is liable to come down with utmost severity not only on the guilty and partly guilty but also on innocent people. It is apt to be felt in particular by those who put into practice the love and righteousness of Jesus, by Christians who want nothing to do with the evil and corruption that is the legitimate object of severity. We sincerely request that it not be assumed or even considered that these misgivings arise from any unfriendliness, much less a treasonable or seditious attitude. Rather, our attitude should be seen in its true light, as springing solely from burning and anxious love—a love concerned for the truth, a love that earnestly believes and hopes for what is good and right and is ready to bear any hardship. It is a love that warmly embraces all opponents and is genuinely ready to be corrected by God's word and truth whenever its representatives may have erred because of man's inevitably limited insight.

We know we are completely free of any hostility to the government, the state, or the nation; we are innocent of giving support (even in thought) to any movement or group that is hostile to the present state. Even though we are not, and can never be, National Socialists, we cite our Reichskanzler as our authority. We understand that our Reichskanzler has emphasized that good Germans who do not profess National Socialism may be given time to find their way in relation to the new government; beyond that, in special cases they may be allowed explicit exemption, especially when they represent "positive" Christianity.

This clarification took up half of the letter; the rest of the letter discussed more specific practical questions:

Trusting in that assurance, we have asked, urgently and persistently since the day our District Administrator Dr. Burkhardt took office, that he come to us for a comprehensive discussion about our concerns. We hoped on the one hand to be able to speak out candidly all that stirs our conscience, and on the other hand, to be given an authoritative, official, and detailed personal briefing on the highest goals and ultimate ideals of the National Socialist government and about practical ways to achieve them.

Instead, when we inquired about allegations concerning us in the Schlüchtern district, we were informed by the government representative in Fulda, Dr. Stachels, that if we conducted ourselves in a way displeasing to the authorities at the election and plebiscite of November 12, we should expect our Bruderhof life to be drastically interfered with. Rumors went round that such intervention might even take the form of dissolving the Bruderhof. In response to the rumors, Dr. Karl Heim, the renowned theologian, wrote the enclosed letter as a testimony on our behalf; it is especially reliable because Karl Heim does not share our position.

Over against all that, the detailed ascertainments of the Gestapo in Kassel emphasize the influence of our educational work as the decisive factor. May we point out that just that aspect of our communal life touches a vital nerve of the task committed to our community. Without our educational work we cannot live. If we have understood the demands of the state correctly, our school is to be dissolved or placed under National Socialist direction. We would find dissolution unacceptable, for as things are around here, the long distance to the nearest school in Eichenried presents problems, especially for less robust children. Besides, the upbringing and instruction of children in the spirit of the Christian church known as Hutterian must remain a moral necessity for us. That is why we request that the interests of the state be combined with our Christian concerns. Perhaps the state could designate a not too expensive teacher for our school, a portion (to be determined by the state) of whose salary would be paid by us and under whose supervision our own teachers could share in the instruction. Maybe our small Hutterian church could come to an agreement with the state along the lines of the concordats concluded by the large churches, just as in times past Prussian kings and Russian empresses and tsars granted the Mennonites and our brethren an existence morally acceptable to them and at the same time serving the interests of the state.

We expect the leaders of the North American Bruderhofs (who are all ethnic Germans) to submit a petition to the Reich government similar to the one they sent to President Wilson during the World War, when they had to suffer terrible hardships for being Germans and Christians. Not one of the Hutterian brothers took part in the war against Germany; many were imprisoned for that, and some lost their lives. The Hutterites in the United States opposed the wartime propaganda against Germany, and for that even the oldest and most respected members suffered insults and injuries. For that reason almost all of them emigrated to Canada, where they were assured more freedom of conscience than in the United States.

Though it is the last thing we would want to do, we will also have to emigrate if the German Reich and the Prussian state denies our request to continue the beneficial work that we have undertaken at great sacrifice: rural settlement work, mission among the people, and educating our children. It would be unbearably painful for us to leave our homes and fatherland and to give up our work to help meet the needs of our beloved nation. But if we cannot follow our consciences to live in brotherly community here, we must and will make that sacrifice. The difficulties of such an exodus would be considerable ... We would have to dispose of our German Bruderhof at a price sufficient to recover the more than 130,000 marks our German brethren in America and our German-Swiss members have invested in it and to provide us with the funds necessary for resettling and accommodating our 110 adults and children. We would have to obtain permission to immigrate ... As such preparations would require considerable time, we ask the government, in case such an emigration would prove to be unavoidable, to be kind enough to make the time of transition tolerable, taking into consideration both the inner demands of our conscience and our outward need to make a living.

We face serious problems. Since the raid by the Gestapo, which has become public knowledge, there has been a significant loss in our business transactions. We would be grateful if the authorities would refute the untrue allegations that are circulating about the Bruderhof and causing us serious harm. These false rumors charge us with being *Edelbolschewisten* (idealistic bolshevists), with being involved in a conspiracy with revolutionary communists or political pacifists, and with possessing arms ...

For more than fourteen years of careful management, we have built up a relationship of trust with our many business friends. If that is shattered, we will no longer be able to support our twenty hard-working families and seventy co-workers, whose dedication to the common good has been thoroughly tested. For the sake of our faith, we would have to leave immediately, abandoning all we have, and face the unknown. Without the necessary time and quiet to dissolve our communal household in an orderly way, we would have to let our creditors have everything just as it stands …

Finally, to come back to the main point, the statements made in this letter, and especially in the reports of our brotherhood meetings, can readily be confirmed by these seventy attentive witnesses, for whom absolute truthfulness has been and will always be a main and basic concern in their life together. To underline the factual correctness and thoroughness of our presentation, we enclose our brochure "Light and Fire" … It was written in September of this year, and a first copy was sent to our Reichskanzler Adolf Hitler.

In openhearted trust we lay our future into the hands of the governments of the German Reich and the Prussian state. With sincere love and respect we continue to hold ourselves fully at their disposal.

On behalf of the German Bruderhof—the church called Hutterian—and with its unanimous agreement, its minister and spokesman,

[signed] Eberhard Arnold

There is no evidence that the Bruderhof was ever told the results of that December 11 meeting. However, word of the Gestapo raid of November 16 reached England. Otto Piper, who had known and respected Eberhard for years and was currently teaching at Woodbrooke College in Birmingham, wrote to the German embassy in London, who in turn questioned the German foreign ministry. On January 5, 1934, a member of the SA of Hanau turned up at the Bruderhof in a grand car and asked what had caused the "horror propaganda in England to the effect that the Bruderhof had been dissolved."[7] Evidently the Nazi government did not wish to create martyrs; perhaps the community could be obliterated by other means.

A letter of December 14 was addressed to Dr. Conrad, the Advisor for Church Affairs in the Reich ministry of the interior, following up the earlier letter of introduction of November 7. Now Eberhard wrote to tell him about the "visit" of the Gestapo, making an effort to keep the officer informed about the Bruderhof's action in regard to the plebiscite:

> Faithful to our four-centuries-old tradition, we abstained from taking an active political part in the parliamentary election at the time of the plebiscite. Nevertheless, answering the question that our Reichskanzler Adolf Hitler put to the whole nation, and therefore also to us, was a duty of love and respect that we were happy to fulfill—not in the sense of taking part in the plebiscite as demanded, but in the sense of a thankful, personal reply to the question asked us. Each brotherhood member who was eligible to vote signed the following statement.

The statement was quoted in full in this and most of the letters sent to government agencies. The letter continued:

> Meanwhile the Gestapo in Kassel have gone through all our records, including minutes of our internal brotherhood meetings. To elucidate these, we have submitted to the regional governor in Kassel, to the chief of the Gestapo in Kassel, and to the district administrator a formal statement, a copy of which is enclosed here.
>
> We herewith request the Reich minister of the interior to decide what our fate is to be—whether and under what conditions the four-centuries-old Hutterian church, related to the Mennonites, will be permitted to live in the German Reich according to its professed faith. As an objective description of our way of life, we take the liberty to enclose for your attention a letter of support written by Karl Heim, well-known professor of theology in Tübingen. Through the two brothers we are sending to Berlin we are making ourselves personally available to you; we will be further at your disposal at any time.

On December 16, Eberhard wrote a long letter to Baron von Neurath, minister of foreign affairs. Here he emphasized the Bruderhof's contacts abroad.

> The Bruderhof is a branch of the communities known as Hutterian. They have early Christian as well as centuries-old German roots, and their main body of about four thousand people live in South Dakota and Canada. The Bruderhof asks respectfully that the Reich minister of foreign affairs take a kindly interest in the cause of the Bruderhof as a branch in Germany of that church of expatriate Germans. We request the minister's attention because after the plebiscite and parliamentary election of November 12, 1933, the Bruderhof's single-mindedly religious attitude has been subject to political censure. We take the liberty of submitting our account of what took place with enclosures of

our official letters of November 7 and December 14 to the Reich minister of the interior and the regional governor in Kassel. We also enclose a theological opinion by Dr. Karl Heim, well-known university professor.

Eberhard mentioned that the Bruderhof felt threatened with being forced to emigrate, "for the sake of our Christian conscience." He emphasized their connection with countries abroad:

> Our reason for asking the foreign ministry to consider our situation is not only that we have to reckon with the possibility—a most undesirable one for us—that our 110 members will all have to emigrate for the sake of our Christian conscience. Nor is it the fact that foreign nationals, i.e. Swiss Germans and Swedes, form about a quarter of our village community. Our main reason for appealing to the foreign ministry is that our community, with its deep roots in old German ways and early Christianity, is carried on in the name of and on behalf of the ethnic German communities in North America known as Hutterites, who in their origins are closely related to the strictest of the Mennonites...

Should the Bruderhof be forced to emigrate: "We would ask the Reich minister of foreign affairs to support us with advice and practical help as we prepare responsibly for our collective exodus." After an appeal that the community's land and buildings remain intact for some form of group use, even if its members had to emigrate, the letter ended characteristically, in the name of the Hutterian church in North America.

In a last-ditch effort to save the Bruderhof school, on December 19, 1933, Eberhard addressed another official letter directly to the education minister, Bernhard Rust. With that letter, Eberhard enclosed a copy of a pamphlet that he had written two years earlier: "The Children's Community of the Bruderhof and the Spirit of Its Education."

Trip to Berlin

By the middle of December, Eberhard could be up for a few hours each day and hobble around on his crutches. He was a big man and probably diabetic;[8] he was still so weak that brothers had to walk in front and behind him to support him in case he should fall. As he was not yet able to travel, two Swiss brothers, Hans Meier and Hannes Boller, were sent to Berlin on December 18 to visit the various ministries and hand-deliver the Bruderhof's most recent official letters. They also called at the

Gestapo's national headquarters to find out what they intended to do with the Bruderhof. Hans Meier kept careful notes, partly in shorthand:

> December 18, 1933: With Dr. Conrad [advisor for church affairs], from about 12:10 to 12:30 p.m., on a street by the Königsplatz (near the Victory Column). He did not seem to know anything yet [of the raid of November 16], asked us what had actually happened, and explained that it must have been initiated by Prussia (i.e., the Prussian Gestapo, which the Kassel office was under); they (i.e., the Reich ministry of the interior) had not initiated anything. We asked where that Prussian office was so that we could go straight there. He arranged for us to see Government Assessor Wittig at the Prussian Gestapo, Prinz Albrecht Straße, 2nd floor, room 215.
>
> We were with Wittig from about 1:00 to 1:30 p.m. We passed on regards from Dr. Eberhard Arnold and apologized that Dr. Arnold could not come himself. We handed him our letters to the Gestapo of November 20 and December 6, which he glanced through. He asked, "You were investigated?" and asked why the Gestapo had proceeded against us. We replied that the district administrator's office in Fulda had received denunciations against us from Schlüchtern, which proved to be completely unfounded ...
>
> There was a long phone call, during which a file was brought in. Then Wittig opened it and read aloud a telegram from Veitsteinbach about our non-participation in the plebiscite. That seems to have been the immediate reason for the Gestapo's intervention. Then he read us extracts from the minutes [of our meetings] of March 7, 17, and 25 and June 10, 1933. He said that in Frau Emmy Arnold's history of Sannerz it says, among other things, something about Christian communism. What was most serious in the minutes was the sentence that today the state again clearly shows its predatory nature and that communism at least has an ultimate goal which is lacking in National Socialism ... Several times Wittig was a bit disconcerted, but he always came back to the telltale passages he had in his file. Among other things he declared, "Gentlemen, this material would be quite sufficient for a dissolution, and I cannot represent a more lenient approach. The decision is in the hands of the regional governor in Kassel." ...
>
> Wittig stated further that a lot of Marxist literature was apparently found, including a letter to and from Max Hölz [a well-known communist from Saxony]; there was also mention of immoral and dirty literature. We replied that we had a number of

art portfolios that had been given to Eberhard Arnold when he was the literary editor of the Furche-Verlag. Then, too, woodcuts by Masereel* were said to have been found.

As regards the political question and the goal of National Socialism, we said we had repeatedly asked the district administrator of Fulda to visit us and give us precise information about the aims of the National Socialist government. The assessor replied that that was not the district administrator's task.

As to the question what decision is going to be made, the reply was again that we should wait and see. The question of our emigration was raised. We said we did not want to emigrate but were convinced that we could render a service to the German nation through our witness of a true people's community, however small. Wittig replied that he really could not give any advice, so again we were told to wait. We asked him about our connections abroad—the brethren in North America and the capital investments from Switzerland. As this question was combined with the question what was to happen now, we got no answer other than to wait for the decision [of the governor in Kassel]. Wittig added that with such subversive communist and radically pacifist ideas, we could not possibly educate children properly for the state. We again protested against the reproach that we held communist ideas and declared that what we confess is the gospel and the church of Christ. In that context we asked to have explained to us just what the National Socialist Party means by "positive Christianity." There had to be something opposite, which was rejected as "negative." He answered that an attitude as hostile to the state as was evident from our minutes could not be positive . . .

Wittig excused himself for a moment and left the room, leaving the file open on the desk. While he was gone we saw in the file a letter from the German consul in Winnipeg to the foreign ministry in Berlin, in which he expressed the great concern of the Hutterian Brethren about our situation in Germany. When Wittig returned, he simply closed the file and dismissed us without any further comment.⁹

Hans Meier and Hannes Boller also called on other people who they hoped would offer the Bruderhof some support. One of these was Benjamin H. Unruh (1881–1959), a Mennonite teacher and writer who was instrumental in helping Russian Mennonites emigrate. Hans Meier's report continues:

---

* Frans Masereel (1889–1972), an artist whose woodcuts portrayed the lives of ordinary people. He was condemned by the Nazis.

> Our second task in Berlin was to call on Professor Benjamin Unruh, to see if there was any possibility of our standing with the Mennonites in a joint witness. We met Unruh at the home of his fellow Mennonite, Dr. Ernst Crous in Berlin. But we did not find a sympathetic ear for a joint witness based on our common roots in the Anabaptist movement. Unruh, well acquainted with the history of the Anabaptists, understood our concern immediately, but declared that the present-day German Mennonites had a different attitude to the state and government: now they were willing to obey the state, including performing military service.[10]

Benjamin Unruh did, however, express willingness to help the Bruderhof emigrate to Canada.

Hans and Hannes also visited Martin Niemöller, who with Dietrich Bonhoeffer and others had begun the Pastors' Emergency League in response to the rapid nazification of the church. Niemöller would later be taken to the concentration camp in Sachsenhausen where he suffered brutality and humiliation. But he was not a pacifist; he had commanded a submarine during the First World War and offered to join the navy again at the outbreak of war in 1939. He was not willing to stand in solidarity with the Bruderhof. Hans reported:

> We visited Martin Niemöller at his home in Dahlem. Our question was again whether we could stand together in the escalating spiritual fight and make a united Christian witness against the dark powers of National Socialism. But he refused to have anything to do with us because we were not obedient to the government's order to do military service. Niemöller said that in obedience to a call from the government he would again take charge of a submarine, but he would not obey if Hitler forbade him to proclaim the pure word of God. We spoke at length about obeying the pure word of God that bids us love our enemy, and what that obedience implies. But he remained adamant; he couldn't agree.
>
> We tried to see another member of the Pastors' Emergency League, Pastor Günther Jacob. But his wife asked us fearfully at the door of their apartment to go away quickly before the Gestapo spied us there. They were having enough trouble already, she said.[11]

The Bruderhof stood alone. Neither the English Quakers, the Swiss Religious Socialists, the German Mennonites, nor Lutherans who opposed Hitler would join them in the witness they wished to give.

Chapter 8—November to December 1933

The Hutterian Brethren in North America addressed a letter of petition to the Reich government. It may have been drafted by Eberhard himself but copied and signed by the Hutterian elders and dated December 16, 1933. It was a long letter; only a few paragraphs can be reproduced here. The letter was taken seriously, at least by the ministry of foreign affairs.

> Petition of the Brothers called Hutterites to the German government in Berlin, Reich president Hindenburg, Reichskanzler Adolf Hitler, and their co-workers:
>
> The Hutterian Brethren have at present thirty-six Bruderhofs with about four thousand members in Canada and the United States. Together with the Bruderhof near Neuhof in Germany, they form a church that lives in full community in the spirit of Christ. For the sake of that complete unity, we, the American Bruderhofs, desire to make known to the German government and its co-workers our attitude, arising from our faith in Christ, and the situation of people and nations, in particular of our Bruderhof in Germany. Our attitude is the same as that of our forefathers of the sixteenth century—and ultimately of the early Christian church...
>
> Life means being united in one living body with God, with all his children, and his creation... We humans must unite in love under the sole leading of God's Holy Spirit. For the sake of Christ, who is the way and the life, we can no longer seek our own advantage. None of us claims any longer any property as his own; we hold everything in common and share with the poor. In short, urged by the spirit of Christ, we say, "What is mine is also to be yours" (whereas a non-Christian says, "What is yours is to be mine, too"). Such mutual service in love leads necessarily to full community of all life and all work.
>
> Thus we can truly serve God only if we can live together on our Bruderhofs in complete peace and social justice and strict Christian discipline, if we can educate for such a life of service the children entrusted to us, and if we can meet all our guests with love, regardless of their race and birth. With God's help, we would take upon ourselves any suffering—even physical death—rather than give up that witness to God's love. For the sake of that love we cannot go to court or be part of any military organization or any other institution that uses violence. Because of these basic principles we do not demand sacrifices from others but can only sacrifice ourselves for the sake of Christ. We have in our possession the accounts of more than two thousand persons of our

faith who sacrificed their lives and died a martyr's death, without having demanded any sacrifice from others ...

We ask the supreme government authorities of Germany to appreciate that such an example of a Christian life of practical brotherhood is necessary and is a blessing for the German people, especially at the present difficult time. We plead with you not to impede the carrying out of that task. What should make it easier for you is the fact that we take no part whatever in politics; we want to live only as instruments of the love of Christ.

Christmas

The raid of November 16 had created quite a stir locally and damaged the Bruderhof's business relationships. Word went around that the sale of books and craft items, the children's home, and the Bruderhof school were being closed down. It became known, too, that the Bruderhof's open door and lively guest traffic would be ended. All their sources of income were now being choked off; basically the only income left came from farming.

The swiftly spreading news and rumors had an alarming effect on the community's creditors; they came in droves to claim their money. One even brought with him an armed storm trooper who stood over Hans Zumpe while he demanded immediate payment. The coal merchant refused to deliver any more coal and demanded his money.[12] But Emmy was determined to celebrate Christmas. She wrote to her sister-in-law:

> You will have heard from Mama that we are really struggling economically this year. We have a request: Could you send us red or white Christmas candles? Even for that we have no cash. The [political] difficulties have damaged us financially. But in spite of that we will celebrate Christmas, in true poverty this year. It does not depend on gifts—Jesus was born in a stable—and perhaps this year Christmas will be especially blessed. We are happy. But if you could help us by providing a little light with a few packs of Christmas candles it would give us great joy and be a service to the whole community. Moni would love some poppy seeds, as that means Christmas to her.[13]

Six weeks had passed since Eberhard had broken his leg, and he saw his doctor again. The doctor was not happy. Eberhard was still in pain and had lost weight. But he was given a walking cast, and slowly he began to use his leg again. He wrote to his sons, Hardy in England and Hans-Hermann in Switzerland, who would not be home for Christmas. (He could not spell out his thoughts specifically but wrote in symbolic language):

> Mary, whom we remember during this serious time of Advent, cherished the word for months within her heart before the miraculous birth took place. We too want to take hold of this serious time of waiting, in the expectation that afterwards a new Bruderhof life will be born, serving the glory of God even better through the living word and the Holy Spirit.
>
> Otherwise we don't know what the future will bring. A new decision will be made in Kassel on December 11. The newborn Christ child was immediately taken out of the land of his birth to escape from Herod the king, in order to be spared for something greater, even the greatness of the cross.[14]

Though there was little money for Christmas gifts this year, Alfred managed to bake a Christmas *Stollen*. The group gathered often in the evenings by candlelight. They sang their favorite Christmas carols and thought of the baby Jesus, born in the poverty of a stable.

On December 20, Emy-Margret gave birth to a little boy, Eberhard and Emmy's first grandson. He was called Ben. In a meeting of dedication for this child his grandfather expressed his faith that the Bruderhof would survive the present crisis:

> I am infinitely happy that Emmy's and my second grandchild, the first son and second child of our Emy-Margret and our Hans, can be presented to the church today. We ask God the Almighty, and Jesus Christ, through the Holy Spirit, that this beloved child may be raised in the discipline of God in Christ and his spirit from his early age onwards. We ask that with awakening consciousness he may be introduced into the service of the church, into the love of Christ, and into the calling of his kingdom. We believe that during this child's whole lifetime (to the year 2000 if he remains strong and healthy) the church of Jesus Christ will be protected against all danger from the tyrannical, rapacious beast with its military and judicial power, so that the way of love and unity will be preserved.[15]

After Christmas, Edith traveled to Kees Boeke's Brotherhood House in Bilthoven in the Netherlands where Hardy, her fiancé, met her from

England. Hardy and Edith were to tell their pacifist friends of the danger the Rhön Bruderhof was under.

Edith brought a letter that Eberhard had drafted to the Hutterites in America. The letter shows that he was exploring all possibilities, knowing that sooner or later they would have to leave Germany. Hardy and Edith copied it out ten times and mailed it to ministers of various Hutterite communities.

Bruderhof, Germany
December 1933

Dearly beloved brother,

May the peace of God, the love of Jesus Christ, and the community of the Holy Spirit be with you and all of you dear brothers and sisters.

Your letters have refreshed us again and again and given us deep joy. I have been confined to bed since the beginning of November because I broke my leg and have it in plaster, and my letters have been hindered by the trouble of the times as was the case with Jakob Hutter in 1535 ...

We have been notified in writing that the Bruderhof "can no longer be maintained to the same extent as before, since it gives no guarantee that its education will be in the national interest or according to a recognized church." We suffer this tribulation on account of the articles of faith, as set down in Peter Riedemann's *Confession of Faith* of 1540 ...

Our schoolchildren and their teachers have been invited to Switzerland by a group similar to the Rappists, who live in community of goods and await Christ and his future.† They would probably be ready to accept part of our community, as many as thirty-five souls immediately. These would be the school children with their parents, and would form our daughter community. But the Swiss government is making difficulties with the immigration, since they do not want so many foreigners. We would much rather be all together on one new Bruderhof. In spite of some increases we are only 110 people, because some unbaptized novices have broken their word and become unfaithful in the face of tribulation, and children whom we loved and cared for over a long period have been taken away. We would only divide such a small Bruderhof reluctantly. If we emigrated quickly with the

---

† This was the Essertine community Hans Meier had visited (see above, 111). Unfortunately it did not work out for them to take the Bruderhof children.

whole community, we would have to sell at such low prices that we would lose the little money and goods we have and could not even pay our passage to Canada. The German Mennonites help us with their advice. Their Professor Unruh, who arranged the emigration of the Russian Mennonites to America, is prepared to travel to the government in Canada, if we will pay the fare. There he would arrange our journey and entry into Canada with the help of the Canadian Pacific Company.

We plead for your counsel and help in all these questions . . . Would you be able to get permission for our immigration into Canada? Could you send us money? We have to make many journeys to the government and need to have money on hand in order to undertake the emigration from Germany, which we do not wish for but which will probably soon prove necessary. We want to do this with the friendly agreement of the German authorities. But we would rather see our almost seventy baptized members without house and home, without bed or shelter, than do anything against our faith. We want to do everything we can to preserve for the church of Jesus Christ the little property we have obtained with loving help from you and our Swiss brothers. We often have not a cent in hand, for all the community's assets are tied up in our houses, while our own harvest provides our food as long as we can remain here. We beseech you, in spite of your own poverty, to send us sufficient funds to help us do what is necessary for our children and prepare for emigration.

We know of no way to help ourselves without a large gift of money. However, God gives our hearts courage and joy in spite of many tears. He can also change everything, providing for us so that we can continue with a clear conscience in the service of the church in full community, proclaiming the gospel and educating our children.

May God's Holy Spirit lead both you and us and keep us all in the discipleship and poverty of the love of Jesus Christ, that we may be found faithful to the end in all things. These are great and serious times, and just such periods of severe affliction are given to the church as a blessing. Our faith grows all the more deeply and we find it all the more to be true that "Joy in the Lord is your strength." At the beginning of the Sermon on the Mount in Matthew 5, which I ask you to read again, Jesus said, "Rejoice and be glad!"

We greet you in this joy of the suffering and cross of Jesus Christ and with the kiss of fellowship in the Holy Spirit of God.

From your brothers and sisters in Germany and their lowly servant, who loves you with all his heart as his brothers and sisters. Your faithful

Eberhard Arnold

9

January to February 1934

JUST AS HE HAD asked Professor Karl Heim for a letter of support, Hardy Arnold had written to Professor Jakob Wilhelm Hauer. Early in January his answer came, written on the stationery of the German Faith Movement. Hauer's letter shows the delusion that he, and presumably many other Germans, was under, that National Socialism was really not so bad and things would eventually shake out. And like many others, he was not willing to take a personal risk on behalf of the Bruderhof.

> You will be wondering why you haven't heard from me yet. It was not indifference but an overload of work, particularly unanswered correspondence. In addition it is of course very difficult for me to make a decision in this matter. I considered it this way and that and have unfortunately not found a solution.
> Perhaps you do not understand the situation. It is impossible today to stop official measures. It is a matter of directives from the very top, and these directives have to be followed. For example, I tried to intervene in a situation where a worker was summarily laid off because in 1931 he had been a member of the Communist Party for six weeks. I took the matter all the way up to the Department of the Interior with the help of a National Socialist official whom I knew well. It was all in vain. We have to wait until the details of the amnesty that has been promised are clear. Then such individual situations can be taken up. I hope, by the way, that in your case the worst has been avoided. I am ready at any time to answer questions about your father and his whole endeavor. But I have to wait until the government demands such a statement from me, or it will be seen as interference in official matters. If you can arrange for me to be asked, I will express my conviction that your community has nothing to do with communism as such, that is, with bolshevist communism, but

stands in opposition to it because it is based on a firm Christian foundation.

Please write to me about your situation because, as I said, I see no way to intervene.

With the German greeting*
your J. W. Hauer[1]

Flight of the School Children

As the New Year began, danger threatened from all sides. On the last day of the year, December 31, 1933, the mail brought an official notice from the department of education in Kassel. In 1928 their school had been approved and over the next five years received government funding. This was now withdrawn.

> To the board of directors of the Neuwerk Bruderhof:
>
> In reply to your petition of November 22, 1933: I am not in a position to assign the requested teacher to the elementary and middle school of the Bruderhof. Instead, the events that have become public knowledge oblige me to withdraw the permission to operate a private elementary school and middle school that was granted by the government decree B IV 7420a of January 30, 1928; this withdrawal to take effect immediately. The school inspector in conjunction with the district administrator will shortly send you further directions as to the schooling of your school-age children.

The Bruderhof had to act quickly. Christmas holidays would last until January 8; before that date the twenty German children of school age had to be off the property. As an immediate step, they were sent to various friends or relatives who offered to take them. Lene Schulz, a single woman in her thirties, took three children who had passports to the home of Margrit Meier's parents in Switzerland. They left early on January 3. Gertrud, who was twelve at the time, recalled: "We did not know whether we would ever see our parents again. We spent the first night in a hotel in Basel, and I cried into my pillow. Lene sat at the foot of my bed and comforted me, assuring me that God would be with us and with our families at home."

---

* The German greeting, "Heil Hitler" accompanied by the Hitler salute, became compulsory in July 1933 (Evans, *The Third Reich in Power*, 123).

Police Officer Weigand appeared on January 12 and asked about the school. He was told: "There are no school children of German parents here, only foreign children who are being tutored."

Hans Meier knew a woman who directed a children's home called Morning Light, in Trogen, in the canton of Appenzell. He begged her to help. She answered: "Send the children. God will provide."[2]

Lene took the three children in her care to Trogen, and soon the other children joined them from the temporary homes they had found. Eberhard wrote her an encouraging note:

> You bear on your shoulders the great and wonderful task of representing the spirit of Christ's true church in its unity and purity as the cause of the coming kingdom. All you do and say should now be determined by this task, so that you form a genuine educational community with the beloved children in the spirit of Jesus Christ. We hope it will not be months, but at the most a few weeks, until we can build up an ordered community with you there... Be faithful at your post. The spirit of the church will lead and strengthen you. We all stand with you and carry you in our daily thoughts.[3]

Both at home and in Morning Light they were desperate for cash and often went hungry. In England, Hardy did what he could to raise money. Living in the home of John Stephens, he felt guilty that he was eating so well and living so comfortably when the rest of the community was struggling to survive. A wealthy Quaker had set up a fund for his upkeep. Hardy asked John Stephens whether he could have that money to send to Liechtenstein. John Stephens was indignant. "That money has nothing to do with you. I pay for your books, your food and clothing from that fund." But Hardy insisted. "Okay," Stephens said. "You can have the money. But then you have to leave my house."[4]

So Hardy moved out. A newly married couple, Arnold and Gladys Mason, took him for a week. They introduced him to friends of theirs, and he moved from home to home, staying about a week in each place. At the same time he gave lectures telling about the community and pleaded for financial help. It was a strenuous way to live as he was still taking classes.

The children at Morning Light were generally quite happy. Wolfgang, thirteen years old, wrote to Hardy:

> We received the donation from Doris Lester and wrote her a thank you in English. Now I want to write to you too. We built fantastic snow houses. They have long dark passageways and bright rooms. It was very difficult to build them. We got completely wet. We have a lot of snow. The view is beautiful. When the weather is clear you can see the Alps. Sledding is great. We write tons of letters: several every day.[5]

On January 25, Adolf Braun, father of two of the girls, was sent to Switzerland. He was to sell homemade craft items and books and spend what time he could with the children in Morning Light. Lene wrote to Hardy:

> Yesterday we received 3 pounds, 10 shillings from you. Thank you very much! Adolf arrived yesterday. If he gets permission, he will stay in Switzerland and sell books in order to provide for the children.
>
> The children are doing well. Here we often sense our bond even more strongly than at home. I hardly dare say it, but—because of that—this time has its special joy. We are very happy that we will see Adolf often here in Morning Light and hope that soon someone else will come, perhaps Annemarie.
>
> Most of the children enjoy the mountains and climb up to see the views. We try to hold strictly to our schedule of classes, but we have a lot of housework, and we get up late in order to save light, so our day is shortened. In addition we have to write thank you letters. In the evenings we read together—legends or Tolstoy's short stories.[6]

At the end of January, Annemarie Wächter arrived to support Lene, bringing two more children with her. Now they were about fifteen in Morning Light. It was not an easy task. Apart from their lessons, the children and counselors had to do their own cooking, cleaning, and laundry. The woman in charge of the home, Tante Laura, was very strict. Everything had to be just so, and they were not allowed to make any noise. They felt far away and lonely and looked forward to the weekends when Adolf joined them.

On February 6, 1934, the district administrator in Fulda sent notice that the Bruderhof's children's home was dissolved, in addition to the private school. The community was now forbidden to take in foster children in Germany. It was painful to give up the work with children, and the loss of government funding for the school and children's home was also a tremendous financial setback.

Emil Möller's Property

At the end of 1933, the former owner of one of the tracts of land being cultivated by the Rhön Bruderhof decided to take advantage of a new law to take back his land. This was a particularly heavy blow, because the community had made great investments in this property. The property of the Rhön Bruderhof was purchased at the end of 1926. At an altitude of over 2000 feet, it was cold and windswept. The *Sparhof*, as it was called, had once been a large farm of about 250 acres.[7] Ownership had changed hands many times over the years and the land had been divided and sold in smaller plots. Because the buildings were dilapidated and the fields neglected, the community was able to purchase it at a relatively low price. They initially purchased ninety-five acres. These ninety-five acres, however, were made up of many small lots and the fields were not even contiguous. Interspersed among these lots were fields and meadows owned by two other farmers: Isidor Schäfer and Emil Möller. Eberhard hoped that they could eventually buy the Schäfer and Möller properties so that the land would support a hundred people or more. He envisioned the Bruderhof as a self-sufficient farming community. Over the next several years, they made large investments of money and labor. Adolf Braun, Arno Martin, Walter Hüssy, and Heiner Arnold were sent to the agricultural school in Fulda so that they would be able to oversee the work.

During the first winter, the main project was to renovate the buildings in order to provide adequate living accommodation, as well as space for the children's house and the publishing house. The community moved over from the villa in Sannerz in 1927.

In September 1928, Schäfer sold them his property. Then in 1930 and 1931, Emil Möller expressed interest in selling his piece, the Upper Klösshof, so that he could buy another tract that would be more suitable for his needs.[8] On July 26, 1932, the Rhön Bruderhof signed the contract for the Upper Klösshof, seventy-three acres. Now the community owned about 175 acres of contiguous fields, which they could finally cultivate as one farm. Eberhard used the occasion of this purchase to describe his vision for the building up of the Rhön Bruderhof:

> Today is a special day for us because we have acquired the third section of our Bruderhof property. We are, in fact, not buying a third farm, but the third section of our whole Bruderhof farm. Originally this entire piece of land was one farm ... The step that was taken yesterday was so particularly welcome because the natural interconnections of buildings, meadows, and paths are now restored, which were previously interrupted by Emil Möller's property lying between them. It was a great drawback that we had to cross his land to reach our farmyard. The same applied to his herd of cows and the herders coming through our fields.[9]

A month later he spoke about it again:

> The accession of the third piece of our property and our cultivation of it is tremendously important. It is already noticeable how quickly the crop of oats was brought in. In spite of a horse being sick, we accomplished much more than last year. We had a large number of guests and co-workers who helped us very much. Likewise the garden has improved considerably. We are thankful for what we will be able to preserve and for what we have already canned. There, too, the work has been carried out in a proper and competent way. We have done very well this year.
>
> When land is entrusted to us it is to be developed for the brothers and sisters, for the community, for our children and grandchildren. From the start we should feel the responsibility of having obtained this third piece, and we have to make the best use of it for the cause. We should cultivate the garden that will be given to us, otherwise we sin against an elementary commandment—for it was the first command that God gave to man to cultivate the garden and take care of it. With the purchase of this third plot we have undertaken a serious obligation, that we have incorporated this ground into our small enterprise.[10]

He went on to describe his plans for a windbreak and an orchard. Three thousand trees were to be planted that fall and the following spring. He described the buildings and the layout of a community for 250 people. Water lines and ditches needed to be dug so that swampy fields could be drained. In the fall of 1932, the community hosted a work camp. Thirty young Baptists came for six weeks and planted thousands of trees and dug ditches. An article about this project was printed in a Baptist periodical:

> The Bruderhof has a good reputation with local officials and in the neighborhood and is highly respected. People do not share

the Bruderhof members' perspective on life, but respect their industry, integrity, and honesty. A recent example occurred when the Bruderhof wanted to set up a work camp for voluntary service in reforestation and in planting an orchard. The labor office in Fulda recognized the public benefit of the project, gave permission for the materials, and assigned the organization and supervision of the work to the Bruderhof. All this went very quickly and smoothly, so there was no need for a long interval between the application and the beginning of the project.

But where were the voluntary workers to come from? The labor exchange could easily have provided the necessary thirty men from the immediate neighborhood, and would gladly have done so. But the Bruderhof preferred a group of young men bound by a common faith. When the preference in this direction was expressed, it was immediately understood, and the request granted. That is how it came about that today we have on the Bruderhof a first work camp for Baptists. Our young people's association cooperated with the Bruderhof and circulated a request for volunteers among our membership. Soon they had enough applicants from many parts of the country. After overcoming difficulties such as always crop up at the start of a new project, the work got under way September 26. Not all the thirty had arrived, but more than half of them were there. The general conditions for the work camp are favorable in every way. There was a good spirit among the participants from the start. Everyone felt the love that had prepared a place for them for several months and supplied them with work.[11]

Throughout 1933, the Bruderhof worked to cultivate the land. But on September 29, 1933, a new *Erbhofgesetz* (Reich Entailed Farm Law) was passed. Farms between 7.5 and 125 hectares could no longer be bought or sold, divided, or foreclosed because of debt. In some parts of Germany it was customary for a farmer to divide his property among his sons when he died. Over the years, this had led to the creation of smaller and smaller farms to the point that they were too small to support a family. Now the new Nazi minister of agriculture, Richard Walther Darré, attempted to win the support of the peasantry by introducing new inheritance laws with the aim of preserving farms large enough to be self sufficient.

Unfortunately, the transaction for Emil Möller's land had not yet been completed. His lawyer, Dr. P. Selig, was an ardent Nazi and opposed to the Bruderhof. He suggested to Emil Möller that he could get his land back, with the improvements the Bruderhof had made, by means of this new law. He wrote to the Bruderhof on December 6, 1933, asking if they would vacate the land on repayment of the sum they had paid.

Eberhard realized that fighting Dr. Selig would be difficult. He wrote directly to Dr. Darré himself on December 14, asking that an exception to the new law be made in this case. He appealed to Darré's ideals: "To the best of our knowledge, the Bruderhof is the only communal settlement that in the fourteen years of its existence has gradually developed into a medieval German village community on a small scale." He went on to describe the faith and life of the community and the improvements they had made on the land:

> On these grounds we plead with the Reich minister of agriculture for a special decision regarding our communal settlement, since ours is not an individual, property-owning family but a four-centuries-old religious community in which all work is organized and carried out communally and all capital is given in for the common good, any claims to its return being relinquished . . . If the three combined farms (which in earlier times formed one unit) were to be divided, the buildings erected at considerable cost could not be utilized, and the drainage, reforestation, and windbreak, all developed with hard labor and at great expense, would be largely destroyed.
>
> Unfortunately by pleading the Entailed Farm Law the former owner is pressing for such a breaking up, while we are of the opinion that we have placed him in the position to claim some other and better land under that law. We ask that we be allowed to retain the property intact and enlarge it, inasmuch as our brethren (ethnic Germans living in North America as well as Swiss Germans) have invested 130,000 German marks in it.[12]

In a long letter to Dr. Selig, who was also the lawyer of the district farmers' organization in Fulda, Eberhard gave full details of the property, the community's acquisition of it, and the work they had done on it:

> A few months after acquiring [Emil Möller's farm], with the help of a voluntary labor service, fifteen acres of wasteland were reforested and a further eight acres were planted with fruit trees. These measures by themselves meant an expenditure of 4000 marks . . . Whereas before we took it over, the Sparhof provided a livelihood for 22 persons, the Bruderhof with its industrial workshops today supports 110 persons.[13]

Chapter 9—January to February 1934

In the first week of January 1934, a sympathetic reply came from the Reich ministry for food and agriculture in Berlin, advising the community how to appeal the case.[14] But this would be expensive. Eberhard wrote to Hardy:

> Our Bruderhof has come into most serious economic danger through the action of Emil Möller. We are trying to get a permit so that our contract of purchase for the Upper Klösshof is recognized as an exception to the Reich Entailed Farm Law. To achieve this, we must put down a deposit of 15,000 marks cash. If we don't manage this, all our work of cultivating the land and putting up buildings during the last two years will be lost and the saleable value of the whole Bruderhof will be reduced to a minimum. We would probably get next to nothing.[15]

How could they raise 15,000 marks? They could only beg from friends and family. Emmy traveled to Breslau where Eberhard's family lived; Annemarie went to her mother in Keilhau; Hans Zumpe went to Berlin where he had connections with a publishing house. Eberhard wrote to Hardy: "Here on our Bruderhof we are in the severest economic struggle and cannot raise any funds. Our bread ration is curtailed to almost nothing, and we have experienced again and again in our fourteen years that a breadless diet is detrimental! The Lord's Prayer says with good reason, 'Give us this day our daily *bread*.'"[16]

Apart from the expense, they needed an "expert opinion" from the regional office of agriculture to validate their purchase. But the local office was unsympathetic. Hans Zumpe, who helped Eberhard with the paperwork, described a visit he and Eberhard made to the office of Farmers' Leader Metz and his lawyer Dr. Selig:

> They expounded the idea of "blood and soil" and explained in heart-stirring tones how the peasant was intimately bound to his soil through generations. Eberhard retorted that this was nonsense, that the people and lands of the Sparhof were in a neglected and derelict condition when we had taken over.[17]

A few days later two ominous inspections of the Bruderhof took place. On January 31, a government assessor named Claus arrived, wishing to determine how the Bruderhof houses and land could best be used. Then, representatives of the Reich Farmers' Union appeared. Heiner knew them personally from his agricultural training in Fulda, and they had always been friendly and helpful. Now they seemed cool. It felt like plans were already being made for the liquidation of the Bruderhof.[18]

In fact, documents obtained from the German National Archives express quite clearly that in spring 1934 the Gestapo had intended to dissolve the Bruderhof. A letter from the Office of Church Affairs to the governor of Hessen-Nasau dated July 29, 1936, says:

> I am enclosing a copy of the reports by the secret state police [of June 16 and 19] for your information and opinion.
>
> The matter was submitted already in March 1934 as LK 460 G Nr. III 227; however at that time it was decided not to dissolve the Bruderhof.[19]

The report of the agricultural inspection must have been quite positive. Apparently on the basis of that report, Governor Jerschke himself intervened on behalf of the Bruderhof to defer dissolution. It is worth noting, however, that only two years later in December 1936, the same Governor Jerschke was to reverse his position and ultimately approve plans for dissolving the community.

> As early in 1934 I saw the matter concerning the Hutterian brotherhood as a reason to probe the affairs of this brotherhood. Since at that time the brotherhood's agricultural work was judged favorably, in the report of March 7, 1934, submitted by my agricultural development department (LK 460 G Nr. III 227) I suggested to the Prussian minister for agriculture that the brotherhood's rights not be infringed, and by his decree of May 25, 1934, the Prussian minister for agriculture decided accordingly.[20]

Hospitality Forbidden

In early January another blow came in the form of a letter from Dr. Burkhardt, the district administrator:

> In accordance with paragraphs 14 and 40 of the Police Administration Law, I herewith forbid you to extend hospitality on the Bruderhof to strangers and transients and any person not a member of the Bruderhof or a close relative of one. I further direct you to provide me, within twenty-four hours after their arrival, the names and accurate particulars of new Bruderhof members or of members' relatives. Non-compliance with this injunction would compel me to adopt stringent police measures. You are entitled

to enter a protest against this police injunction with the regional governor in Kassel within two weeks after notification.[21]

Eberhard wrote to Kassel, as recommended. He asked that they be permitted to continue to proclaim the gospel and protested the accusation that their hospitality endangered public safety:

> We request that we be allowed to comply with the injunction against giving hospitality to strangers and those passing through in such a way that, according to our commission, we can continue proclaiming the gospel of Jesus Christ to earnest seekers and those ready to follow the call, all the more so since the injunction assumes the entry of new members.
>
> Our objection lies in the citing of paragraph 14 of the Police Administration Law as the reason for the injunction, since we are firmly committed to confronting anything that might imperil public order or safety. We are determined to be increasingly careful to reject and refute any thoughtless word, so that nothing may arise at our Bruderhof to violate the respect and Christian loyalty we owe and wish to show the government, state, and nation. As regards the basis and content of this stand of ours, we beg you to refer to the numerous petitions and statements we submitted in 1933. With our whole brotherhood known as Hutterian, we continue to represent what is stated therein.
>
> I plead with respect and love that both our objection and our readiness to comply be taken into account.[22]

Just at that time a visitor came, Kaspar Keller from the Werkhof in Switzerland. Two days after his arrival a policeman came up and read out the official notice: the community could no longer offer overnight hospitality to guests. Anyone wishing to stay had to become a "member" and commit to six months. "Will you stay for six months?" Kaspar was asked, "or should we find you lodging in the next village?" He was ready to stay.

In those years of unemployment, there were many tramps. The community had always given them a bed—or at least a place in the shed. This was no longer allowed. The Bruderhof informed the district administrator and mayors of the neighboring towns:

> Because our district administrator has ordered that our Bruderhof can no longer take in people who are passing through, and because the Bruderhof itself only desires to accept as new members those who feel God's call to the gospel and to true Christian com-

munity, and because homeless people are repeatedly directed to our Bruderhof from numerous villages, who have no inclination or vocation to our life of community (simply because here they will receive a roof and a free meal), and because it would be cruel to send people away after sunset, specially in bad weather (several have gotten lost)—we ask the mayor to distribute this message to all houses. It should not happen again that homeless people are sent here against our wishes. All too often they have no desire to convert from serving private good to the common good, from selfish roaming to people's community, and from godlessness to positive Christianity. On the basis of our peace-loving, Germanic, Christian brotherhood, we wish to support the German and the Prussian government, according to our conscience, bound to Christ as our Führer...

With best wishes for your work as mayor and for the welfare of your region, all the best for Hitler and *Heil* in Christ.[23]

From now on, every visitor had to report to Police Officer Weigand immediately on arrival and again when he left. When a member of the community went on a trip, he had to report, giving details of where he was going and for how long. From this time on Police Officer Weigand was the Bruderhof's most regular visitor, paying weekly visits to inquire who was there and what work was being done.

On January 20, Eberhard saw the doctor again. The cast was removed, but his leg was still swollen and painful.[24] The stress of the last months was wearing on him, and the doctor said it might be a long time before he was really well again.[25]

As outward conditions grew more and more difficult, Eberhard tried to establish the church more firmly. On January 11, he baptized eleven new members. Karl Keiderling described the service in a letter to Lene:

> Eberhard proclaimed clearly again that whoever enters the church and is baptized cannot expect comfort. He makes a complete break with all his former relationships; his old life is buried and forgiven, and now he lives in the strength and in the future of the risen one. He promises to die rather than sin consciously, and he has to be ready to abandon house, home, and all possessions for the sake of his faith. These are outrageous demands that can only be fulfilled through faith in the strength of the living Spirit...

How those being baptized kneeled down, how Eberhard laid his hands on them and what he said to each of them in the authority of the Holy Spirit—all this I will not try to describe out of reverence for this powerful experience. I am unable to convey the essence and depth of this experience. Those who were baptized gave their personal testimonies freely and joyfully.²⁶

On February 11, he ordained Hans Zumpe and Hannes Boller as ministers or "servants of the Word," as he liked to say, using the old Hutterian terminology. It was clear by now that a second Bruderhof would have to be started outside of Germany. Eberhard also expected sooner or later to be imprisoned and killed, and he wanted to provide for the community's continuance. The ordination was a solemn, festive occasion, and for the week preceding the event, he read from the orders and practices of the Hutterites of the sixteenth century. Eberhard hoped Hans Zumpe would take primary responsibility for the Rhön Bruderhof in Germany as he was familiar with the local authorities. Hannes Boller, who had been a pastor, would move to the new place once it was established. Eberhard himself would oversee both communities and travel often between them. Edith's letters to Hardy describe those days:

> We are experiencing very important days. Through the readings in preparation for the service of the Word we are being led deeply into the spirit of mission, into the nature of the true apostolic church. We feel how far we still are from the capability of sending out apostles to go from town to town on foot, without purse or money. Yet we feel with great gratitude that we are coming closer and closer to this, through no doing of our own. More painfully than ever we feel our poverty; we grown-ups take it with joy and as a gift of grace, but it fills us with worry for our very youngest . . .
> We realize more and more clearly how alien we necessarily are on this earth in its present spiritual condition; nowhere can we feel at home here.²⁷
>
> We hope the confirmation of the service of the Word will soon be held; unfortunately there are constant delays. This confirmation by the laying on of hands is the greatest that can be given us in this hour. It is a symbol of the living stream of power that has been passed on from hand to hand through the centuries, a power of the Spirit that has moved through history to the present day and is laid into our hands as a responsibility to see that the commission of apostolic mission is handed on at this point of

development in history. It is hard to grasp completely the great significance of this action. An enormous responsibility rests upon Papa, and one always has the feeling that he does not have enough help. Unfortunately his leg is still giving him more pain than it should.[28]

Hannes Boller wrote:

If I think of our experiences of the past weeks, I can only compare it to the rushing of a powerful river; in its bed are small bowls that are constantly filled to overflowing. Although they are filled to the brim, they remain insignificant vessels that can only be distinguished from other humble vessels by the fact that the river has flooded them ... Through this event we can expect new gifts to be given to the church—perhaps to those who are sent out, perhaps here, perhaps in many places.[29]

Eberhard and Emmy Arnold with their children in their home in Berlin

The Arnold family in Sannerz. From left to right: Hans-Hermann, Emy-Margret, Emmy, Monika, Eberhard, Heiner, Hardy

Eberhard Arnold

Emmy Arnold

The Rhön Bruderhof

Folk dancing at the Rhön Bruderhof

Dining Hall at the Rhön Bruderhof

Eberhard Arnold (center) with members of the Rhön Bruderhof

The community meets for lunch outside

Emmy Arnold and Arno Martin on the harvest wagon, October 1933

The Alm Bruderhof

Wedding of Hardy Arnold and Edith Boeker
at the Alm Bruderhof, August 1934

Escaped from prison, the three men are reunited with their wives in England. (Bearded men from left to right: Adolf Braun, Hannes Boller, Karl Keiderling, Hans Meier)

Der Reichsbischof   Berlin-Charlottenburg 2   den 11.10.33.
                           Jebensstraße 3
                           C 1 Steinplatz 5231

Herrn

Dr. Eberhard Arnold.

B r u d e r h o f
bei Fulda a.d. Rhön.

Es würde den Herrn Reichsbischof interessieren von Ihnen zu erfahren, wie Sie und Ihre Gemeinschaft zum Christentum und zur Kirche stehen. Für Uebersendung entsprechender Unterlagen wären wir dankbar.

Im Auftrage

[signature]

Letter from Reich Bishop Ludwig Müller to Eberhard Arnold, asking for a statement. See p. 81.

First draft of Eberhard Arnold's letter to Adolf Hitler. See p. 88.

Abschrift.   00237

Staatspolizeiliche Anordnung.

Gemäss §§ 1, 4 der Verordnung des Reichspräsidenten zum Schutze von Volk und Staat vom 28. 2. 1933 (RGBl. I. S. 83) wird der Verein

" Neuwerk - Bruderhof e. V. ", Veitsteinbach, Krs. Fulda,

aus staatspolizeilichen Gründen mit sofortiger Wirkung aufgelöst. Das gesamte Vereinsvermögen wird beschlagnahmt.

Zuwiderhandlungen gegen diese Anordnung - insbesondere eine Weiterbetätigung im Sinne des aufgelösten Vereins - sind gemäss § 4 der genannten Verordnung strafbar.

Ein Rechtsmittel gegen diese Anordnung ist nicht gegeben. Es bleibt jedoch überlassen, sich mit der Dienstaufsichtsbeschwerde an das Geheime Staatspolizeiamt in Berlin zu wenden.

K a s s e l , den 9. April 1937
Geheime Staatspolizei
Staatspolizeistelle für den Reg.Bez.Kassel:

gez. H e r r m a n n .

Für richtige Abschrift:
Kassel, den 15. 5. 1937

I/1 B. 2526/36.

Kanzleiangestellte.

Order of the Gestapo dissolving the Rhön Bruderhof. See above, 1.

10

February to May 1934

Founding the Alm Bruderhof

EBERHARD AND EMMY WANTED to travel to Switzerland. Their son Hans-Hermann was still in Switzerland, recuperating from tuberculosis. But they were even more concerned for the children, who were starting to get homesick. A more permanent home had to be found for them, where other community members could also join them. Despite visiting government officials in Bern and the Swiss ambassador in Berlin, they could not get permission to establish a Bruderhof in Switzerland because the men refused to serve in the military. The director of Morning Light said she could only keep the children until March 20.

The brotherhood met to consider the options. Suddenly Eberhard had an inspiration: Liechtenstein. Someone ran for a map. Liechtenstein was a small independent principality, about sixty square miles, bordering on Switzerland and Austria.

Eberhard and Emmy set out at the end of February. Eberhard wrote to Hardy from on board a Swiss ship on Lake Constance—once out of Germany he could write more freely, and he summarized the position of the Rhön Bruderhof.

> The situation at home is getting more and more serious: 1) our school was closed; 2) the foster children were taken away—the last one just two weeks ago; 3) we have been forbidden to take guests and are watched by the police; 4) our charitable status was revoked; 5) our hospitality was declared a menace to public safety; 6) our credit-worthiness is being shattered from all sides—even high official ones—to the point of imminent bankruptcy. Then yesterday, February 26, the main blow fell, making it an unholy

> seven: on the basis of the Reich Entailed Farm Law the authorities are doing their level best to take Emil Möller's farm away from us and thus destroy the last economic basis we have. In doing this they explicitly say they know that then we could not maintain ourselves any longer. The reasons given are our refusal to bear arms and that we do not represent the "blood and soil" requirements under the law for the property in question! Nonetheless, the whole brotherhood remains joyful and brave.[1]

Eberhard and Emmy went first to Morning Light to encourage Lene, Annemarie, and the children. Then they went to Liechtenstein, taking Adolf and Annemarie along. Emmy wrote to Hardy:

> Hans-Hermann seems very well! He looks tanned and healthy; a very nice doctor in Celerina thinks his lung has healed. So we were able to take him with us and let him travel from Chur to Trogen, while we went on further search in Liechtenstein, a tiny principality with altogether about 10,000 inhabitants of Catholic faith situated in the Rhine Valley between Austria and Switzerland! Just now we are sitting in a small café at Schaan near Vaduz, getting a little information. So far we have been told of a castle called "Gutenberg" and of a hotel "Waldhotel" which are available for rent. In spite of his crutches Papa is joyful and courageous. Or would you know of a possible place for us in England?[2]

They spent the night at a village inn, hoping to get acquainted with the local people, and asked if there was a house for rent that they could use as a home for children. Someone mentioned a summer hotel called Silum high on the mountain above the village. It was not heated or insulated, and the road up to it had not been cleared of snow. A friendly farmer offered to take them in his horse-drawn sleigh. Emmy described this trip in a letter to Trudi Hüssy:

> It was rather adventuresome traveling in ice and snow. The last five hundred meters, the horses sank up to their necks in the snow and had to be shoveled out. Our driver said Adolf, Eberhard, and I had to get off. We trudged up to Silum in snow over our knees, without any visible path. Eberhard, supported by Adolf, stepped into my footprints, and the owner's daughter who was on skis exclaimed over and over, "Oh no, oh no, I just hope nobody breaks a leg!" After we had warmed up a bit, looked at everything and talked things over, Eberhard made a verbal agreement to rent the whole house with the surrounding property. Then we went down again—over icy paths, with steep, partly rocky slopes and sharp

curves, and rather fast too! That night in Chur when I lay in bed, the whole decision seemed rather foolhardy to me, just as the trip through the deep snow with Eberhard on crutches had been, and in my dream I saw us tumbling down the mountainside, horses and all.[3]

Eberhard and Emmy visited Julia Lerchy, a single woman who had visited the Rhön Bruderhof a year earlier. She had worked for eleven years in a home for children of dysfunctional families but had fallen down a flight of stairs and was in hospital. She told Eberhard and Emmy that she had decided to join the community. When they said good-bye to her, she pressed an envelope into their hands. It contained 6,500 Swiss Francs, enough for the first installment on the hotel, with money left to take home. Their faith had been rewarded and they felt a clear confirmation of this new venture.

In Morning Light the small brotherhood circle (Eberhard and Emmy, Adolf, Hans-Hermann, Annemarie, and Lene) gathered to consider the new beginning. They would call it the Alm Bruderhof, "alm" meaning alpine pasture, and they suggested some families and single adults to staff it. To support it financially they planned to make craft items for sale and to bring in more foster children.[4] Eberhard had talked to the authorities who agreed to let them stay as long as they didn't take children from Liechtenstein, they didn't try to convert the Catholics, and they conducted no sales in the principality.[5] So they would do their sales work in Switzerland and would have to travel further afield to find children whose families would be able to pay for their care and education.

Within a few days they had packed up their things and moved to the new Alm Bruderhof in Liechtenstein. They were soon joined by Fritz and Sekunda Kleiner, Adolf's wife Martha, Edith Boeker, and several others. The adults would find life there difficult: high on a mountain with no access road, no insulation or heating, and no level land for agriculture. But for the young people it was a great adventure. Edith gave her impressions:

> A mighty world of mountains surrounds us. The force of the earth seems to want to rise above us powerfully! Just so powerful is our task, to be God's vessels through which the spirit of light can illumine the earth. If only we truly understand the reality of this spirit of light, so that we can complete what was begun in Christ, that through bearing the suffering of the world we might

> take part in the cross of Christ, for the sake of the resurrection that God's kingdom brings!⁶

Eberhard and Emmy stayed for a few weeks to help establish the new community in a new country, free from the stifling atmosphere of Nazi Germany. They felt encouraged that people in Switzerland, England, and other countries were taking interest. Hardy came for his Easter vacation, bringing with him a young Englishman, and he told of others who promised to visit. At Easter Eberhard wrote a letter to those left at the Rhön Bruderhof. It was a long letter with a personal word of encouragement to each of them:

> How joyful and grateful we are for the wonderful leading and guidance of the Spirit in these past weeks! Few and insignificant though we are, through us God now holds two places as witness. On the two communities we are more than 115 souls! We have suffered defeats through the closing of the school, the closing of the orphans' home, the forbidding of hospitality to guests, and the serious threats to our economy. But as far as we can see, these defeats have not only been made good, they will in a few months be left far behind through a new spreading of the holy cause. Yet we must be ready for even more intense struggles.
>
> Growing circles in England, Holland, America, Austria, and Switzerland are becoming aware of the significance of true church life. Men proposed to cut us off so that we should have no influence on the world around us. But God has disposed otherwise; the world now takes more notice than ever of what, through God's leading, goes on among us.
>
> Apparently we are entering a period when the community will increase so much that all previous growth will seem small by comparison. A time of great significance for the history of our brotherhood is probably beginning; in many countries the possibility, the reality of true community life will get the attention it deserves.
>
> In the smaller community up here at the Alm, self-forgetting love blossoms in joyful readiness to help. This was our experience at Sannerz. May it be given anew in your larger circle, also in the smallest things. It would make everyone very happy.⁷

Easter fell on April 1 that year, 1934. Emmy Arnold wrote from the Alm Bruderhof to Trudi, still at the Rhön Bruderhof:

> A spirit of joy and trust is reigning here. And it is so beautiful. Our Lord's Supper celebration was completely under the sign of our new start, just like the children of Israel celebrated their Passover standing and ready. On Easter Monday we read all the letters from the Rhön Bruderhof with great inward participation, and on Tuesday we baptized Susi who had been asking for it for a long time.
>
> Nature here is wonderful: the Rhine Valley below us and high, snow-covered mountains all around us. The snow is mostly gone now, at least the meadows are practically free. Snow heather is in full bloom, also crocuses, and here and there one sees gentian buds, cowslips, hepaticas, and violets.[8]

Over the next week the group at the Alm continued to think about their task. Several young people had come from the Rhön. They needed work, and the community needed an income. This small, new, youthful beginning reminded Eberhard of when they first began to live together in 1920. Here, like then in Sannerz, the education of children would be a focal point. Adolf would continue traveling through Switzerland trying to sell craft items and the books they had published. This was to be regarded as mission. But they could not ignore what was happening in the wider world and their real purpose:

> We must see the tragic situation in the world in conjunction with what we discussed this morning. It has to be clear to us that we with our little community cannot change or move anything. Our task is to be really ready for what God wants to do.
>
> We must ask to be filled with the Holy Spirit so that the great event of world history can break in—the kingdom of God. It is a question of the kingdom of God, of the great revolutionary world event to be brought about by God.[9]

From Liechtenstein Eberhard wrote two letters to the Hutterian elders. He described the problems they were facing and once again pleaded for financial help.

> In the first week of March the brotherhood of our German Bruderhof gave me the task of following through on our decision to establish a new Bruderhof for our children and young

people. So in spite of still being on crutches with the broken leg I suffered in autumn 1933, I traveled to Switzerland and afterward to the neighboring land of Liechtenstein. The Swiss rejected our repeated request for immigration because of our poverty and our refusal to take part in war...

Liechtenstein is in the Alps where the Rhine River flows into Lake Constance... The present prince of Liechtenstein is Franz I. His government has no soldiers, so in this very important conscience question we have no difficulties. Freedom is also granted for us to educate our children and to give Christian instruction in our school. There is also no disapproval of our communal economy, in which we all work and hold property in common. So for the time being we have in this little land of Liechtenstein the longed-for place of refuge for about a third of our people. The two houses of the new property are high up on a mountain, far from other dwellings, on the hillside overlooking the Rhine Valley. In addition to the school, we hope to run a cattle and dairy farm and to make handicrafts for sale...

The reason for the founding of a second Bruderhof lies solely in the political upheaval in Germany. We would have been so glad to remain together, and the farewell cost many tears... We love Germany and do not wish to fail her in this hour of need.

In January our school in Germany was closed by the government because we are against war and live in community of goods. For conscience's sake it is impossible for us to accept the state school that the government wanted to set up for our children. The German greeting, "Heil Hitler," is daily practiced everywhere with raised hand and is demanded of all children of public schools. This can be understood to mean that salvation comes from Adolf Hitler, the chancellor of Germany, or as worship of him, almost as if he were a god. But we never make this idolatrous greeting. The Horst Wessel song, which glorifies bloody street fighting, is sung repeatedly in the schools. But we do not sing it. In the Hitler Youth and the SA the entire youth of Germany is instructed in warlike practices and sports. But we do not have so much as a finger in that. Also at present the entire teaching of history in the German schools concentrates on the barbaric and idolatrous worship of German racial blood and holds in highest esteem its military achievements. In all this our children should take no part. For this reason our conscience will not allow us to send our children to a state school...

Lastly our young people stand in serious danger because they cannot and will not take part in training for war. It is to be feared that they will be thrown into an evil prison as they refuse to wear any military uniform, to sing warlike songs, or to take part in army preparatory exercises in sport or shooting practice. Already today every student in Germany in the higher grades and universities is obliged to join these martial activities, and it looks as if soon all young men of Germany will be forced into it. Therefore it is possible that we servants of the Word and our young men will one day be imprisoned, as has already been threatened...

Brothers! The need and affliction which have come over us are great... Do not forget for a single day or night that, for the sake of your faith and ours, the brothers and sisters have fled to the mountains with the helpless children, and that they are there without real work and almost without hope of subsistence. They depend on your love... In such dangerous times no one should say, "The richer communities should do it. Our community is too poor," or "We will wait till we hear what the other communities are going to do." The poor widow did not think in such terms, but gave everything she had. She did not wait long, but simply gave. And so according to the words of Jesus Christ she gave more than the others who were rich. Forgive me for speaking so openly. I am led by my heartfelt sympathy for the poor children and their faithful parents. The honor of God, the name of Jesus Christ, and my love for you drives me to beseech you earnestly: Help, help, help, before it is too late! Help like the widow with your last cent! What you do for our children you do for Christ! The light of truth entrusted by God to our church communities must not be quenched![10]

Little by little, many things that the Nazis might seize were moved to safety at the Alm. This included the community's most valuable papers and documents: Hutterian manuscripts from the sixteenth and seventeenth centuries that Eberhard had collected as well as minutes and transcripts of his meetings and lectures. The printed signatures of *Innerland*, which had been sealed in metal containers and buried, were dug out and brought to Liechtenstein.

Early in May, Eberhard returned to the Rhön Bruderhof. (Emmy had come home earlier.) He planned a trip to Celle in northern Germany where the main court for Entailed Farm Law cases was located. On his way home, he stopped in Fulda to see his doctor about his leg, which was still causing him much pain. He needed another operation. Emmy wrote a full report to his mother:

You will be anxious to hear details of how Eberhard is doing, and I want to give you a full report. We brought him home three days after Pentecost because we couldn't afford the hospital expenses. He had a fever for two days but that is passed and we are very thankful. But I believe we need to do all we can that his leg really heals so that we don't have a repeat of what we've just been through.

I had noticed already in Silum that he was complaining of pain when he walked. We thought it was the nerve irritated by the wire that was holding the bones. When Ebbo came home from the Alm Bruderhof, we all noticed that his leg was crooked when he walked, and in the month since I had seen him he seemed to have gotten worse. Ebbo had to take a trip to Celle near Hannover to deal with property issues. I didn't want to let him travel alone, but because of the cost he didn't let me go with him.

He returned Wednesday before Pentecost [May 16] and phoned me from Fulda, asking me to come because he had been admitted to the hospital. I was in bed that day because the infection of my right leg was worse. At noon there was a call from the hospital that he needed a small operation. I traveled immediately and spent the night with him. I also spoke with the doctor who said that it probably was the wire, that there was no callus formation and the leg had not healed properly. He was surprised that Ebbo had been able to walk at all. The leg would remain crooked if he did not operate.

The operation didn't seem as bad as the first one. He was only in the operating room one hour, whereas last time it took three hours. He woke up soon from the anesthesia, and I was allowed to sit next to him until evening, when he was fully awake. The next day he had a high fever and they didn't know what caused it. The third day he still had a fever, but on Sunday the fever was gone . . . He asked the doctor to discharge him on Tuesday. So he is really home now, and I and the whole community are very happy after the long separation. The brothers carried him on a stretcher into our meeting. He had been gone from the Rhön Bruderhof for three months.

Beloved, faithful Mama, you have helped us so much in the past difficult year, but because we need it so badly, I plead to your mother's heart and beg you to help us again. For the operation, the cast, the anesthesia, the hospital, the trips to Fulda and back we need 300 to 500 marks.[11]

Eberhard had spent Pentecost in the hospital. Ten days later he spoke about that great event in Jerusalem when the church was born.

> Pentecost came down to an expectant group in Jerusalem, a small group, but one that was decisive for the world because it was inspired by the faith of expectation. What did the first church expect? It expected the kingdom of God; it expected the revolution of all things and the revaluation of all values.
>
> The church acknowledges the necessity for the powers that reign in today's world. But that which is entrusted to the church itself is something completely different from the sovereignty of these powers which are foreign to it. What is entrusted to it is the kingly embassy of the last kingdom. Every kingdom maintains an embassy in Paris, Petersburg, Berlin, Rome, or elsewhere. The ground of the embassy building is sacrosanct territory. There, no one can be subjected to the law of the state in which the ambassador lives, but, rather, in the embassy building only the law of the state which has sent this embassy is in effect.
>
> It is exactly the same with the embassy of Jesus Christ through the Holy Spirit of his church. Here only the law of life of the last kingdom counts. Therefore the church may not simply subordinate itself to the laws of the government in power today. It should honor them, but it should not be subject to them in a slavish way. The church of Christ demands for its actions the sovereign freedom of the final kingdom. What is decisive for the church and for its entire conduct of life is and remains only the character of the kingdom of God.
>
> The church is placed into this world and into the history of its powers for the purpose of allowing the heart of God, the innermost depths of his love, to triumph over the iron step of all powers. Thus the church confesses that the final goal of God's kingdom is her way in the present time. The way of God's church goes straight into the midst of God's judgment; it goes directly through God's anger, but it stands alone under the sign of mercy and of love—the love of God which loves its enemies. The church loves her actual opponents. Even in them she recognizes an ideal which they hold before them; even in them she feels the pulse of an awakened conscience; them, too, she may acknowledge as being called.[12]

11

June to July 1934

Dietrich Bonhoeffer

Increasingly, Protestants were growing concerned about the German church under Reich Bishop Müller. The Pastors' Emergency League had grown to nearly 6000 members by the end of 1933. At the end of May 1934, 138 pastors and lay people, representatives from all over Germany, met in a synod in Barmen for the founding of the Confessing Church.[1] After hours of discussion, they agreed on a declaration that came to be known as the Barmen Confession, drawn up by Karl Barth. The declaration rejected the subordination of church to state and the "Aryan Paragraph" which demanded pastors to expel non-Aryans from the church.

Dietrich Bonhoeffer, who is one of the best-known members of the Confessing Church, was in London and did not attend the Barmen Synod. Deeply troubled by developments in Germany, he was still considering what his role and that of the church should be. Hardy Arnold in Birmingham was surprised by a call from him one day. He introduced himself and asked if they could get together. Hardy met with him and two of his friends. They talked about community and Bonhoeffer's plans to travel to India to talk with Gandhi, in particular to get advice on how to overthrow a hostile government nonviolently—a trip that never materialized. Later Hardy recalled:

> It was clear that Bonhoeffer was a pastor and could not imagine a Christianity outside of the denominations. So it was difficult for him to understand why the Bruderhof had separated from the national Protestant Church. Being a Christian for him meant

working in and for the church. Again and again he emphasized how urgent it was to get rid of Hitler without using force.²

Such a position is explained by John Conway in *The Nazi Persecution of the Churches*. He points out that the Barmen Confession was never intended as a program of political protest, and neither did the Confessing Church aim to become a resistance organization. They did not take a stand against wanton violence, the persecution of Jews, or the erection of concentration camps. He says:

> The Lutheran tradition of respect for the ruling power was too deeply engrafted to be lightly overthrown. The popular image of the pastor in German society was one of loyal support to the ruling classes, never of dissent or opposition.³

This attitude seems evident in Bonhoeffer's reaction to Hardy, and stands in sharp contrast to the radical position adopted by Eberhard and the Bruderhof community. Hardy continues:

> I phoned Papa (probably the only time I called him from England) because I felt the meeting with Bonhoeffer was important. Papa felt the same. He remembered Dietrich Bonhoeffer's father who had been a professor of psychiatry in Breslau [where Papa's family lived]. Papa asked me to invite Bonhoeffer urgently. I passed this invitation on to him.⁴

From Birmingham, Hardy wrote a report of his encounter with Bonhoeffer to his father:

> I met Pastor Bonhoeffer in London; he has two German churches there. He has been here [in England] since October, and before that was a private lecturer in systematic theology in Berlin. When he had the opportunity, for obvious reasons he came over to London.
>
> A short time ago he wrote to me asking that I arrange a meeting with him either here [in Birmingham] or there [in London]. He intends to found a brotherhood with some of his students, solely on the basis of the Sermon on the Mount. He heard about us from Niemöller and wanted to hear about our experiences. So I met with him and two of his friends and heard more about their plans.
>
> The idea is to have an evangelical cloister with religious exercises, confessions, etc. It is assumed that we do not know God's will for our time, but nevertheless they will try to live accord-

ing to the words of Jesus and to learn the will of God by means of thorough Bible study and religious practices. Unfortunately Bonhoeffer draws a distinction between theologians and laymen, who would also be accepted. Although not absolutely rejecting marriage, he is critical enough to fear that the love between two and the care of a family would cause married people to digress from what is essential.

These are all points which must be discussed in the deepest way. Unfortunately the time was so short that he and I had to limit ourselves to listening to each other. It seems important to me that there is a group of sixty to seventy people following Bonhoeffer's ideas, who earnestly seek to know and do the will of God in this time. For this they are ready to take anything upon themselves. There are such groups in Berlin, Bonn, and Tübingen.

In the middle of next week Dietrich Bonhoeffer wants to visit the Bruderhof. For this reason he is traveling to Germany, and on the same trip will confer with the pastors' association which shows a deep-going interest in his plans.

He will phone you from Berlin, probably on Wednesday, to speak shortly with you about when and how he can best come to you. I think the whole matter is very important. It would be wonderful if we could become united with this group. At any rate we must be ready. They look up to the Bruderhof very much. His other two friends, who return to Germany sometime next month, have also agreed to visit.

In fall Bonhoeffer plans to go to India for half a year with one of the two, Dr. Jehle, to live in Gandhi's community, which, as you surely know, has complete community of goods but is strongly monastic and ascetic. It seems to me that Bonhoeffer hopes for much from this contact. In the essential points we agree with him: 1) no private property but the communal management of property, and 2) nonviolence. But it appears that he has not yet grasped the church as the circle led by the spirit of God. Perhaps you can help him. I gave him the chapter about the Holy Spirit from *Innerland*.[5]

Eberhard Bethge's biography of Dietrich Bonhoeffer confirms the fact that at this stage in Bonhoeffer's life he was contemplating a life of community. Bethge writes:

> At that time it would have seemed unthinkable to Bonhoeffer to take part in a conspiracy against Hitler. What he sought was a prototype for passive resistance that could induce changes without violence . . . What he was aiming at, therefore, was a means

of combating Hitler that went beyond the aims and methods of the church struggle while remaining legitimate from a Christian standpoint.[6]

In many ways, his position seemed similar to the Bruderhof's, and it is not surprising that Hardy was enthused. Eberhard, however, was more cautious. He answered Hardy:

> The belief in a united church is almost unknown because the third article of the Apostles' Creed (faith in the Holy Spirit and his working in the whole of Christendom) has become entirely lost. This is also true for Dietrich Bonhoeffer—who has not yet arrived here, although I phoned his house. It appears to me that with him, as with others, the attitude to poverty, the communal management of property, and nonviolence is far removed from the commission given to the church through the spirit of Jesus Christ. Although following the Sermon on the Mount and living according to the words of Jesus is significant for them too, everything is put into question by their thoughts on the cloistered life of monks and their inclination to eastern Indian religion. This was true also for Leo Tolstoy and others ...
>
> I believe that in these days of political world crisis the hour is near when many will turn away from state politics to seek a better way of justice, people's community, and peace for mankind. They will turn to the *politeia* which recognizes only one kingdom that is truly God's. May it also be given to us in this strength to come together here with Dietrich Bonhoeffer or perhaps with Dr. Jehle and also get to know their circles in Berlin, Bonn, and Tübingen. But after some experiences which I have just had at the universities, with similar hopes, I can hardly expect that as many as sixty to seventy young people would be ready to risk everything for the life shown by Jesus. Write to me immediately whether we should write again to Dietrich Bonhoeffer in Berlin even after phoning his mother, who perhaps did not pass on our message.[7]

Unfortunately Bonhoeffer spent a very short time in Berlin and did not visit the Bruderhof. Hardy wrote to his father again on July 3:

> I will meet Bonhoeffer and Dr. Jehle in London. I have a clear feeling that the latter is drawing closer to us; he will visit us in August, either at the Alm or the Rhön Bruderhof, whichever works out best. I'm looking forward to spending time with him ... I will meet Pastor Bonhoeffer, Dr. Jehle, and the young Pastor Weckerling of the group of young cloistered evangelicals on

> Tuesday. I spoke with Bonhoeffer on the phone, and he told me that his pastoral duties did not allow him to stay away from London for more than four days. He was in Berlin barely three days and was not able to come to us. But he wants to make up for it in August.[8]

Herbert Jehle did visit the Alm Bruderhof later that summer. Bonhoeffer spoke of his plans for community at the Ecumenical Youth Commission in Paris the following January:

> A group of young Christians are seriously considering the possibility of starting a small Christian community in the form of a settlement or any other form on the basis of the Sermon on the Mount. It is felt that only by a clear and uncompromising stand Christianity can be a vital force for our people. It is also felt that the developments of the church disputed in Germany are tending more and more towards a sort of conservative Christianity which of course would go very well with the rather conservative spirit which is steadily growing under the present Reichswehr and Industry regime. This group would also make a definite stand for peace by conscientious objection.[9]

The seminary community he founded lasted only about two years before it folded under pressure from the government. Bonhoeffer agonized over the spiritual decline of his country. He left Germany several times over the next years, but ultimately felt he had to return, accepting responsibility and guilt for his people. As he wrote to Reinhold Niebuhr:

> I must live through this difficult period of our national history with the Christian people of Germany. I will have no right to participate in the reconstruction of Christian life in Germany after the war if I do not share the trials of this time with my people . . . Christians in Germany will face the terrible alternative of either willing the defeat of their nation in order that Christian civilization may survive, or willing the victory of their nation and thereby destroying our civilization. I know which of these alternatives I must choose; but I cannot make that choice in security.[10]

He was ultimately arrested for his participation in the movement to resist Hitler. He was hanged on April 4, 1945.

Chapter 11—June to July 1934

At the end of June 1934 Hitler directed a massacre that came to be known as "The Night of the Long Knives." Rivalry had developed between the two paramilitary organizations, the SA *(Sturmabteilung)* and the SS *(Schutzstaffel).* The SA, also called storm troopers or brownshirts because of the color of their uniforms, were the paramilitary wing of the Nazi Party, built up by Ernst Röhm since 1921. They were primarily responsible for Hitler's rise to power and for widespread violence against Jews and communists. After Hitler was appointed Reichskanzler, their brutal violence had been given free rein. The brownshirts

> visited "the bloody terror of unrestrained hordes" upon their enemies. Their violence was the expression of long-nurtured hatred, their actions directed against individual "Marxists" and Communists often known to them personally. There was no coordinated plan, no further ambition on their part than the wreaking of terrible physical aggression on men and women they feared and hated.[11]

The SA pledged allegiance to the Nazi Party, not to Hitler personally. The SS, on the other hand, had its origins in a small unit formed in 1923 as Hitler's bodyguard. Under Heinrich Himmler's leadership since 1929, it increased in strength and become an independent body with its own black uniform. In spring and early summer 1934, Hitler began to fear that he could no longer control the storm troopers. When he heard rumors that they were planning a coup, he struck with a vengeance that shocked even those closest to him.

Early in the morning of June 30, he assembled a group of SS and police and drove in convoy to the hotel where Ernst Röhm and other storm troopers were still asleep. They were dragged out of bed to prison. Unwilling to kill Röhm himself, Hitler sent two officers to bring him a revolver to shoot himself. When he refused, they shot him at point-blank range. Over the next few days more than eighty others were summarily killed. These included Erich Klausener, leader of the Catholic Action, Adalbert Probst, director of the Catholic Youth Sports Association, and other conservatives. The "Night of the Long Knives" marked the end of any pretense at legality. Hitler defended his actions in a speech before the Reichstag on July 13:

> If anyone reproaches me and asks why we did not call upon the regular courts for sentencing, my only answer is this: in that hour, I was responsible for the fate of the German nation and was thus the Supreme Justiciar of the German people! ... I gave the order to shoot those parties mainly responsible for this treason ... The nation should know that no one can threaten its existence—which is guaranteed by inner law and order—and escape unpunished! And every person should know for all time that if he raises his hand to strike out at the state certain death will be his lot.[12]

Members of the Bruderhof read about these events with trembling. Eberhard said that the "socialist" aspect of National Socialism was eradicated with brutal murder. Hitler murdered anyone who still tried to represent decency and honor.[13]

Eberhard wanted to finish his book *Innerland* and had also committed to several other publishing projects. The largest of these was the second volume of the Hutterian chronicle, *Das Klein-Geschichtsbuch*. He had been working with several Anabaptist scholars, notably Johann Loserth and Robert Friedmann, both in Vienna.

In spite of the long days of intense physical work, both communities met each evening to focus on what was truly important. Ultimately, all they had to oppose the Nazi spirit was prayer.

> We meet each evening to plead that the kingdom of God might descend and come near to this earth, to pray for the Holy Spirit to come and bring the church down to us. After the burden and heat of the day, after work, worries, and failings, unconscious or unintentional, it is something wonderful to be able to come before God.
>
> I thank God from the bottom of my heart when I see how hard and concentrated everyone works. Everyone is giving his or her best to help uphold the church in this time of need. But surely I may say that we must not let the work become a tyrant. The shattering need in the world should make us realize every day the burning necessity of opposing the horrors of murder, of impurity, of mammon, and of lying with the outpouring of the Holy Spirit, the proclamation of the kingdom of God, and the coming of his rulership. That is why we meet for worship, to ask God that his name be hallowed, that his kingdom come, and that his will be done on earth as it is in heaven.

Let us stand together in protecting what God gives us, making pure vessels of our hearts to guard it. Let us carry the light home in our hands, not allowing it to be blown out on the way. Let us ask God that he may newly kindle the holy light in our hearts through the descending flame of his Holy Spirit. Let us ask him to fit us into his great future, into his kingdom, into the creative powers that transform all things so that the old creation passes away. We ask for the powers of God's great future to come to us more and more so that we are enabled to live accordingly and to spread this message to all people. Then, in the midst of the old nature but having no part in its sinfulness and degradation, our whole life, day and night, will be a witness to the new creation.

Let us ask God that in the horrors of the present time people awake, not only in tens and hundreds but in thousands upon thousands, so that their hearts turn from the "abomination of desolation which stands in holy places" (Matt 24:15). Let us ask that many awake and search their hearts and turn to God, who created them; that they become one with the death of Christ, suffering death rather than killing others; that they become one with the life in Christ and his love so that they surrender all their powers, gifts, and means of livelihood rather than keeping anything for themselves; that they become one with the truth of God so that they break with the whole web of lies that enmeshes the world; that they become one with the heart of Jesus and reject all unclean spirits.

This evening we also want to think of our brothers who are on journeys, our brothers in America, and all scattered people whom God alone knows. Let us ask God for his Holy Spirit so that we can answer for our decision with the last drop of our blood.[14]

Blood and Soil

In connection with negotiations for the Emil Möller property, the community's lawyer recommended that members prove their "Aryan" descent, since the minister of agriculture, Walter Darré, had popularized the phrase "blood and soil"—the idea that German racial identity was essentially tied to the land. One of the clauses of the Entailed Farm Law defined eligibility: A farmer, in the sense of this law, had to be of German blood, with no Jewish or colored blood in his line on either his mother's or his father's side.[15] Eberhard researched his genealogy; he came from a line of educators, theologians, and professors of church history. He traced Emmy's family back to the seventeenth century when the von Hollanders were the ruling family in Riga. He ended his long and detailed genealogy with the words:

> I hardly need to mention but will summarize expressly in conclusion that all families of the ancestors of Eberhard and Emmy Arnold (nee von Hollander), the spokesman and housemother of the Bruderhof, can prove their pure German blood through the centuries without the smallest trace of anything else.[16]

He also used the opportunity to acknowledge his rich spiritual heritage, as he wrote to his mother:

> How wonderful all this is for us on the Bruderhofs, who feel ourselves to be true spiritual heirs of all that was given to these ancestors moved by Christ ... Our firmly united life of discipleship, founded only on complete faith and complete love, appears to us to be a necessary fulfillment of the direction given us by our parents and forefathers.[17]

Of course he made no mention of the fact that many members could not boast such pedigrees. His lawyer, Dr. Blanke, submitted to the Entailed Farm Law office:

> I am pleased to enclose with this a complete survey of the Bruderhof members' descent, in particular of their ancestors' blood lines and occupations. In my opinion, this information will be of considerable significance for the decision of the Entailed Farm Law. It shows that the Bruderhof members represent human material that is genuinely German and of a specially high quality at that—which is also a guarantee that the Bruderhof's work on the land it has purchased will bring forth good fruit for National Socialist Germany.[18]

~

The community decided to expand the sales trips that Adolf Braun was taking in Switzerland as a means to raise money. Several other men were sent on similar trips in Germany as well. They were to see this as a mission task, an opportunity to witness to the truth of Jesus. At the same time, Hardy and Adolf were looking for children who could join the school and children's home at the Alm Bruderhof to bring in some income. Eberhard pleaded with the members to look beyond the frustrations of daily life to the world beyond:

> We cannot think only of Germany, we cannot think only of Europe; we must think of the whole big world and what an enormous need there is, a judgment evident to all, with these remarkable phenomena like earthquakes, plagues of grasshoppers, and many other things.* I wish so much that God may put our mission—however modest it may be—into this large context for us. In this tremendous context of the world's great need, we need to be aware of how very small our work is, in view of great historical events. All the more are we dependent on the prayer that, in the face of the world with its thousand million people, our tiny business of publishing and wooden products nevertheless has an effect that moves the world in ways known only to God. But it is quite certain that this small, mustard-seed-like faith that we have taken hold of in contrast to our weakness will be proven as a living, productive faith.
>
> So we are now sending out our beloved Georg Barth and our beloved Alfred Gneiting. At the same time we remember Adolf in Switzerland, Hardy in England, and the Alm Bruderhof. We pray as Jesus taught us, by asking for what is greatest of all, for God's kingdom to come, for God's name to be honored. We also ask for our daily bread and that the sale of wooden articles and books and this Franciscan begging may serve to help us in our indescribable need and that we may be allowed to continue our communal life. We ask for forgiveness for all unintentional and unplanned transgressions, just as we whole-heartily forgive all transgressions against us. And we ask God that in the great historical hour of temptation that has now come over the whole world, we may be protected, and that the world may be redeemed and rescued from the devil.[19]

As a result of the sales trips a number of people visited the Rhön Bruderhof from a community called Ziegelwald near the German city of Eisenach. Several decided to stay. For these new people Eberhard spoke of what it meant to be a church living for the kingdom of God.

> What do the four Gospels, the letters of the Apostles and the Revelation of John mean by the kingdom of God? A kingdom is a system of government; a kingdom is the organization of a nation,

---

* A powerful earthquake struck India on 15 January 1934, causing the deaths of some 30,000 people. There was also a terrible plague of locusts in Africa and western Asia in 1934.

in work done by the people and in mutual social relationships. A kingdom is a joining of the national community in justice, in solidarity. This is the kind of government system that the prophet envisions when he speaks of God's kingdom. It exists only when real national community is attained, an enduring, binding justice in mutual relationships, when a new order comes about in all relationships and conditions.

Here God alone has the rulership, God and God only is the king! That is God's kingdom. We know, of course, that in the present world this kingdom has not yet taken shape. Apart from God, the mighty national governments have a very large say. Apart from God, lying and impurity have a very large say. Apart from God, those powers that are in complete discord with God have their say. God's kingdom has not materialized yet, for its materialization would mean that nothing else counts anymore. John says that this earth will be so transformed in the new realm of God's rulership that it will no longer need sun, for it will be all light (Rev 22:5). We are not living in that yet.

Then comes the question of the church. Paul says that this is a completely new revelation; that all nations of the world shall be gathered together in this church; that all fences and walls that are erected between the peoples, nations, classes, ranks, and strata of men are to be broken down. Not only shall the whole world be conquered for God, but the church shall show forth life in full unity, right in the world. The mystery is great, but I am speaking of Christ and the church.

Paul continues to say that the church is an embassy of the future kingdom. The members of the church, then, are the king's ambassadors. So we are ambassadors of God in the place of his king, and so we come to the whole world bringing the call: Be united![2]

12

Romans 13

IN AUGUST 1934, EBERHARD spoke at length about Paul's exhortation in Romans 13: "Let every person be subject to the governing authorities." He sensed more and more strongly that they were living in the end times and that the state was the beast of the abyss spoken of in Revelations. He started his talk with an overview of the political situation of Europe and the fascist states of Austria under Dollfuss, Italy under Mussolini, and Germany under Hitler.

> In no state ruled by absolute monarchy has there been such centralization as there is today in this fascist state. Just as the monarch was supposed to represent the whole state, in the same way present-day centralism has to sum up everything in one person: in the dictators Mussolini, Hitler, and Dolfuss. It calls to mind imperial Rome. But no emperor claimed such idolatry, such a deification of his own person, as do present-day dictators. For Nero and other emperors little incense altars were erected here and there, where little balls of incense had to be offered to testify to the religious significance of the unified imperial power, to the genius of the emperor: not to the emperor in person, but to the genius of the emperor...
>
> But apart from these little altars, never did Nero or any other Roman emperor bring matters to such a state that at every street corner "Hail, Nero!" was called out. The dictator of today is so utterly without all religious or supernatural impulses and spirits that he does not even believe in the genius of the dictator, but only in the little person of the dictator. Thus idolatry is today coarsened in the most vulgar way. It is the loud voice, the hair, and the nose of the dictator that is worshiped. It is simply the human being who is made into an idol. As a result authority is also

robbed of all genius. What the dictator says is done. Thinking is forbidden. He who thinks is hanged.

Modern fascism is such that one could weep about it day and night. Freedom of thought is forbidden. Objective justice is abolished. Goebbels says, "If we are right, it follows that no one else is right. For us there is no other justice than that which serves our interests." Thus there is absolutely no justice. Stupidity reigns. That is appalling in the twentieth century. Who still believes in progress?

I do not believe that such an unspiritual conception ever ruled or was dominant among the American Indians or the primitive Germanic races of Europe. There the chieftain or duke was bound to observe the decisions of the legislative assembly or the gathering; he was bound to the place of gathering and to the legal conception of the order of the body politic. Today, however, national egotism and the self-assertion of the present dictator-group control law and justice and all thought.

What power opposes this force? What is England's parliamentary monarchy doing? What are the other countries with great spiritual traditions doing? What are the churches doing? What are the great philosophies and the great spiritual movements doing? What position results from this for the churches and the intellectual movements in Germany? The Pope signs one concordat after another with Hitler. Raids on the bishop's palace, the murder of two of the most outstanding Catholic priests, priests arrested and taken to concentration camps—none of this prevents the Pope from dealing reasonably and respectfully with Hitler again and again. The Protestants are led by a cleric [Ludwig Müller] with an ignorance unprecedented in thousands of years ... It seems that one established church after another is succumbing to brutal violence and base deceit.

It is interesting to note that the Confessing Church Synods have issued the slogan, "No separation from the church!" But this paralyzes all energy. For when the church becomes godless one cannot say, "We protest, but we remain in the church." When the church is ruled by demons and idolatry, one cannot say, "We protest, but we remain in the church." Even the protesting groups in the Catholic and Protestant Churches render unconditional homage to the present state. They make the offering of "Heil Hitler!" They are prepared to take active part in the functions of government. So what good is it if, from within the church hierarchy they protest isolated incidents that lead to suppression of free speech, brutal murder, and all manner of other horrors, while at the same time supporting the overall application of this evil system?

The reason for this weak and feeble attitude is clear. It is the retribution following the fact that the reformed church has never taken up the clear attitude to the state and to society that the early Christians did. It is the retribution for its historical sin, in that during the Peasants' War it joined the princely authorities and committed a crime against the popular Anabaptist movement—just as in England at and after the time of Oliver Cromwell, Christianity sold itself to the state. The cause of Oliver Cromwell's error also lies in a misunderstanding of Paul's words to the Romans (chapter 13): "Let each person be subject to the governing authorities." The great churches always use verses 1–5 to defend their interests in the state:

> Let every person be subject to the governing authorities. For there is no authority except from God, and those that exist have been instituted by God. Therefore he who resists the authorities resists what God has appointed, and those who resist will incur judgment. For rulers are not a terror to good conduct, but to bad. Would you have no fear of him who is in authority? Then do what is good, and you will receive his approval, for he is God's servant for your good. But if you do wrong, be afraid, for he does not bear the sword in vain; he is the servant of God to execute his wrath on the wrongdoer. Therefore one must be subject, not only to avoid God's wrath but also for the sake of conscience.

They use verses 6–7 to say that consequently the Christian should pay taxes.

> For the same reason you also pay taxes, for the authorities are ministers of God, attending to this very thing. Pay all of them their dues, taxes to whom taxes are due, revenue to whom revenue is due, respect to whom respect is due, honor to whom honor is due.

Then, however, comes Paul's answer to the tasks of government, the answer of *love* (verses 8–10):

> Owe no one anything, except to love one another; for he who loves his neighbor has fulfilled the law. The commandments, "You shall not commit adultery, you shall not kill, you shall not steal, you shall not covet," and any other commandment, are summed up in this sentence: "You shall love your neighbor as

yourself." Love does no wrong to a neighbor; therefore love is the fulfilling of the law.

There is no state without police force and the sword. Thus God has in the state an order of wrath of the sword. That has been ordained by God in the unchristian world so that evil might not gain the upper hand. Rapists and murderers are not to be permitted to kill all little girls. That is God's order for hell. God has also an order in hell; God has also an order for the evil and unjust—that we are not to forget. With regard to evil God must also be *relative*—for as long as evil exists. Therefore the state and the police force are God's order in the world of *evil*, not in the world of *good*. In the world of evil God's *relativity* reigns. We cannot stand up in London and preach, "Away with all policemen!" We have no quarrel with the necessity of order maintained by the governmental authorities for the world of evil. That would be wrong.

But now comes the absolutism of God in *love* (verses 8–10). In the absolute sphere of love there is no active part taken in the force of the state. In the absolute sphere of God there is no order of police and military. There are two regions. The one region is that of evil and of political power. The other region is that of love and of the Holy Spirit without active participation in state power ... The world of pure light and pure love has nothing to do with violence.

Hitler is a God-appointed lord of hell. Pharaoh was an instrument of God. He was an instrument of God's wrath ... God does not utterly forsake humankind, and therefore he gives them a relative order. Should he utterly forsake them, they would not breathe even for a moment more. They would also have no more to eat. Therefore God permits his sun to shine and his rain to fall on the evil and the good. No human being exists in whom there is *nothing* of God left. Even in a prostitute there is still a trace of God ... Even in a brothel God has still his order: even in an army. But it is an order of hell.

Now something more about the devilish origin of the state, as described by John in Revelations 13: "And to it the dragon gave his power and his throne and great authority." This means that the dragon gives the state his might. "Men worshiped the dragon." Men worship the beast in Hitler and say, "Who is like Hitler? Who can oppose Hitler and the SA? Who is his equal?" "They worshiped the beast, saying, 'Who is like the beast, and who can fight against it?'" (Rev 13:4). This does not only apply to Hitler.

It applies also to the parliamentary British state. Look at India, Ireland, and Palestine!

> And the beast was given a mouth uttering haughty and blasphemous words, and it was allowed to exercise authority for forty-two months; it opened its mouth to utter blasphemies against God, blaspheming his name and his dwelling, that is, those who dwell in heaven (Rev 13:5-6).

Therefore it is given to all great powers to speak blasphemies against God.

> All who dwell on earth worshiped it, every one whose name has not been written before the foundation of the world in the book of life of the Lamb that was slain (verse 8). Anyone who takes others captive shall himself be taken into captivity; if anyone slays with the sword, with the sword must he be slain. Here is a call for the endurance and faith of the saints (verse 10).

Christians have no active part in this. You cannot serve two masters. Anyone who kills with the sword must be killed with the sword. The holy church suffers death by the sword and has faith in God without revenge. "Here is a call for the endurance and faith of the saints." That is a patient bearing. The Lamb is slain, but the state slays.

The most fearful thing, however, is expressed in verses 11-17:

> Then I saw another beast which rose out of the earth; it had two horns like a lamb and it spoke like a dragon. It exercises all the authority of the first beast in its presence, and makes the earth and its inhabitants worship the first beast, whose mortal wound was healed. It works great signs, even making fire come down from heaven to earth in the sight of men; and by the signs which it is allowed to work in the presence of the beast, it deceives those who dwell on earth, bidding them make an image for the beast which was wounded by the sword and yet lived: and it was allowed to give breath to the image of the beast so that the image of the beast should even speak, and to cause those who will not worship the image of the beast to be slain. Also it causes all, both small and great, both rich and poor, both free and slave, to be marked on the right hand or the forehead, so that no one can buy or sell unless he has the mark, that is, the name of the beast or the number of its name.

The second beast is the institutional church. It is the Protestant and Catholic world church! Revolution is the constant wound of the first beast, of the state. But it dies of no revolution, for it is part of the very nature of the state that it constantly falls and is healed again. But it is the world church that "makes the earth and its inhabitants worship the first beast." Ludwig Müller does this every day. He says people should hang pictures of Hitler in every room and place them on the altars. Verse 15 says: "It was allowed to give breath to the image of the beast." Hitler receives some spirit through the church: " . . . and to cause those who will not worship the image of the beast to be slain." Whoever refuses to say "Heil Hitler" is killed. Further (verses 16–18) all the people, small and great, rich and poor, free and slave, all accepted the sign on their right hand or on their forehead: the free and the slave, the capitalist and the proletarian. The proletarians and capitalists accept a sign: on their forehead, the swastika on their military cap; on their right hand, the swastika on their right arm—and where it is not the swastika, then the equivalent badge of the other nations. Most terrible of all is the economic consequence. Everything is numbered. No one can buy or sell without the number. And the world church is to blame. It comes to this: the whole state leads to the deification of man, of his might and power! To help in this is the great sin of the church. It helps to idolize man.

Now, however, Paul in the very same thirteenth chapter of his Epistle to the Romans gives yet a second answer to the matter of government, the answer of God's *future* (verses 11–14).

> This warning I give to you because you know what hour it is: the hour has come when you must wake from sleep. For salvation is nearer to us now than when we first believed; the night is far gone, the day is at hand. Let us then cast off the works of darkness and put on the armor of light; let us conduct ourselves with decency as in the day, not in reveling and drunkenness, not in debauchery and licentiousness, not in quarreling and jealousy. But put on the Lord Jesus Christ, and do not care for the body in such a way that evil desires are awakened.

The kingdom of God is approaching: the day has come! The works of darkness, these are the weapons of killing. Hatred and unchastity belong to darkness just as killing does. The conclusion of the whole is to live like Jesus Christ.[1]

13

July to August 1934

Cousin Hermann

Hermann Arnold was the son of Eberhard's brother, who had died in World War I before Hermann's birth. Hermann did not know the Bruderhof, but he had met some of his cousins when they visited their grandmother, and he decided to visit the Alm Bruderhof on his vacation. He was a member of the SA, however, and before his arrival Eberhard warned the community that he might be a spy. From Hermann's memoirs:

> I was quite nationalistic. My father had given his life for Germany, for his fatherland, and I thought that was my duty too. In 1933, the year Hitler came to power, I was seventeen. Hitler promised that Germany would be better off again and would take its place with the other nations in the world and come to power again. He really was quite successful in this. Unemployment fell off, and the economy improved. My whole high school class joined the Hitler Youth except for one boy who was a Catholic. I joined with enthusiasm.
>
> On my visit to the Alm Bruderhof Eberhard gave me a pile of newspapers to read every day. In Germany the newspapers were censored and you had no idea of what was going on. At the Alm Bruderhof in Liechtenstein they got newspapers from Switzerland, so they knew what Hitler was really doing. Eberhard wanted me to know what the Nazi regime was all about without having to say it himself.[1]

Hermann met Eberhard and Emmy, who were returning from Germany, and arrived with them. His diary gives a vivid picture of life at the Alm Bruderhof:

Monday, July 9: Left Munich at 9 a.m. Wonderful journey by express train through the Bavarian plateau and Allgäu to Lindau, wonderful crossing over Lake Constance in bright sunshine. By express train into the magnificent Alps to Buchs. I have no words to describe how beautiful it is here!

On leaving the train in Buchs, I met Aunt Emmy and Uncle Ebbo. Uncle Ebbo's leg is unfortunately still in plaster of Paris, but he is very cheerful. Ride by bus to Vaduz, a nice residential village ... We went by private car to Triesenberg, and a bit farther. There the whole household welcomed us with a song. Uncle Eberhard was taken up to the house in a vehicle drawn by cows surrounded by children and grown-up Bruderhof members. Then in the evening I was introduced with some heartwarming words by Uncle Ebbo. I sleep in a small house in a little room with Heiner.

It is so wonderful here that I cannot find words to describe it. The Rhine flows in the valley and high mountains rise steeply on both sides. The fairly wide Rhine valley is 500 meters high, and grapes even grow there. Up here, only a few hundred meters away as the crow flies, we are at a height of 1500 meters. Many high mountains surround us, forming with their naked peaks an imposing frame for the lovely picture of the Alm meadows with their huts.

Wednesday, July 11: My day is generally like this: get up 6:30 a.m., wash at the well, 7:00 breakfast—oatmeal or some similar cereal with bread. Until midday, work in the hay, garden, or on the potato field. 12:00 dinner, then again agricultural work. 3:00 p.m. snack, which is taken in the families. Then agricultural work until evening. Supper between 6:00 p.m. and 7:00 p.m. Then, for me, mostly free time as I don't take part in the members' meetings. I enjoy the physical work. This morning the Zeppelin flew along the Rhine valley below us!

Friday, July 13: I am completely and tremendously moved by the life here. I liked it very much from the first day. Even the outer life is fine with me as the physical work suits me very well. But it is not only that, nor the beautiful landscape, which gives me such pleasure, but I enjoy so much being able to live here in this unique community. I cannot describe the unity and love to one another. One just has to experience it. For me, at least, being here is a tremendous experience. Perhaps it is *the* experience—I do not know yet. Then there is the awful uncertainty of the political situation in Germany. Germany seems to be on the rocks economically. I am in a hard fight and do not know yet how it will end. It would be best if Mother would get to know the life here. That would be a great joy and relief to me.

The people come from all sorts of backgrounds and situations, but all are driven by the one faith in God: Father, Son, and Holy Spirit. All they do, including the lowliest work, is ultimately carried by this faith. They do nothing for themselves and earn nothing for themselves but do everything for others. That is the great thing. In addition, here at the head stands the really significant figure of Uncle Eberhard, who with his tremendous intellectual vigor carries everything along with him.

The decision for my future from now on does not lie in my hands. It is very, very difficult. I hope with God's help to find the right way. I will need a long time to think things over. My future with the storm troopers is not at all clear to me. I was never wholeheartedly in it. God will show me the right way.

Wednesday, July 18: Worked hard in the hay from morning to evening until I was really tired. In the evening, fetched Uncle Ebbo who was at the doctor's because of his leg. Unfortunately he must be in plaster of Paris for four more weeks. I had a long conversation with Monika. Like all Bruderhof members, she has a highly educated mind. In spite of her youth she is amazingly quick in the uptake, has a keen and penetrating mind largely owing to the mental and spiritual education by Uncle Eberhard. Indeed, I am struck by the mental and spiritual training of all Bruderhof members. Even the children can answer wonderfully to the point when Uncle Ebbo, with his fabulous pedagogic mind, suddenly interrupts with a question at table—something he is very fond of doing.

Monday, July 23: Worked during the day in different places, but nothing was really right. The hard struggle I am in and the decision facing me occupy me so much that I could not sleep. I had an indescribably tense feeling, which only slowly relaxed. What my way will be now is still completely unclear to me. I am quite certain I am facing an important decision for my whole life. God will help me.

In the evening I spoke with Heiner and Emy-Margret, first about all my questions, and then I walked up and down with Monika and spoke with her for a considerable time. Then late in the evening, I still went for a long walk with Hans-Hermann.

This Monday seems to me to be the most important day of my stay here. From day to day the points which separated me from people here have grown fewer. All my objections disappeared before the one great fact that here in this community there is true Christianity. What my relatives in Breslau and my mother feared has happened: I am "infected," I am "contaminated" by the spirit of community in Christ. A difficult time lies ahead of me, however the decision falls—at any rate, I shall have a very hard time before me at home, in school, and with the storm troopers. I am subject to God in all I do, and I must obey him more than men. I only ask that a clear decision may be given me, strength for the hard fight, and that truth may win.

Sunday, July 29: I described this day in a letter of August 1 to my mother—this day, in every way the most important and most wonderful day of my whole life here, and perhaps of my whole life.[2]

From Hermann's memoirs:

Then came the moment, two or three days before I was supposed to go back again, when I was standing on the balcony outside the dining room. Eberhard was there, and I went to him and said, "Uncle Ebbo, I have decided. You know that I always wanted to follow Jesus, and this is the only place I can really do that. I want to give my life together with you." Eberhard put his arm around me. At first he could not speak, and then he said, "My only brother's only son." He embraced me and said, "You should not call me Uncle Ebbo any more. Call me Papa. I want to be your father."

It was not easy to face the Nazis when I got back. I wrote an open letter, withdrawing from the Nazi Party. I said I could not agree with the principles of National Socialism any longer. Eberhard was actually shocked when he heard that I had written such a letter, because it could have landed me in prison or concentration camp. But there was a lot of internal strife in the Hitler regime right at that moment and no one was watching too closely. I returned my uniform and dagger and my gun. I still had six months of school, and this was hard because most of the teachers were Nazis.[3]

The night before Hermann left, Eberhard spoke directly to him in the worship meeting:

It is an immensely wonderful thing when a human heart is touched and moved by God. Only God himself can move a human heart. As truly as God is God, no human strength can move a heart for God . . .

The future kingdom receives form in the church. This is why the church lives in perfect peace and perfect justice. This is why it cannot shed blood or tolerate private property. This is why the church cannot lie or take an oath. This is why it cannot tolerate the destruction of bridal purity and of faithfulness in the marriage of two people in the church. This is why it also must be free of all actions by which man is made great. This is why the church lives for this: that God will bring everything under his rule on the throne of his kingdom. This is why there can be no idolatry in the church. Nobody must think that the individual is a second or a third or fourth Christ. The church in its whole corporeal being, not the individual in the church, is the incarnation of Christ . . .

The most widespread error is that of mixing this specific task of the church with public affairs . . . Yet Paul shows clearly that it is not the task of this body of Christ to attain prominence in the political power structure of this world. According to the apostolic truth there is no such thing as a Christian state. A Christian church does not fight for the interests of the state. Nor does a church fight against the interests of the state. There is no such thing as Christian politics in the League of Nations, and so on. No head of a state can wield the sword in the name of Christ. No church can say that it agrees to this. Nor can a League of Nations decide to organize an armed punitive police force and say that this is done in the name of Christ.

There are two distinct and separate spheres of life; one is the state and the other is the church. The Christian therefore is not active in German or British national politics or any international politics, such as the League of Nations. The Apostle says that our politics is in heaven, from where we expect our Lord Jesus Christ to come (Phil 3:20). Our politics is that of the kingdom of God.

Therefore, beloved Hermann, I want to entrust you with the very highest and greatest thing which can exist for a man in this world. You are asked whether you can take upon yourself the task of an ambassador of God's kingdom. The Apostle says we are ambassadors of the kingdom of God (2 Cor 5:18–20). We must understand this word in the sense of high politics. When the British ambassador is in the British Embassy in Berlin, he is not subject to the laws of the German Reich. The grounds of the embassy are inviolable. In the residence of the ambassador, only the laws of the country he represents are valid.

The Apostle says that we are ambassadors of God, representing Christ, the Messiah King, the regent of that last kingdom, which is not represented by any state or government of this world, but by the church. We are ambassadors of the kingdom of God. This is something tremendous. It means that we do nothing at all except what the King of God's kingdom would himself do for his kingdom. And this will of the King is the will to unite. This is why the Apostle says we are God's ambassadors on behalf of Christ, appealing to all men, "Be reconciled to God." Our task is reconciliation and uniting, and nothing else. There is nothing else we have to do in this world.

When we take this service upon ourselves we enter into mortal danger. Whoever goes the way of Christ goes the way of the cross; for the world, the state, society is not willing to follow this call of Christ. Nevertheless, there is in every human heart the certainty that this is the only way of truth. Paul also says that our testimony bears witness to every human conscience that it is the truth. This then gives us the courage of love ... There is no greater bravery than that of faith. There is no greater courage than that of love.[4]

What Does Pacifism Mean?

While Eberhard and Emmy were in Germany the previous month, the men and women at the Alm Bruderhof had become discouraged. Hannes Boller had laid down strict rules for the young people. Some of them had reacted with boisterous pranks, and he had come down hard on them. When Eberhard and Emmy arrived, they found the community depressed and confused. Hannes and Else returned to the Rhön Bruderhof. After the specific instances were spoken about and cleared up, Eberhard tried to direct the thoughts of those left at the Alm beyond their personal problems and remind them of the purpose to which they had all committed their lives:

> We are the heralds of the last kingdom; we stand here and go out as bearers of the cause, as envoys, as messengers of God's kingdom. The turning of all things is near; everything else must collapse. God's love alone shall triumph! With this task, we must always be so turned toward the outside world that we have a word from God to say to it in regard to world history; a word that is coined and weighed for the present historical situation; a word that proclaims to all countries alike a message of the supra-political kingdom of God, a message that is true for all ... We have no time for self-centeredness and self-contemplation.[5]

Hardy had come home to the Alm Bruderhof from England; he and Edith were to be married on August 24. At the same time a number of people had come from England to visit the community as well as four who had decided to stay: Arnold and Gladys Mason, a newly married couple, and two single women, Winifred Bridgwater and Kathleen Hamilton. To Eberhard this influx from England was a confirmation both of Hardy's missionary role and of God's continued blessing on the community's venture. They were becoming an international group with members from Germany, Switzerland, Sweden, and now England. As he wrote in a Christmas letter to friends at the end of the year:

> The things we experience with the new people who come to us are often amazing. In one instance a sick woman leaves her bed in a hospital in Switzerland, hands her small assets over to the church, and from now on shows herself to be of one spirit with all Bruderhof members, a wonderful healing being given. In another instance, an old acquaintance finds his home on the Bruderhof on the basis of an experience of Christ that has at last transformed him, after following the wrong track many times. Another time, three people who tried earnestly in one of those vain attempts at community find among us the home of true unity they have longed for. Or again, another who had deep leanings toward Buddhism awakens for the task of Christ's church and sees how it turns toward a declining world with God's whole interest. I wish you could have experienced all this with us, and also the coming of those little groups from Zurich, Tübingen, England, and Eisenach! . . .
>
> A particular confirmation was given to us in England, so that one could speak of a movement there, very small to be sure, but constantly developing. There are at the moment six members of the community at the Alm Bruderhof who have come over from England, Scotland and Ireland; all of them have grown very close to our hearts. A number of others have visited us, and more intend to follow. What an inner moving of hearts binds us with them all! What a vital connection there was here between the faith in Christ and in his spirit on the one hand, and social responsibility, the peace task of God's kingdom, and all problems of world redemption on the other! And how much do we expect for the future building up of our work from these novices from England and Scotland, who include capable workers and several trained as teachers. Will perhaps something similar arise now in one of the larger Swiss cities where several of our young brotherhood members have the task of preparing for their service in the church later? We do not know. But we feel that the spirit of the future is broadening our vision and that the responsibility of God's love has laid on us a task for all people.[6]

One of the visitors, Godfrey Payne, was part of a pacifist group in England. He had worked with Doris and Muriel Lester in the slums of London and then lived with a small communal group in Birmingham. Eberhard welcomed him and told him how they anticipated this encounter after what they had heard from Hardy. He encouraged him to think beyond a utilitarian pacifism to the ultimate causes of war and the true peacemaking Christ demanded of his followers. His own convictions on peace had deepened in the fifteen years since he had first met the pacifist movement in Kees Boeke and the Fellowship of Reconciliation.

> We do not represent a pacifism that believes there will be no more war from now on. That is not true, for there is war right up to the present day. Nor do we represent the kind of pacifism that says better nations should have such an influence over others that war would be abolished. We do not represent the League of Nations and the armed forces of the League of Nations that are supposed to keep the unruly nations in check.
>
> We disagree with a pacifism that holds on to the root causes of war—property and capitalism—in the delusion that there can be peace in the midst of social injustice. We disagree with pacifism that seeks peace through treaties while nations are fighting each other. We do not believe in a pacifism of business competition. Neither do we believe in that pacifism whose amiable representatives cannot even live in peace and love with their own wives. We do not believe in any selfish pacifism. We do not believe in any utilitarian pacifism that pursues the advantages of a nation or business. We do not believe in the pacifism of unchristian states and nations. We do not believe in the pacifism of unrenewed people who are not led by the Holy Spirit.
>
> And because we cannot believe in so many kinds of pacifism we would rather not use the word "pacifism." But we are friends of peace and we want to work for peace. Jesus said, "Blessed are the peacemakers." If we really want peace we must represent it in all things. We may not do anything that contradicts love. Therefore, we cannot kill anyone, either with poison gas or with weapons. We cannot harm anyone in business; we cannot have a hand in a system by which the manual worker is poorer than the educated. We must remove our hands from anything that brings hate or unpeace. We must live like Jesus. He helped everyone in body and soul. We cannot take part in anything that harms people. As friends of peace we should take our hands off all business and all politics that are not as Jesus would have them. Our whole life must be dedicated to love.[7]

Chapter 13—July to August 1934

In a second meeting he spoke to Godfrey Payne's endeavors to try to stop a war between Germany and England:

> I really believe that much good is being said and done in the cause of peace and for the uniting of nations. But I don't think it is enough. If you feel urged to try to prevent or postpone a serious European war, we can only rejoice. But what troubles us is whether you will have much success in opposing the war spirit that exists right now.
>
> Isn't it war, if in Hitler-Germany many hundreds of people are killed unjustly? Isn't it war, if hundreds of thousands of people in concentration camps are robbed of their freedom and stripped of all human dignity? Isn't it war if hundreds of thousands are sent to Siberia and freeze to death while at work felling trees? Isn't it war if in China and Russia millions of people starve to death while in Argentina or the United States millions of tons of wheat are stockpiled? Isn't it war if thousands of women's bodies are ruined for the sake of money in prostitution? Isn't it war if millions of babies are killed annually in their mothers' wombs before they are born? Isn't it war when people are forced to work like slaves because they can hardly provide milk and bread for their children? Isn't it war when wealthy classes live in villas and parks while some families don't have a room to themselves? Isn't it war when some people assume the right to build up a capital of half a million, while others can scarcely earn a dollar for the most necessary things? Isn't it war if automobiles, driven at a speed agreeable to the owner, kill many thousands of people every year in America?
>
> These questions could be increased a hundredfold, but most of us will have already put them to ourselves and have felt that pacifism is something very weak that has no clear solution for this war. We believe, therefore, that Jesus did not speak about the warfare between nations. Jesus always represented the whole, all-embracing truth and had no interest in partial truth. He did not put value on improving any one area through any kind of compulsion. The reason is clear enough: an attack upon one area is only an apparent success.
>
> We experienced in Germany, at the beginning of the [last] war, that a great many friends of peace and pacifism disappeared without a trace. What will happen if war breaks out again—and the governments tell us with clever words and well-considered motives and reasoning that a war is necessary? What happened in 1914 to the pacifist movement, to all movements with socialist interests? They all disappeared, apart from a very few who were strongly convinced . . .

> The Sermon on the Mount is concerned not only with questions of peace and war—although it certainly says, "Love your enemies," and "Turn the other cheek." But at the same time it also says, "Do not go to law or the judge to complain, but rather allow all to be taken from you." The same sermon also says, "Do not speak great or long words; give no oath but say yes or no. Kill no one; humiliate and despise no person. Take no part in the despising of any soul." The Sermon on the Mount says further, "You may have no property—gather no treasures unto yourself. You can own nothing if you want to go the way of Jesus—otherwise you will take part in war and injustice. Your hearts must be completely directed to the kingdom of God and his justice in all matters. You have no other goal, no other meaning in life, than the kingdom of God and his justice."[8]

Godfrey Payne felt that his entire outlook on life was being challenged by what he experienced at the Alm Bruderhof. He said in a meeting before he left:

> I always felt that the only thing worth living for is the kingdom of God. But I want to tell you that I am still afraid to give up my possessions. Up till now I believed that Christ is present in movements such as pacifism, and I wanted to work for unification of the churches and sects to one great world church. It would be very hard for me to give this up. The Bruderhof is a shining light to me. But how can the whole world live like this?[9]

He returned to England and worked with young people, encouraging them in pacifism and community. He remained a good friend to the Bruderhof.

A Second Plebiscite

On August 2, 1934, eighty-seven-year-old Reich president Hindenburg died. He had been a respected conservative, and to many his death meant the end of an age. Anticipating his death, Hitler had convened a cabinet meeting the night before at which the offices of president and chancellor were merged. Hitler announced that the title of Reich president was "inseparably united with the name of the great deceased." From now on, Hitler would be known as Führer and Reich chancellor. With this, Hitler also became supreme commander of the armed forces. All Germany's troops were made to swear a new oath, pledging allegiance not to the Constitution but "unconditional obedience to the Führer of the German

Reich and people, Adolf Hitler."[10] The law to decree Adolf Hitler as Germany's Führer was to be ratified by a plebiscite on August 19.

Another plebiscite on August 19. What should they do? This time Eberhard was in Liechtenstein. He wrote a note to Hans Zumpe at the Rhön Bruderhof:

> It is clear that we do not take part in nor confirm the government, that is, we cannot participate in any such action. We recognize the government that has been established by God without instating or confirming it. Our way is not an authoritarian way but the humble way of being killed. For that reason, too, we can in no way appoint or confirm the commander in chief of a great army. So we should this time too send letters to that effect to Herr Meissner in Berlin [Otto Meissner, State Secretary] and to Herr Bernhard in Fulda [Burkhard, the district administrator]; but not do anything beyond that. This situation is even clearer and more definite than last time [November 12, 1933], for what is demanded of us now concerns the supreme command of the army, that is, the authorization of more killing to come. This is an opportunity to witness to the one way of Jesus Christ and his love.[11]

Eberhard spoke further on this theme in a meeting.

> We recognize Adolf Hitler as the governmental authority by whom we are ruled. But we know we are called not to practice any governmental force, for we are called to live the life of Jesus, who only loved. If we were to take part in the plebiscite we would be ruling over Adolf Hitler by confirming his use of governmental force. We do not want to rule over Adolf Hitler; we will allow ourselves to be ruled by him. Adolf Hitler has the task of governmental force and the sword. We Christians do not have this task. Therefore we cannot put the sword into Hitler's hand by voting. We recognize that the sword will exist as long as the world is not Christian. But as Christians we are called not to hand the sword to anyone. We have no active part in the government, for we are called to a life of love and nothing else.
>
> It should be recognized by our life what Jesus meant and what the heart of God is. The heart of God will not kill. The government will not survive without the sword. Adolf Hitler has been appointed by God as commander in chief of hell. We recognize him as such. But we will not join in ruling this government of hell, rather we belong to the king of heaven's kingdom, and so we must live as this king of heaven's kingdom lives. The question is: Will you go the way of the cross or not? Will you be baptized with my baptism? Will you drink the cup from which I have drunk?[12]

Hans Zumpe wrote the letters Eberhard suggested. Copies went to the office of the Reichskanzler in Berlin, the Gestapo in Berlin, and to the district administrator of Fulda, signed by every member of the brotherhood. As in the case of the earlier letter to the Reich president (of November 10, 1933) a courteous acknowledgment of receipt arrived from the Reich president's office, with the information that the petition had been passed on to the ministry of the interior.

Before the plebiscite, a printed announcement was delivered to the Rhön Bruderhof:

> The Right to Vote is a Duty to Vote!
>
> As a citizen you have claim to certain rights, but please fulfill also your duty to your nation and your leader ADOLF HITLER! He keeps faith with the German people, and that includes you! Do you? On August 19, 1934, after 12 o'clock noon I will take the liberty to inquire whether you have fulfilled your highest civic duty. If you are prevented by sickness from visiting the local polling station, please report to the nearest office of the National Socialist Party.

Refusal to vote was dangerous. Polling stations were surrounded by brownshirts, creating an atmosphere of fear. Anyone who did not participate risked being pilloried as an opponent of the Nazi state.

This time the Bruderhof members did not enter the polling booths. At noon, all those of German nationality disappeared by various routes into the nearby woods where they remained until dark. They took with them the *Chronicle of the Hutterian Brethren* and read stories of the Anabaptist martyrs of the sixteenth century.[13]

Hardy and Edith's Wedding

Hardy and Edith were married on August 26. Trudi Hüssy described the wedding:

> The preparation time for this wedding was very special. Hardy had studied in England for a year or so. He had been eager to tell young people there about our life in community. Through the increasing devilish power of Nazism, people in Europe, especially England, were inwardly alive. There were courageous young people who resisted the evil spirit which was already ruling over most Germans. Four English people had been deeply

moved by Hardy's witness, Arnold and Gladys Mason, Winifred Bridgwater, and Kathleen Hamilton, and they had come to the Alm Bruderhof to experience the community. They were so struck by what they found that they all soon asked to become members and put all they owned into the hands of the church. They had many questions about the Bruderhof's understanding of marriage. Thus every evening for two or three weeks Eberhard let them ask their questions.

On the Saturday before the wedding Eberhard and Emmy went with the young couple to Triesenberg where the registrar lived. He was a Catholic priest, and Eberhard presented him with a number of Hutterian documents on marriage. On their return Eberhard told us that this man was deeply impressed by the clarity of this witness.

The wedding itself was a very joyful occasion. The beauty of the mountains around us, the wedding procession along the Alpine footpaths, the meadows on both sides covered with flowers, the wide view into the Rhine Valley were overwhelming. A courageous spirit was alive again, the joy that can be given when a serious fight is waged. We sensed that we were resisting the Nazi spirit, although some of us were unaware of how serious the situation was. We still hoped that we would hold out longer, as Eberhard used to say (that Hitler might soon collapse), and that in a few years we would all be reunited on the Rhön Bruderhof. It is a grace that the future is hidden from us!

At the wedding dinner some of the young people danced for us. There was great joy. The young couple left for Italy—hitchhiking with very little money—and the beautiful August evening spread its peace over the landscape.[14]

After their wedding, Hardy and Edith moved to Zurich where they were both to continue their studies. Hardy's brothers, Heiner and Hans-Hermann, joined them; Heiner was attending an agricultural school and Hans-Hermann preparing to study medicine. The four of them were to be a small community. Men from the Alm occasionally stopped in at the small Zurich community while traveling door to door in Switzerland selling books and homemade craft items. On his return home, one described the circumstances of those living in Zurich:

> They have two rooms: the sitting room, which is also Hardy and Edith's bedroom, and the kitchen, which is Hans-Hermann's bedroom. They sleep on mattresses on the floor. In the sitting room there is a round table and a chair without a seat, but they have

> made one of rope and made a cushion. For books there is a board on two boxes, but the room looks quite nice as a curtain covers the boxes, etc. Edith gets home from the university at about 7:30 in the evening, and has to set to, to cook the big meal of the day. She also makes the breakfast porridge as there is just time to heat it in the morning.[15]

Hans Zumpe traveled to the Alm Bruderhof in time for Hardy and Edith's wedding (his wife Emy-Margret was already there with the children). Eberhard and Emmy returned to Germany on September 25. In a farewell meeting the night before leaving, Eberhard asked Hans Zumpe to take on responsibility for the Alm Bruderhof.

> In the name of the brothers called Hutterians and of both our communities I give you full responsibility for the Alm Bruderhof until we decide on a different arrangement. We do not know if political events will cut us off from each other. This hour is a historic one in which the Word Leader* hands the Alm Bruderhof over to its servant of the Word, with full responsibility and complete joy. Hans Zumpe and the whole Alm Bruderhof are accountable to me as the Word Leader; they have to give me frequent and truthful reports, while I on my part commit myself to keeping Hans Zumpe most carefully posted.[16]

At dinner that night he said:

> Our deepest belief is that the ultimate meaning of life is worldwide unity. But we are not under the illusion that this is achieved in the present political and social life. Our faith is in a cosmic order of unity still to come. From this tension we must face the disorder of our time with the future order, even if only in a small community.
>
> We live from the powers of the future world. The inner source of our strength seems to lie in the future, but actually it is at work in this present time. The Holy Spirit creates unity among us, unity that exists in all areas of life. First of all in the heart-to-heart relationships, but just as much in the material world around us. For the mainspring of our life is love. Love is joy in one another, a joy that wells up from the fountain of unity and enables us to surrender everything. Community in the Spirit becomes community

---

* Word Leader (*Wortführer*): The term has usually been translated as "spokesman" but is here translated literally as Eberhard gave it the meaning of "one who leads in the Word [of God]" or gives expression to that which is moving in the church. It was used to refer to Eberhard Arnold as the leader of the Bruderhof movement.

of education and work, and community of work quite naturally becomes community of goods without private property.

Giving up money means nothing compared with the surrender of all one's strength. We share both the goods of the earth and our working strength, but we do not want to live in collective egoism. We bear witness that people can and do live in community, not in words, but in deeds. We bear witness to this reality which lies in the future kingdom of God. By living in this way we hope to say something to the world, not in words, but in deeds.

At this farewell my wish for us all is that with our every word and every deed we express what we stand for.[17]

14

September to December 1934

BACK IN GERMANY AFTER spending the summer in Liechtenstein, there was much for Eberhard and Emmy to do. Eberhard saw to reprinting chapters of his earlier book *The Early Christians After the Death of the Apostles* to sell as small pamphlets. Since the community was divided into two now, he was missing some of the people who usually helped him. With Hans Zumpe at the Alm Bruderhof, it was left for him to oversee the daily accounting and questions of taxes that had come up as new laws were passed and the community lost its tax-exempt status. There was sickness among both children and adults, and in general people seemed weary. Again and again he reminded them of the historic hour they faced. As he wrote to Hans Zumpe at the Alm Bruderhof: "I am suffering under the fact that on this Bruderhof we are extremely lacking in inwardly stimulated minds. All here are very faithful brothers and sisters, but there should be more stimulation from the living Spirit."[1] In a members' meeting he called the church members to wakefulness:

> How can you help me so that we do not have any more sleepy or absentminded participants in our worship meetings? I can no longer be responsible for reading or saying anything essential or vital if some people are sleeping. What is the cause of this? How can it be overcome? . . .
>
> We may not surrender to sleepiness. Our worship meetings must be the heart of our whole day. The spiritual struggle for which we live all day begins in our meetings. All brotherhood members must take responsibility for the wakefulness of the circle. We are not sufficiently aware that a decisive struggle is taking place, a struggle between spirits encompassing the whole world. We do not want to make pious exercises; we are called to a decisive spiritual struggle between lies and truth, between

mammon and the justice of God's kingdom, between purity and impurity. We must keep this before our eyes in opposition to the spirit of sleepiness. If necessary, people should take a rest during the day so that they can be fresh for prayer and worship, for the spiritual battle.[2]

Only insofar as members of the church are faithful in their daily lives will they be prepared to withstand temptation. And only insofar as they are ready to serve God and his holy cause in their daily work will they also be ready to sacrifice their lives at the last hour for Christ and his kingdom. To the degree that we are prepared to die a martyr's death for Christ in the time of terrors to come, to the same degree will we also be prepared to withstand sin and defy false prophecy, even to the last drop of blood. If we are ready to die *physically*, we will also be ready to commit the entire strength of our lives—day by day, hour by hour—for the justice and peace of the kingdom of God. For the barrage of hostile powers which storm against us is always the same, and so is our defense, whether it be in times of peace or in times of murder and destruction.

We are thankful that today we may live in a time of mortal danger, because this question has now become practical and real for us: Are you ready? We want to answer with the affirmative "yes" of prayer and worship, thanking God that he has called us to the holy way of the cross, the way of dedication to Christ, and asking him to protect us and give us the strength to die with Christ in the manner that he died. As we reflect on the redemption of the cross, let us pray that Christ keep us as his disciples unto death. May God give us the power of true discipleship and the influence of the Spirit.[3]

August and Gertrud Dyroff expressed what the brotherhood was thinking in a letter to the Alm Bruderhof:

In the last days we have experienced so much...We feel distinctly that something is occurring in the atmospheres; two poles are approaching each other. When will they meet? We do not know. But I must say we are all filled with a great thankfulness and joy that we can give a witness for this life.

We also feel very clearly that the hour is here when it is no longer a matter of people but of world concepts, that is, of the existing government order and the church of the future world order of God's kingdom. Hans Meier read from the early Christians in our worship meeting today. What happened then is still happening today, and we feel strongly bound with the church above and all witnesses to truth who fought this struggle of love and sacrificed their lives for it.

These days for the first time we really understood what Eberhard has so often said: we must all be won for the greatness of God's cause. We feel clearly that we are under God's protection and that only that will take place which he allows and is his will. We must be watchful and listen to what the voice says to us in this hour. The financial help we have received from you shows us clearly that we must continue to build up, and our hearts are thankful for this. We must not let anything frighten and distract us but must look with open eyes at the signs of the times, which point out to us the immediate causes of the judgment that is breaking in and the coming of God's kingdom. For us this means readiness to sacrifice, and at the same time building for the future.

In this joyful expectation of God's kingdom, and in faith in the victory of Christ's love over all darkness, we greet you.[4]

~

At the end of October, Eberhard traveled to Berlin to call on several offices. On the whole, his trip was encouraging. "I bring comparatively favorable information from Berlin," he wrote. "A certain understanding has been found in important places. And we have good advocates in some government offices."[5] His visit to the foreign ministry went well; Germany was still concerned to preserve a positive image abroad, and he told them of the investments to the Rhön Bruderhof made by friends in England, Switzerland, and the United States. About his visit to the office of finance he reported: "Even though we are recognized as a charitable foundation, our farm operation is still subject to taxation . . . Our farming must be geared strictly to our consumption needs."[6] Then he described an incident:

> When I was in the Foreign Office I saw the Russian ambassador. I was sitting and waiting, and a young man came in and announced, "The Russian ambassador is coming." He was a small man with gray-black hair and beard.
>
> There I had an illustration of what it means when a powerful country dispatches its ambassador. I experienced that an ambassador of a country represents the entire power, the entire

authority of that country. Wherever he goes he must be shown the respect that is given to his country.

We are sent out as ambassadors of God's kingdom. We do not desire worldly reverence and worldly respect. When an ambassador of the Messiah-king comes, of the kingdom of God's justice and unity, when an ambassador of the church comes, he is a representative of God's kingdom. Regardless of the character of a worldly kingdom, diplomacy senses the power behind it. What do we sense when an ambassador of the kingdom of God comes? The ambassador is the church that is sent into the world. The ambassador might be unpretentious, but he represents a power. The small church might look very unpretentious, but it is an ambassador. For this reason we should not forget what the church, as embassy of the kingdom of God, has to say. It says, "Be united."[7]

As time went on, Eberhard emphasized more and more the spiritual aspect of the confrontation with Nazism. Living for God's glory alone and denying any human veneration was the only power that could counter the idolatry of the Führer cult. This, Eberhard believed, was the witness he and the Bruderhof were called to give in Germany. In this sense he wrote a very personal letter to his three sons in Zurich.

To you Hardy, but also to your dear, faithful Edith, to Heiner, and to Hans-Hermann, I want to write as is possible only for a father to his son or a friend to his friend. I feel urged to tell you very personally some things about myself. First, I want to tell you that unfortunately it took me decades, in spite of the most decisive Christianity, to gradually overcome the touchiness of a sensitive soul, the fretful struggle for the desired love of beloved persons, and the overestimation of self which passionately imposes one's own influence, supposedly good, and one's own gifts, supposedly exceptional. This inability to listen to others and to be open to others with gifts of a different kind, who could have spoken to me, gradually subsided. I should describe to you once in detail how deeply my Emmy, your mother, helped me with the instinctive certainty of her simple nearness to Christ, her motherliness, and her healthy attitude. Here I only want to emphasize how long this inner process lasted, and unfortunately had to last, because of the stubbornness of my heart!

The result of these often very difficult decades was emotionally remarkable. I now think only seldom and unwillingly of my person. It seems to have almost faded away in what fills and surrounds me. My greatest happiness is a work of love in which I forget that I am there and that I am active. Often for a long time I feel about my person as everyone feels about his hand or his foot. Both are used constantly. But the more they become accustomed to being used and get practice in it, the more they lose their own importance. Other members of the same body are just as useable in their way, perhaps much more useable than it seems at first sight from the limited view of the "I." But this remains clear: it is not a matter of indifference how I or my hand, or other I's and other hands, are used. The greatness which fills and surrounds my smallness and other smallnesses wishes to use everything, including the most humble, if only it is put at his disposal with the right proportion of values!

It took a long time, oh, such a very long time, until this redeeming from the morbidly exaggerated ego (which in the end seems such a matter of course) began very, very slowly to penetrate in a practical way. It is just what the apostolic word, echoed faintly by Goethe, describes so clearly: a dying of oneself and a coming into being of the other! What a cruelly slow dying! And yet, what a real resurrection! The love of the one who loves becomes all the more glowing and true-hearted when it has had to lose and bury much, so very much, that was domineering, when it has learned to forget more and more the power-thirsty desire to be loved itself. A man's spirit becomes more alive, more active and all-embracing, the further and further it removes itself from the fearful, proud urge for self-assertion and from the greedy and restless urge for expansion and power of the human soul.

Many will believe this is impossible, and it is clear that we men can experience this all-too-slow transformation only if we are very close to God, only in the light of Christ, and only when we are listening to the voice of the Holy Spirit. In this way alone will we learn the true objectivity of God's love, so that we no longer see our relatives or other people with an emotional love that makes emotional demands again and again, but instead as organs of the church. The clear love of God sees in these organs of the church what they essentially are: instruments of God and his clarity.

In our closeness to the loving God, that truly happens which appears too marvelous, yet is objectively real: we forget more and more the touchiness of our so-often-offended feelings and now carry on our hearts the much greater, widespread need of the whole inhabited world. We carry it as God himself carries it. Within this great encircling world need, we take upon ourselves quite specifically the poverty and affliction of the church as Christ has done and continues to do. In this way we become sober and responsible, austere and objective, also in the affairs of mammon entrusted to us.⁸

～

On November 21, 1934, Germany's annual national Day of Repentance and Prayer, Eberhard presented a sweeping review of the world situation in a meeting at the Rhön Bruderhof:

> The state of the world is altogether frightening. Worldwide we find an intellectual decline in all movements of genuine social significance. This is true of bolshevism and of those movements that worked for peace through disarmament—the League of Nations and Gandhi's movement in India. We are especially distressed that the Religious Socialists—Christian Socialists—though they try to maintain their social welfare work, have lost depth and greatness.
>
> Just a few years ago there was worldwide a living expectation of God's kingdom. This has receded throughout the world. A true, active expectation of a kingdom of justice and peace can be found only in very small circles today.
>
> The reason for this will be clear to anyone who reflects on the idea of the final kingdom. Eschatological expectation has been forced into the background by a different kingdom to which the promises of a thousand-year reign are now connected. Everywhere the ultimate human goal of true, perfect love is degraded. Mutual help between men—full community—is devalued. In bolshevist Russia, in fascist Italy, and above all in Germany, there is a lot of talk about the common good, but this idea has not penetrated life to the extent that humankind's genuine goal of mutual help and full community overcomes self-interest or even causes it to recede.
>
> At the same time movements have arisen across the globe that give a shocking overall picture in the sphere of religion. On the one hand personal piety has become very widespread, but unfortunately only in the sense of a private experience of the Savior and a personal sanctification. We regret this phenomenon because of its narrowness. However much we rejoice when people are awakened to a love for Jesus and experience forgiveness of sin in his death on the cross, we have to say that the true significance of love to Christ and the meaning of his crucifixion is not grasped if it is restricted to the heart's subjective experience of salvation. There is something great in recent theology in

> showing that God is completely different from any movement of social activity or personal piety. But the one-sided emphasis on this fact—removing the living God to a great distance—has resulted in repressing or extinguishing social responsibility. The result is that in the great confessional movement of the Pastors' Emergency League you feel practically nothing of a deeper calling or strong social responsibility for the desperately oppressed groups.
>
> But this is only one side of the picture. At the same time, in Russia we have seen a historically unprecedented rise of crass unbelief. And all over the world we find an unexpected recurrence of paganism. Today's exaggerated nationalism is wedded to this new paganism ...
>
> How much justice is left in the world? How much love and mutual service exists among the peoples? How much genuine social responsibility remains for the impoverished, oppressed masses? This is the crucial question, and it is connected with what people call religion. In this present situation, what is our task?

Eberhad then compared the present time with the Reformation when there was similar oppression and despair. In the Hutterian communities of the sixteenth century social justice was realized.

> The center of this church was the living Christ, the ruler of God's kingdom. The kingdom of God gave direction to the life of the church. This was not a human, idealistic enterprise, not a socialist, revolutionary matter. And yet it embodied what was best in those idealistic, revolutionary endeavors: God's will for justice. This representation of God's kingdom knew and acknowledged obedience to government authority, but only to the extent that this did not violate the love of Christ.
>
> Our task today, amidst the extremely oppressive worldwide need, is to grow in numbers and influence, in inwardness, significance, and spiritual vitality. Unfortunately, we have been forced to divide into two Bruderhofs.
>
> Our Christ-centered life, attuned to God's kingdom, must be enlarged in every department. Our livelihood—handicrafts, farming, and gardening—must be carried on more intensively and extensively. The writing and marketing of books must continue to grow, with all brotherhood members increasingly moved inwardly and participating more and more actively. In the raising of our children, in inner sharing, in brotherhood and worship meetings, the life of the church must grow more alert and active than ever before. We must alert all mankind to who God is and

what he wills, that through Jesus Christ he brings perfect love, that this love lives in genuine community today—in full social justice and brotherliness. Our chief task is to call the whole world to recognize that the goal that humankind longs for, but has almost forgotten, is truly possible. We must call those in high places as well as the masses of the lowly.[9]

When one of the young men moved from the Rhön to the Alm, Eberhard sent him off with the following words:

> You are being sent to a mission church. You will have to put everything into the task, heart and head, hands and feet, with full responsibility. You are commissioned as a living message, a letter, a book from one church to another. That is why you should be received with exceptional love, just as we entrust you with special love to go from our midst to the arms of the other brotherhood and church.
>
> There is one who took on himself the whole suffering of the world on the cross and overcame it. If we take the suffering of the world on ourselves as Christ did, so that the word is fulfilled in us, "Blessed are those who bear suffering," if we accept the place which Christ accepted on the cross at Golgotha, then we shall have the mission of Christ, then we will approach the world with the outstretched arms of complete love, then we will have words of reconciliation to proclaim. For we are messengers of this Christ, messengers of God representing this king—the messengers who are to say to the world: Let yourselves be reconciled with God, let yourselves be united with God, find unity! The standpoint of the cross and the hour of Golgotha: this is the decisive point from which we look at all the suffering in the world and take it upon ourselves. From the center of the gospel we have to embrace the whole world anew with the outstretched arms of Christ.
>
> For this we are placed in the world. Therefore we ask God to reveal this last depth of the gospel to us and give it into our open empty hands as a commission.[10]

～

At Christmas 1934—no one dreamed that it was to be Eberhard's last Christmas—Eberhard and Emmy celebrated their twenty-fifth wedding anniversary and Emmy's fiftieth birthday. It was a season to reflect on how God had led and protected them over the years. But it was also an occasion to look forward with joy and faith to the future:

on Christmas day their son Heiner called from the Alm Bruderhof: Annemarie Wächter had accepted his proposal of marriage. Emmy wrote to her mother-in-law:

> On my fiftieth birthday we had a big surprise. During the midday we had a phone call from Silum. Just imagine, our Heiner became engaged to dear Annemarie Wächter on Christmas Eve. They have been friends for a long time ... Ebbo and I love Annemarie very much, as do all the brothers and sisters. We are sure that there can be no better wife for Heiner. She has a deep inner faith and at the same time works hard and is very practical. Heiner will do very well by her. We were told on the phone that they are both overjoyed. I believe you can give them your blessing; they would be very happy if you would write to them. We can't plan the wedding yet since Heiner first has to finish school, which will be another year and a quarter.[11]

As 1934 drew to a close, the community sent a Christmas letter to their friends in the form of a pamphlet of thirty-two pages, relating the events of the past year.

> Christmas 1934! In the midst of the unrest of all humankind that encircles our planet from Japan to America, from America to Russia, from the northern hemisphere all the way to South America and Africa, we send you the greeting of the expectation of peace in which we believe in the final kingdom. Come what may, God's kingdom will lead to true peace coming from the throne of Jesus Christ, a peace that no human efforts can attain. With this peace we greet you! ...
>
> We offer you the peace of God. What we offer you is the call to gathering in the unity of a church led by the Spirit. This gathering is the embodiment of a unity which is invisible. It is communal life and communal work. We believe that the actual existence of this life is of utmost significance in a time when there is no peace. It is a lamp on its stand, a city on a hill: the material witness to unity in the life of the church ... Certainly we know that our community is weak and small, yet it is a testimony that full community is possible, that true community of peoples, that the unity of peace, that unselfish sharing and brotherhood is possible.
>
> What we experience here and now points to the great future of things to come. That which is lived out and witnessed by a small, humble handful today will in God's future attain rulership over all worlds as the government of his kingdom. The church proclaims to all people the peace of God's ultimate future, the

final new creation of the whole world and all humankind. Jesus Christ will reveal himself above all worldly kingdoms as the king of peace and of justice. The Son of Mary is the newborn God-King.

In the faith of this joyful expectation, we at the Alm and Rhön Bruderhofs are living in the midst of a deeply moving, even shattering, Advent. Already last Christmas we felt the sharpness of God's language in the history of this momentous time. Again this year, we sense that our continued existence is an undeserved miracle of God. In the midst of the bitter sufferings and passionate struggles that have seized the whole world, the communal work which has been undertaken in God's name has been preserved and can expand ...

Eberhard went on to describe the community's response to the plebiscite of November 12, 1933, and quoted the statement they had pasted to the ballot sheet. He told how the children had fled Germany and how the Alm Bruderhof was begun. Then he continued:

But just what humans planned for evil purposes, God used for good. What humans planned to cause our downfall, God used for building up his little work. One Bruderhof became two. Our influence abroad expanded in an undreamed-of way to wide circles in several countries ...

Thanks to the political events and the division of our community, two or three brothers are sent out to the villages and towns almost every week by each of the two Bruderhofs. Their task is to convey the news that community based on the gospel is really possible. Their message is that the kingdom of justice and peace has come closer than ever before to a perishing world. But these messengers also have to help provide for the living of the community that sends them out. The two Bruderhofs could not possibly get along without our publishing and printing and our handicraft workshops. We now have four lathes, and on these we produce wooden bowls, boxes, candle-holders, and other articles ...

Into how many present-day problems and struggles the spirit of truth and love had to shine with the authority of the word this past year! How rich in content are our meetings! We have been concerned with the light-victory of faith, as it once blazed in Persia; with the struggle of the two spirits among men; with the call of Jesus that has placed the church in the midst of this wrestling between light and darkness. As the embassy of the coming kingdom, the church stands in opposition to all the powers of the great world. At other times we have been specifically concerned with the question of violence and bloodshed by the state, with the enthusiasm of nationalism and the completely different spirit of loving discipleship of Christ...

It was around the turn of the year 1933–34 that the serious question presented itself to us forcefully: Shall we stay in our homeland? Do we have a place in Europe? What is to happen to our mission to the whole world and all nations? What is our task in regard to our children and the people who speak our native language? Before the political upheaval, countless guests and temporary helpers passed through our house. Perhaps now we must go out to many more people, because they cannot come to us.

The brotherhood, then, is standing directly before new decisions of faith. We cannot avoid them. In comparison with the smallness of our development hitherto, something great must take place. Never before has an age needed the practical witness of true community so urgently as ours. There is no turning back, only an uninterrupted forwards![12]

15

January to March 1935

THE NEW YEAR 1935 started with an encouraging event for the community. The Entailed Farm Law Court in Celle sent a five-page document announcing that the five judges had ruled in favor of the Bruderhof that the Upper Klösshof belonged to them and not to Emil Möller. Eberhard read the letter to the community before lunch on January 5. After lunch, the members met to consider the ramifications of this decision. It seemed to be a sign that they should remain in Germany, but they would have to pay 25,000 marks, the remainder of the purchase price, within three months. Eberhard passed around pictures of what the place had looked like when they acquired it and reminded them of how the houses had been built over the past eight years. Then he asked each to speak.

> *Georg Barth:* The fact that we can keep the Emil Möller property gives us hope that our two Bruderhofs could move together again on the Rhön Bruderhof, even though the question is still open as to whether we could set up the school again. Now we have to see how to obtain the money that we have promised to pay.
>
> *Hannes Boller:* It is a deep joy to me that the decision fell this way. I am thinking especially about the significance of the position that the government took toward us. I have a quiet hope that the terrible judgment of God might be averted once more. I don't know how we will procure the means, but I have faith that it will be given.
>
> *Emmy Arnold:* Humanly we cannot grasp it, that the judgment was made in our favor. It is unbelievable.
>
> *Arno Martin:* We see clearly that human strength can do nothing but everything depends on God. With this decision, something

tremendous has been given to us that touches especially on our agriculture. It is good that we didn't lose heart when things were difficult.

Alfred Gneiting: It is a miracle. It is as if this place has been given to us anew.

Hans Meier: The result of this decision is that we need more workers. We need to advertise for people and for money.

Ludwig Kleine: I see in this ruling respect for our convictions. If we had made compromises to the state in other questions, this decision would not have been made and we might not be here anymore. It is also a sign that there is still justice, and we should be thankful for that.

Eberhard: Through this ruling of the Entailed Farm Law Court, we are firmly bound to this land. It means that we have to practice the most intensive agriculture and that we can also build. We need to recruit more people. Our begging for money also needs to be more intensive.

Two billion people live on earth today, only four thousand of whom live in community. God does not look only on these four thousand but on all people. His interest is not directed only to the churches. God has a burning interest in all peoples. There are many vocations in the world, all of which need to be fulfilled, just as Pharaoh, bolshevism, Buddha, nationalism, Gandhi, and other people and movements fulfill their mission. Pharaoh was an instrument of God in that he drove the Israelites out of the fleshpots of Egypt. We cannot be narrow-minded. God's grace that forgives sin is there for all people, not only for Christians. The church has a special task to represent the purity of Christ as God's heart of love: harmony and community of goods, that they all may be one in order to fulfill God's mission. But not everyone is called to this.[1]

One of the newer members wrote in a letter to his family:

Our attitude to the government can be expressed much more positively than I was able to express it [before I came]. We recently had an interesting experience. Because of a suspicion, Dr. Eberhard Arnold was summoned to defend our political and economic suitability. He won recognition in a wonderful way: "We love Adolf Hitler, we love the German people and Germany—and we love and respect you, Herr Landrat. We are happy to be subject to those in authority."

"What about your refusal to bear arms?"

"Please get to know our life better and consider us a religious order. Priests and members of religious orders have always been allowed to refuse the shedding of blood for reasons of conscience. Our brothers and sisters have consecrated their lives to a spiritual vocation."

After our economic success was satisfactorily recognized, the district administrator promised to inspect our premises and represent to the government that our work is productive for the nation. Eberhard answered the "German greeting" with "All the best for Hitler and *Heil* for us all through Christ"—and received a warm handshake in farewell! Even if the gentlemen laughed and shook their heads after he left, it was a demonstration that love is victorious.[2]

A New Threat

On January 11, Eberhard appointed Georg Barth and reappointed Hannes Boller to the service of the Word. The needs of the two communities were not being adequately covered by Hans Zumpe and himself, and he trusted that in the power of the Holy Spirit, Georg and Hannes would be given strength to provide leadership. In preparation for this ordination, he held several meetings on the topic of mission during the first week of January, recalling how Christ sent his disciples out. Those entrusted with this task should see themselves as "servants," not as rulers, and must be ready for martyrdom.

> Jesus' missionary words in the tenth chapter of the Gospel of Matthew are very important for a servant of the Word, because they make clear that the picture of Jesus Christ is not the heroic ideal. Jesus does not wish that his servants and church seek to become famous martyrs, whose heroism in death is proclaimed. Certainly, they must be prepared to die for the sake of the witness, but they should be as unassuming as possible. The important thing is that the truth is testified to, unbroken and unchanged, by the servant who is sent out, even if he should be put to death. He must represent the truth to the end, neither weakened nor exaggerated, neither adding to it nor subtracting, and always in love. Only through this is his martyrdom consecrated, through the objective loyalty and modesty in the representation of the truth. That is a very deep lesson, and not every one will immediately understand why Jesus expressly says, "Flee from one land into

another." The whole attitude of the church hangs together with this. If we have no permanent place, no permanent Bruderhof in any country, but are always prepared for flight, then we cannot cling to property, nor think we have a comfortable place in the work we are responsible for. Then we will be prepared to do the lowest service, like Jesus did. We will not consider whether our work is particularly important or successful, but we will be prepared to clean shoes all day long or change jobs repeatedly. We will be prepared to be moved from one job to another, even as our whole life is a pilgrimage.

It must be clear to us that especially a servant of the Word must in no way become more than that which Jesus lived and demonstrated. He would not be a true servant if his name is not dishonored, if he is not deeply insulted. As it happened to Jesus, so it should happen to the servants of the Word.

We need not worry. We need not fear. A comfort is given to us: The Son of Man is coming, the hour is near when he will come again. We shall not finish our proclamation, we shall not have traversed our whole planet, and Jesus will be there. Our pilgrimage will stretch from Germany to England, from England to America, to Japan and Russia, and back again to Germany. While we are thus traveling, Jesus will be there—not for our small brotherhood, but for the whole of Christianity.

The service of the Word and apostolic mission are placed under Christ's return. That is the encouragement we receive in our need: the arrival of Jesus Christ. The coming of his kingdom is near! near! near! Therefore let us be courageous and brave, even to the smallest detail, prepared for whatever is laid upon us, for the time is near.

We will praise God for this, and ask him for true humility and endurance of simplicity, and the endowing of the true service of the Word, not only for our servants of the Word, but for all of us, who are called to this way.[3]

In the middle of February, Eberhard met Dr. Jerschke, the deputy governor in Kassel. Jerschke respected Eberhard and had signed a favorable report on behalf of the minister of agriculture. Now he said that compulsory military service was in sight and would be enforced in a few weeks. When Eberhard told him the community would not comply, he strode excitedly up and down the room saying, "What will become of you? There are no exceptions to this law!"[4]

Emmy heard the same from Baron von Gagern's wife, with whom she remained in touch even after von Gagern's transfer from Fulda to

Melsungen.⁵ A serious question faced the community: Should they remain in Germany and prepare to die, or should they flee? If they left the country, it should not be out of cowardice but in order to continue the witness of community and love.

Eberhard was to go to Switzerland to meet with Leonhard Ragaz and other Religious Socialists. He arrived at the Alm Bruderhof on March 2, carried up the mountain through the snow by eight men.⁶ Here he told them of the situation and they discussed the question. Annemarie described the meeting in a letter to Heiner:

> Papa told mainly about his visits in Kassel and Fulda. At three different places he got the same warning about military service for our men. The punishment for refusal is either immediate death or life imprisonment; in most cases the first will be carried out right away.
>
> Hardy told us of some wonderful brotherhood meetings in which all the brothers stated their readiness for anything—for death, prison, or possible emigration—and their utmost obedience to the will of Christ and the leading of his spirit. The openness with which Papa spoke to government officials is simply amazing. The district administrator got a strong admonition from Papa; he received it in silence and did not have a word to say. It is a marvelous thing that we never allow ourselves to be silenced, but always speak the truth, cost what it may. Papa has a wonderful way of communicating with all kinds of people.⁷

In another letter the next day she described how the decision had been made:

> Something Mama said at the Rhön Bruderhof has become important to us: We are forced into the situation of our families having to emigrate from Germany because if our men were to stay there and be handed over to the violent power of the state, we would make ourselves co-guilty of their blood. Death in Germany would be a real martyr's death; they would be regarded as traitors by the people and as such, despised as the most dishonorable, base riffraff. No Nazi German would regard it as a death for Christ's sake but as the just reward for deeply despicable conduct. So the men will come here. We must maintain our livelihood: are we ready?
>
> The necessity of the selling mission exposes our people to spiritual danger: temptations, abuse, slander, and softening. Mama sees this as the test of martyrdom set for us here. For even in martyrdom it is not death itself that is the difficult thing, but

the attempts of people to make the firmness of spirit waver. Thus the trial of selling mission is a test for martyrdom—and up to now we have to say that we have failed this test. We are not mature enough to show the firm and steadfast faith that our brothers in medieval times showed ...

We see ourselves placed again before the decision: for or against. There is no such thing as partial readiness. This is the struggle of martyrdom in which we at the Alm Bruderhof are placed. It has become clear to us afresh—and we were quite unanimous—that we want to dare to send brothers out again, trusting in God's power.[8]

There are no existing transcripts of those meetings, but the discussion continued at a meeting held a few days later.

Annemarie Wächter: We must be ready for what the hour demands of us, for the unstained witness of the church is now at stake. The question is whether the city of light is to stay alive or whether other powers will drag it down into the mire.

Hans Grimm: I believe we must now stand together more faithfully than ever. The military question is one that touches every one of us. It seems as if from all sides everything is to be torn apart, yet time and again the light draws it all back together. The Spirit has never ceased to select his instruments—a small fighting band, ready for any consequences, ready even to seal that willingness by death, if the hour demands it. Not that we take steps in that direction but that we let ourselves be prepared.

Winifred Bridgwater: We who are English nationals want to carry the danger together with you and be completely one with you.

Sekunda Kleiner: We sense that this is a horrible hour and that the whole world wants to kill the truth. It is our task to prevent that. It's important to give one's whole strength, and we feel that the witness must not be thrown to the dogs but be built up here. We stand by the brothers with our whole life.

Liesel Wegner: It is shaking to see how the evil powers want to destroy the life of the church. We know that what is at stake is the future, the light, and that we must testify with our whole life that we are ready. I stand completely with those concerned.

Edith Arnold: Eberhard, when you get to the Rhön Bruderhof tell them that we stand completely with those who remain there. In this hour we sense the task God has for us and that we have to

> carry it out fully or not at all. And we have to face death. We can only speak of readiness if we are willing to take everything upon ourselves, even death. But we cannot do it in our own strength.
>
> *Eberhard:* Only when death comes actually close does it become clear that in ourselves we do not have the strength for martyrdom. The threat of death makes martyrdom much more real. Jesus said, "If it is possible, let this cup pass me by. My God, why hast thou forsaken me?" The agony of death became revealed in the death of Jesus. It was no heroic pose but a true death. So I, too, feel we should sense at both our communities that what we are facing is no longer a "hero's death" but genuine death. That is why we tremble and shake and cling to faith. We don't push ourselves forward but do hold ourselves in readiness.
>
> *Erna Steenken:* The fact that things are coming to a head helps one to greater firmness. And when the hour of martyrdom comes, it will become clear who is actually ready and who is not.
>
> *Kathleen Hamilton:* In our own strength we simply cannot face the situation, and knowing ourselves so weak and incapable makes me think of Paul's word that man's weakness lets God's power come in. The hour of decision is entirely in God's hands.
>
> *Eberhard:* "My power shows up best in weak people." That is what Jesus shows us in Gethsemane and on the cross. Are we all united in that?[9]

The following night, Eberhard read to the community an account of persecution of the Anabaptists in the sixteenth century, when 150 men were arrested. Then he said:

> We know that we cannot hold out in times as hard as those if we do not have a very strong and living relationship to God, if we are not clothed with the armor of God, if this spiritual armor does not give us the strength to remain faithful in all things, in suffering as well as in reaching out. So today, too, we have every reason to unite very deeply in the request that God may keep us together in all tribulation and danger, so that none of us may have to be separated. May we form a solid wall against all the attacks of the enemy! We do not know what the next days will bring, but one thing we do know: Where men have something evil in mind, we know ourselves in the hand of God, who turns hostile designs around and changes their outcome. Remember how through persecution we were led on to mission! Let us ask that the truth may grip all members of our household that their

hearts are moved and they are led fully and completely to the cause of the kingdom.[10]

Annemarie wrote again to Heiner:

> We came to a clear understanding that it is very shortsighted to think that we here [in Liechtenstein] are more secure from the danger than those at the Rhön Bruderhof; above all, the brothers and sisters who remain there, whose menfolk are to take to flight on the suggestion of those not affected by conscription—these brothers and sisters are in very great danger. We will not and cannot make ourselves guilty of shedding their blood. For it is very possible that the Nazis will take revenge on those who remain and that they will make Papa responsible more than anyone.
>
> The whole departure from Germany is an extremely difficult decision and means a very difficult situation for both communities. Here we only know theoretically that we might suddenly have to support ninety people. And we do not know how long this little Liechtenstein will remain so peaceful. If a world war begins now, the whole globe will be set on fire, and we will not find one spot where the church can build up its work in peace. So it has become quite clear to us not only that martyrdom is close at hand for us, but that martyrdom has begun. The reality of preparing for death with all the bitter struggle of dying is thus placed before our very eyes and demands our ultimate inner readiness. It demands alertness and intense movement of heart, filling our hearts with the life-giving spirit of Christ. Then the wisdom and the true inspiration of his spirit will be given us as to what we must do or not do in all practical matters during the next days and weeks, in order to let ourselves be guided rightly and be led to the right place at the given time and hour. We asked God for this in a very special way, for we have no idea what will happen in the future or what may come to us through a sudden political development or what will be demanded of us. One thing is quite clear to us, that the witness of the living city of light on the hill is in acute danger and is marked for destruction by all dark powers ...
>
> This morning it again became very clear to us that our task is that of the fully dedicated love of Jesus Christ which can hate no one but must love evil, turning it into good. This must find expression in Papa's next tasks in Zurich. That is a hard task, but the only one that is constructive and brings new life.[11]

Confrontation with Religious Socialists

Leonhard Ragaz and others of his Religious Socialist circle and the Werkhof had reacted negatively to the community's Christmas letter. They disagreed with two issues: 1) the statement the brotherhood had pasted onto their ballots for the plebiscite of November 12, 1933, and 2) the certainty in which they claimed the presence of the Holy Spirit and the kingdom of God among them. They felt the same attitude in brothers who had come through on their sales mission trips, who had urged them to greater love and unity and full community.

Eberhard and Hans Meier traveled to Zurich to meet with Ragaz and seven of his friends on March 11. Before leaving, Eberhard said, in anticipation of this meeting:

> To the Religious Socialists we have to emphasize: Love your enemies. They label Hitler and Mussolini as devils. I cannot find in the New Testament that Jesus called anyone who opposed him a devil, although he did call some "children of the devil." I do not believe that we can label individual men as devils. Even of Judas it is only said, "He *had* a devil," and that Judas doubtless turned away from the love of Christ. But even our enemies remain our brothers and the objects of our love. Love to the enemy is the true love of Jesus. It would be totally misguided pacifism not to love the enemies of one's country. Jesus says, "Blessed are the peacemakers." If pacifists want to be such men, they have to live in love to their enemies. If they hate them, they might also be capable of killing them. "He who hates his brother is a murderer!" With regards to the Religious Socialists we are commissioned to represent perfect love, also to our enemies. "Love evil until it becomes good!"* For us there are here no boundaries; whoever it is, it makes no difference to whom we offer our love. We love our enemies and want to love them in the right way so that they come to peace. In this we renounce the politics of the great nations.[12]

They met for three hours. To begin with, Ragaz read out a list of eight points against the Bruderhof. Then he and his circle spoke angrily and accusingly.

> *Eva Lezzi:* I was indignant about your statement in the plebiscite. It has nothing to do with the Holy Spirit.

---

* *"Liebt das Böse gut"* is a line from Christian Morgenstern's poem *"Brüder! hört das Wort!"* included in *Sonnenlieder*, 144.

Pastor Goetz: I have supported and helped you for a long time, but I was shocked at the presumption of the Christmas letter.

Clärli Grotz: Christian said I would have to surrender everything to become a follower of Christ. If he had said right at the start that he only wanted to sell some turned bowls, then our conversation would have been finished in five minutes.

Eberhard Arnold: How can we answer all these questions? Such mistrust of our words has been expressed. Therefore our words have no meaning now. If we are accused of untruthfulness from the beginning, there is no use talking anymore.

The testimony of Religious Socialism is a grace of God for us, and I have never doubted it. My attitude concerning the church remains the same as I wrote in that letter to Ragaz [March 1933]. There is only one task for the church: the nonviolent love of Christ, according to which one cannot accept any government office. We can only practice the active love that leads to social justice. The testimony of the Religious Socialists seems to us to be a prophetic testimony, which is bound to protest against every kind of barbarity. We always welcomed it with great thankfulness and reverence; you should know this. Our Bruderhof would not have been possible if this movement had not existed.

We never asserted that we are the church. The testimony of life in community is a decisive witness at the present time, but this does not mean that no other testimonies exist. Regarding the Werkhof: Unity and unanimity are at stake. Community of goods alone is not the proof, but the complete unanimity and unity of hearts. We are not without mistakes, and if there were no sin among us, we would not ask for forgiveness every evening. The gift of unity through Christ is an unmerited grace every day anew.

I am sorry that you consider our testimony to Adolf Hitler to be a defection.

Ragaz: Yes, that is a defection.

Eberhard: We follow Paul's word, that every government is from God, and that we should help all our enemies to find the right way through love. We reached the highest officials in our detailed letters, telling them that killing the innocent provokes God's wrath. Governmental authority has to bear arms, but it should not misuse them. Yet even if the authorities use weapons in a just way, they simply follow a different calling or vocation, which does not correspond to perfect love, also toward one's enemies.

We must seek a way to call these people to repentance through love. They are not devils but people, sinful people. They must be challenged to leave their sin. But apart from the sins of our present government, we would refuse to bear arms for any government. A Christian cannot be a government official or a soldier. The Christian can only challenge to love and unity.

We do not claim to be the church of God, but we expect and plead that the upper church will come down to us again and again. We believe in the upper church, and we believe that there are people everywhere to whom the church descends.

I never said that Ragaz should come to the Bruderhof. We cannot have the wish that the witness of Religious Socialism should cease to exist, for this movement is called by God. We feel that both tasks, of the Bruderhof as well as the Religious Socialists, are from God, and why shouldn't we help one another? It may well be that somebody in hastiness, overpowered by the Spirit and the life witness, went about it in the wrong way. We would reprimand this.

Regarding the behavior of our brothers on sales trips, please understand that this mission is a tremendous burden on them and on all of us. We live in a time of persecution, threatened by death and imprisonment. We are forced to send brothers and sisters out on the road, lest our people starve in this persecution. Six men have to be traveling every day, if we want to support our Bruderhof communities. At the same time we look for an inner encounter with people. Like the early Christians we want to build up community out of love. We want to share the land, the work, and the life with people. We do not want to represent an ideal. We want to be simple Christians united in the love of Jesus Christ, living in real social justice. This is the meaning of our life in the love of Christ. By doing this we do not want to dispute the purpose of the life of another person. We want to live in compliance with our faith without attacking other people who live in accordance with their proclamation and prophecy.

Ragaz: Christ is the foundation for me. I have to object to the explanation of the declaration made to Hitler, because Hitler represents and personifies the totalitarian state that demands everything, and even though he is not the devil himself, he is possessed by him completely. I consider Hitler to be the poorest man on earth, and the most to be pitied. But your declaration will not be understood by anyone in the way you mean it. They will think you mean Hitler's murdering is sent by God. It will even be interpreted as a veneration, like an offering of incense. We know

> it is not easy to stand up and resist Caesar. The form of your declaration seems tremendously questionable to me.
>
> *Eberhard:* We love Hitler, and strangely enough just this declaration you objected to gave rise to Hitler's hostility and hatred against us.[13]

The meeting ended in an impasse. Leonhard Ragaz never visited the Bruderhof, and this was—unfortunately—his last encounter with Eberhard.

Flight

Kurt Zimmermann joined Hans Meier in Switzerland; they did sales work and kept a close eye on political developments. Kurt wrote:

> Every day we read the papers. On Saturday night, March 16, I had the sudden feeling that we should go and check once more whether anything had been posted outside the news office. After picking up mail from the main post office we went to the town hall. A big crowd had gathered outside the display window of the *Baseler National Zeitung* (Basel National News). News had come by telegram from Berlin that nationwide compulsory military service would be introduced in Germany immediately.[14]

Hans Meier later recalled:

> I phoned Eberhard, and as our telephone talks were watched by the Gestapo we had to use a bit of code language. Eberhard asked me, "Is the weather good in Switzerland?" And I said, "Yes, but in the north there is a storm brewing, and our friends from Berlin are going to invite our young men to go there." Eberhard immediately understood what that meant. He said, "Could you come home tonight by train and bring a bit of help?" I called a few friends together in Basel, and they gave me some means to help in this whole situation. I took the midnight train to Fulda.[15]

A special edition of the *Völkischer Beobachter,* the Nazi newspaper, announced:

> Berlin, March 16, 1935
>
> On Saturday, March 16, at 1:00 in the afternoon, the Führer, who had interrupted his sick leave and arrived in Berlin Friday night, gathered the members of his cabinet and presented them with a proclamation to the German people, announcing the decision of

Chapter 15—January to March 1935

the government to introduce military conscription, to be effective immediately. Further details are left to the defense minister.

The National Socialist correspondent writes regarding this proclamation of the Führer's:

This proclamation is a historic event for the German people... Through this proclamation, which is a document of peace but also of resolution, the German nation has been freed from an oppressive humiliation under which it has suffered for sixteen years...

A miracle has taken place. This equality, this freedom, did not fall into our laps. We had to wrestle for it. The Führer won it for us! It is his achievement! He formed the nation anew in fourteen years and welded it together. Within two years of his seizure of power, he won political equality for his people!...

There can only be true peace among free people. We believe, therefore, that March 16, 1935, which is written into the book of German history, stands as the day of German honor and freedom. At the same time it is the beginning of a new epoch of a peaceful cooperation with the nations of Europe.

Eberhard had only just arrived back at the Rhön Bruderhof from his trip to Switzerland that Saturday afternoon. Annemarie, at the Alm, wrote to Heiner how she heard the story:

Papa had arrived at the Rhön Bruderhof at four o'clock in the afternoon on Saturday. At half past six they had dinner. Papa first told about Zurich. Then the telephone rang—Hans Meier was on the phone. Papa went up. Meanwhile they all stayed together. Papa came back, continued eating and telling about his trip. Only after dinner when the brotherhood was alone, Papa said that during this very night all the men must leave; they have received definite news through Hans Meier. At first there was a deathly silence. Then they realized that it must really be true. Arno was sent to Fulda immediately on a bicycle, to hear news on the radio and return as quickly as possible... They had a half-hour pause to pack the most necessary things and say good-bye to their families. Then they met again to discuss the work that had to be done and the practical details. Arno returned with a special edition of a newspaper containing the decree introducing conscription. After that they met once again in innermost unity. Everyone in the circle spoke. All were very thankful for the wonderful leading of God. And then came the farewell. Meanwhile everything had been made ready. Very quietly and softly the individual groups started on their way, so that in the house and outside not a sound was made. Papa had really arrived just in time. He had not even finished reporting his trip when the brothers had to leave.[16]

Emy-Margret had just given birth to her third child a few days earlier; she was at home resting. In her diary she wrote:

> At 4:00 [in the afternoon] I heard the community singing. Papa had arrived. After a few minutes he came up to see me. He looked so happy. He had brought me a piece of chocolate cake. Hans and I ate together, and then Hans went downstairs to hear Papa's report about his trip. At 7:30 Hans Meier phoned from Switzerland. Mama told me about it. Hans came up to me before the brotherhood because he knew I would be worried. I went to sleep. At 12:30 a.m. I heard the brotherhood singing. I knew what it meant. Hans came up to say good-bye to me. By 3:00 he was gone. I could not get back to sleep.[17]

For each brother a bicycle was on hand prepared ahead of time for just such an emergency. Josef Stängl described his escape to the Alm Bruderhof:

> At midnight three of us—Arno Martin, Werner Friedemann, and I—left on our bikes. As we descended the steep slope, I noticed that my brakes were not functioning properly, so I kept close to the roadside ditch, which was safer. Early in the morning I knocked at a door and got the brakes repaired. We cycled on and on, and at about eight o'clock we bumped into a long procession of people marching to the local war memorial. We got off our bikes and walked at a distance of about four yards behind them, and when they turned off toward the memorial, we swung back onto our bikes. No one bothered us at all. We felt relieved to have got out of that tight spot. The same thing happened in the next village; there, too, a crowd of people was marching to the war memorial, and we had to get around them. We just kept on riding, and everything went okay. We rode all day, each with a rucksack and a piece of sausage and bread.
>
> We were tired out, and since we had a little money we boarded a train with our bikes. There were teenagers on that train, and they were talking about the political news—"I bet the French didn't sleep a wink last night," etc. We three looked at each other and thought we had better get out of that atmosphere. So we left the train and mounted our bikes once more.
>
> We got on a train again to cross Lake Constance into Switzerland. The official stamped our passports. We didn't say much

until we got to the other side. At the station, whom should we meet but two of our brothers who had also just crossed the border! We hiked up to the Alm Bruderhof together, three hours uphill.[18]

Eberhard spoke the next day to encourage those left at home:

> Our task is to radiate, to live out the life of love, unity, and justice as a city on a hill in a disunited and torn world …
>
> You must bear in mind that in this time when the German state has decided on conscription, and France, England, and Russia have drawn up huge armies, in this time when the whole world bristles with weapons and awaits the end in bloodshed, now, at this time, nothing is more necessary, nothing more urgent than that a place is maintained where love triumphs in spite of this hatred and murder. This love knows no boundaries, no distances. It is not important where we are; what is decisive is that we live so that the influence of our life reaches out to the whole world.
>
> And just at such a time, in which even our pacifist and socialist friends threaten us, the main thing is that we are loyal, that all brothers and sisters are loyal, that the last drop of life will be surrendered for the brothers and sisters. Not only for them, but for the witness which has to go out to all the world.[19]

At the Alm Bruderhof, preparations were being made to welcome the brothers. Every available bit of space was needed for accommodation. Blankets and bedding were collected wherever they could be spared, floors were scrubbed, and in the kitchen doughnuts were fried to celebrate the arrivals.[20] As soon as the young men came into view from the verandah of the Silum hotel, a shout went up, while at the Rhön, the young wives waited anxiously to hear that their husbands had made it safely across the border. Kathleen Hamilton, one of the new English members, described that day in a letter to her mother:

> Now, darling, this is Sunday, but it is not like a Sunday at all. Late last night we got a phone call from Eberhard, who was only here for a few days, saying that the suspected move on Hitler's part re: conscription had been put into force that very day. So we had a very important meeting to see what we could do. Even if our brothers left immediately they might be stopped at the German frontier. Then there was the question of money. One is not allowed to send more than a very tiny amount from here to Germany owing to the latter's debt to Switzerland, and we had no

> idea how much they had, if any. It was proposed Arnold Mason should leave today taking all we could amass with him. Then we went to bed, knowing those young men to be in desperate danger, but with the one wish that whatever happened God's will might be done. Then this morning we got the news that eleven had left last night—all by different ways: four by train and seven on bicycles (though it is about 350 kilometres to the frontier). They left at 2:00 in the morning, and we have just heard that four are out of Germany. We must do all we can to get the others out. But we believe it is God's will that they should live, and that he can do wonderful things for them. We have just heard that first two and then another two are safe: the first in Switzerland, the second in Liechtenstein. God is good.
>
> I was in the kitchen all morning, which was lovely. All the blankets, etc., we possess were amassed and redistributed to include the eleven, and this afternoon we have been busy, in the faith that they won't be arrested, getting beds, etc., ready for them.
>
> Then there are all the brothers still at the Rhön, and one young man who is studying bookbinding, etc., at Stuttgart. There is also a young cousin of Hardy's, an ex-storm trooper, who means to join us in this life. It will be no simple matter for them, but whatever happens, if it is to God's glory we can rejoice. As for Eberhard, his passport expires in a few days, so he had to go back to Germany. It takes a courage beyond human capacity, knowing that he will be held responsible when it is discovered that the young men have gone. But he went absolutely calmly. He knows that conditions are desperate: he knows only too well what it may mean. Mother darling, this is life! It is one with that experienced by Paul and the early Christians, and with that experienced by people through the ages, who have been driven to live in unity, and therefore community, by the one spirit of God who is truth and love.[21]

A few days later Kathleen wrote again:

> I told you in my last letter of the safe arrival of the first of our brothers. Daily after that as our big cow bell was rung, we rushed to our cellar door—the easiest means of egress owing to the snow—for it meant that other arrivals had been sighted. Three of the cyclists did the entire distance in sixty-five hours—going without sleep all that time. In fact more, for they left after a whole day's work. They are not quite all here yet. Some had considerable difficulty at the frontier, being detained and questioned; others got through easily.

> Silum is the same, and yet different. The spirit reigning there is the same, but what an increase of noise—particularly at meals, you should just hear the singing!!! There is also a great increase in such things as dishwashing, but the work is indeed a joy when one realizes what it means. Two days ago we had a wonderful day in honor of the first birthday of the Alm Bruderhof. At supper the whole story was told—the first arrivals a year ago telling their experiences, and each of us—even those who came much later—added ours. Then there was dancing. My word but the German folk dances are great![22]

Eberhard and Hardy were planning a trip to Holland and England to try to raise the money that was so desperately needed to pay for Emil Möller's property. Before leaving Eberhard held a meeting to dedicate his newest granddaughter Elizabeth to the church. He spoke of Elizabeth, mother of John the Baptist: although she had been barren and was too old to bear children, for God nothing is impossible.

> This is the decisive word in the life of Elizabeth. And just in these very difficult times that our community is experiencing we need this assurance for our little children. As it was for the prophets, so it appears today that it is humanly impossible for our church to continue, for us to carry out our mission. It seems impossible that in ten, twenty, thirty years the children born among us today will be able to represent the prophetic apostolic mission to their children. But we have the faith that with God nothing is impossible. The name Elizabeth points to this: God is my salvation, my security...
>
> I believe that as more children are born into our church it will become clearer to the members of the brotherhood that we are living for a wide future, ultimately for God's future that will be revealed in the establishment of a kingdom of peace. We humans have no concept of time. We do not know what day the new creation will break in. It is possible that our measurement of time breaks down so completely that the need of persecution will be demanded of four more generations for the church to be established on this earth. In any case, we are prepared for the great future, for our entire life is a life of the great future of God. We are completely focused on that which will some day be but is not yet. And just this is the peace that Elizabeth's son prophesied, God's kingdom of peace.
>
> Certainly it often seems to us that our present time contains signs of the end times—and in all modesty we belong to

these signs of the end times. We read yesterday in the Epistola Apostolorum [an early Christian writing]: "When the way of poverty is walked out of love, and when at the same time the injustice of wealth is exposed to the whole world, then the end is near." We are glad that on our Bruderhof the way of poverty is walked out of love, and it is our task to challenge as many people as possible to go the same way of poverty out of love. At the same time we see that throughout the world the injustice of wealth is exposed. The signs of the end are sharp, and in this respect we are reminded of the mother of John the Baptist, who saw the end imminent: the ax was already laid to the root of the tree.[23]

About two weeks later, in early April, the families of the young married men who had fled to Liechtenstein went to join their fathers. Kurt's wife, Marianne, wrote:

> Early in the morning while it was still dark our little band of mothers and small children walked over the hill to meet the bus we had rented. Benches were placed along the sides, and our suitcases were piled in the middle. On top of the suitcases in three big laundry baskets were our greatest treasures, our six babies![24]

It was a long, uncomfortable ride. Some of the children vomited. The customs official closed the door quickly as soon as he had opened it, and they were allowed through.

On its return trip, the bus conveyed a load of non-Germans and German nationals not liable for military service back to the Rhön Bruderhof to fill the vacant work places there and complete the relocation. A letter of April 3, 1935, from Edith to Hardy describes the arrival of the contingent at the Alm:

> Well, all the women and children are here now. It is a very great joy that they arrived safe and sound. We sang "Now thank we all our God" at the noon meal truly from the bottom of our hearts. You should have seen them all coming up the mountain here through the snow. A long caravan, the sleds with the baby baskets holding the very youngest babies. Then the men with the children on their backs, and the many women. We can't be thankful enough that they can all be accommodated, and it is really going well. Everyone has a roof over his head and a bed, and today everybody was able to sit down to eat at one table.[25]

The makeup of both communities was now completely changed.

16

March to October 1935

Holland and England

Ever since the demand was made for payment of the purchase price for Emil Möller's property, there had been talk of a trip to England. Hardy had made amazing contacts the previous year, and people from across the Channel continued to visit both the Alm and Rhön Bruderhofs. As with the sales trips in Switzerland, such a trip was to be seen in the first place as an effort to reach people's hearts and share the news of the gospel, and in the second place as an attempt to raise the money that was so badly needed. It was suggested that Eberhard travel with Hardy for this purpose. Eberhard did not actually want to take this trip. He said, "I really go—this is no exaggeration—with very great trembling. The fact that Hardy in his childlike naiveté was given a great miracle is due to God's grace, and this may not be given to me, because I am no longer so naively childlike."[1] He spoke on the night of his departure:

> In taking leave of the beloved Rhön Bruderhof my heart is deeply moved; in fact, it is frightened. For I see an enormous danger for the task of our church and of our mission in Central Europe. But the faith to which we are called is a faith of courage. The readiness to die and the readiness to flee have been placed clearly before our eyes in the last weeks. We see quite clearly, however, that what we must do is to uphold the witness in Central Europe just as long as it is at all possible.
>
> Whether the trip to England that I am to undertake will lead to an emigration is something we don't know. We don't know either whether it will be granted us to receive money to pay the balance on the Emil Möller property and thus to assure for the time being that our task in Germany can continue. Nor do we

know whether the witness of truth and life entrusted to us will call forth a strong response. We don't know if there are other people in England who will rise up with us to strengthen the life in full community. Certainly this situation brings me considerable anxiety. We have scarcely any footholds in England, and it remains to be seen whether these will hold when the truth is proclaimed clearly.

It is very hard to have to leave just at this time. I have to confess that I expect absolutely nothing to come as a result of my activity, as a result of my words; rather, I regard myself only as an obstacle. But because the brothers and sisters felt this unanimously and because I vowed, when I was appointed and confirmed in the service of the Word, to allow myself to be used at home or abroad, however God wills it, I take this upon myself. I do so trusting in God to make use of my very inadequacy, of the very unfittedness of my nature; in spite of it to knock at human hearts here and there, through his Holy Spirit.

As always, the work is economic and temporal in nature on the one hand, and on the other hand it is spiritual and divine and eternal. The one should be carried out just as earnestly as the other. I ask your intercession for this, for it is nearly as impossible to move people to give large sums of money as it is to move them to leave everything and enter the communal life.[2]

Hardy traveled from Switzerland and met his father in Amsterdam at the end of March. They found sympathy among several leading Mennonites there, including Jan Gleysteen and Teerd Oeds Hylkema, who maintained the traditional witness to peace (whereas many other Mennonites sympathized with Hitler and were willing to serve in the armed forces). This friendship would prove invaluable to the community later when they were forced to leave Germany.

They continued on to London. They met Joan Mary Fry at Friends House; they spoke at a large gathering of the Fellowship of Reconciliation, and then went to Kingsley Hall, a settlement house in the slums founded by Muriel and Doris Lester. From there they took a train to Edinburgh. Wherever they went, Eberhard spoke about the situation in Europe and the predicament of the Bruderhof. Years later, Hardy wrote about this trip:

> I am deeply moved by the wonderful witness Papa gave in personal talks and meetings and by the wonderful gift God gave him to turn around hearts which were indifferent, cold, and even

hostile, and to awaken and arouse the hearts of those who were opening themselves to the light of truth for the first time. Papa said that the places or movements he liked best on his trip were Kingsley Hall, Woodbrooke, and the Gemeentetag movement in Holland. Those were the places where he felt the most response. Papa really was given the arousing prophetic spirit so necessary for mission, and the gift of discerning and separating the spirits. People just responded to him.[3]

He was able to obtain a sizeable loan from the English Quakers for the Alm Bruderhof, but nobody was willing to invest money in Germany when the future there was so tenuous. (Over the next months, some money did come in to pay for the Emil Möller property, but negotiations continued to drag out.) The friendships Hardy and Eberhard forged in England bore fruit for the community later. In anticipation of his return home Eberhard wrote:

> Seen as a whole this mission has led to a public witness which must have reached more than a thousand people, many of whom will have been struck to their innermost core. About fifteen want to come and visit. The financial help has been obtained by much labor and needs further, immediate follow-up and renewed work of long duration. But like this we can expect that it will be a sufficient foundation for the existence of the Alm Bruderhof. For this we have to give honor to God with our whole heart! Our life shall be our thanks![4]

∽

While Eberhard and Hardy were away, Emmy wrote to them of problems at the Alm Bruderhof. Some of the young men who had escaped Germany had lost enthusiasm for the work and didn't seem to grasp the seriousness of the community's position. Eberhard wrote back:

> If the existence of the Alm Bruderhof is to be won for all inner and outer things, all her members without exception must faithfully give themselves completely in the work and be extremely watchful and alert. John Fletcher, one of forty English Quakers who were explicitly threatened with the death sentence and spent years in prison during the World War, told me that the best would be for some of us to accept imprisonment and risk death. To those [young men at the Alm Bruderhof] who do not find a place to work or who do not fulfill their tasks, I am inclined to give the

urgent advice to return to the Rhön Bruderhof to face a test of character in the military question and so prove their loyalty to their vows of faith. Let them have one more opportunity to prove at the Alm whether they can stand this test of character, doing the most vigorous work they are capable of! We must not endanger ninety people because of the laziness of a few.[5]

The position of these young men was becoming more serious. On May 23, 1935, an announcement was made that the following year military conscription would be extended to German men living abroad. This meant that they would no longer be safe in Liechtenstein. After his return Eberhard said:

> The work that we have been commissioned with is more important than prison or concentration camp. In this we differ from the Quakers and others whose lives do not demonstrate an active reality. Although they have meetings, they live in capitalism and personal affluence. In such a case it is better to go to prison. But with us it is different. The strongest witness we can give is not prison or concentration camp; the best witness we can give is in dedicating our lives. We have to prove in daily life that true community and positive unity are possible. Certainly this can also be witnessed to in a martyr's death, and martyrdom is definitely better than years of imprisonment. But best of all is the true sacrifice of one's life for the church, for the cause of the kingdom of God. Our energy should not be lost but should be pledged for the cause of the kingdom of God.
>
> We are all now demanded to sacrifice our strength as perhaps never before. Work production will be demanded, more necessary than ever before. Because we are in greatest danger now, the greatest productivity is demanded of us. If a ship is capsizing in the rough sea, the sailors don't ask if they will get double time for their work. That is our situation now. We are in extreme danger. But the danger does not terrify us. On the contrary, it steels our courage and gives us clarity. We should now prove that we are standing together, that now our utmost is demanded in all areas.
>
> We believe that God is among us and will himself give us strength and be our Führer. He will also give us the money we need. The political pressure emanating from the princes of this world is manifested as the pressure of bloody violence and the pressure of mammon. We have to show that we are equal to these two things through faith. Both questions, bloody violence just as much as mammon, have to be resolved together in total com-

munity and in the building up of the communal life here at the Alm Bruderhof and at the Rhön Bruderhof.

In all of this the gift of faith is urgent; we all have to receive the gift of faith which, as the gift of love, will at the same time enable us to find miraculous ways, unknown ways, and to be inventive in love.[6]

Over the next months, the fight for survival continued. The work was hard and food was scarce. But again and again God provided. Kathleen Hamilton described the arrival of a gift to the Alm Bruderhof:

> What an evening! At supper Alfred Gneiting announced that a tremendous present had come from the community of which I told you—five members of which visited us. He said it would require four tables to hold, so supper was cleared on the spot, people running about with their plates if not already finished— and then package after package was carried in. The wonder of it—eggs, cheese, dried fruit, sugar, ham. Clothes, wonderful baby clothes, shoes, and I don't know what all. The din we made as the entire adult community celebrated the opening of each new sack or box brought the amazed youngsters from their beds to join in the joyful confusion ... The wonder of it—people whom we have seen once, and about whom we knew nothing a few weeks ago!! But where God's will alone is sought, the result cannot but be a life of practical love.[7]

In June, Edith Arnold gave birth to a little boy, Eberhard Claus. She contracted childbed fever and was gravely ill. The church met daily to pray for her recovery, seeing her illness as an attack on yet another front. Slowly she began to regain her strength. Meanwhile, Germany was moving inexorably toward war. Referring to unspecified political developments, Eberhard spoke on July 22:

> As we have just heard from German politics, we in Central Europe find ourselves in a difficult situation. This situation demands us to put aside all human conjecture, all of our own ideas, and ask God himself to intervene. It cannot continue like this, and we have to ask God to arbitrate with his exalted hand so that especially in the German Reich, in Italy, and in all other countries, something powerful may take place that comes from God. Something decisive has to happen—we all feel that. What

> it will be we do not know, but it has to come from God, for only what comes from God can change the course of events. If we look at our own situation, we sense that it is the same as what we experienced with Edith, that through the healing hand of God something miraculous took place. We have to look to the exalted hand of God and see how it draws nearer to stand by us in these dangerous times, to protect us and give us the possibility of life and of living together, of living the witness and the task entrusted to us. We also need God to intervene anew in our communal life, especially for our economic situation—not for any one specific area but in the sense of the potential of the Spirit, so that new, forceful power is given to us for everything that is asked of us.[8]

Visitors continued to come to both communities, bringing both stimulation and challenge. Eberhard explained to them the Bruderhof's task in Germany as witness to brotherhood and nonviolence, love to enemies. Doris Lester came from Kingsley Hall in England and Jack Hoyland, the Quaker director of Woodbrooke, came for a week with several of his students. When Premysl Pitter, a pacifist and educator who later saved many Jewish orphans, came with his companion Olga Fierz from Czechoslovakia, Eberhard said:

> Our position with regard to the refusal to bear arms is well known; our brothers are convinced about refusing any kind of military service, even service in the medical or labor corps. It is quite clear to us that this attitude is very rare and extremely dangerous in Europe these days, and we believe that just because of this we have to uphold this witness in the German Reich and also here in Liechtenstein. In Germany we have mainly citizens of other countries, but it is quite clear to us that both here and there we are continually threatened with the danger of martyrdom.
>
> We are completely united in the readiness of our brothers to give all; but you know that the refusal to bear arms is not our only concern, for it is a negative response. It is more essential to us that we dedicate our whole life to Christ's love and his spirit. We believe that this dedication finds its strongest expression in the common life, where in all things there is understanding, mutual help, and common work. The larger our circle grows, the more certain and joyful we are on this way. We may say that it is a miracle of God that for many years already we have been experiencing over and over again the unanimity of love in practical decisions.
>
> Among us there is no dictatorship of the majority, and certainly not of any Führer. It has been our experience that Christ's

spirit and his abundant love give to each one of us the common conviction which we all represent and the unanimity in all our decisions for all the tasks of our life. We believe that the fact that here and everywhere in the world there are such cells in which full community is alive is the most powerful witness for the world, the most powerful answer to the suffering and injustice in the world. This life is a witness for the future, when God will have attained the reign of his love in this world.

Our attitude toward the National Socialist movement still is this—that we love our enemies. We would find it wrong to oppose our enemy with hatred. In him we see the man whom we should love in such a manner that it helps him to find the way. That is why we want to remain in Germany with part of our circle. On the other hand we feel that the little country of Liechtenstein affords us a splendid opportunity for mission work.[9]

Eberhard hoped most of all for a personal encounter with Adolf Hitler himself in order to appeal to his heart. One night he told the community of a dream he had had.

Last night I dreamt about Hitler. He was trying to daub over, with different colors, a picture I had painted; he said he could do it better. Then he sat down, and I said, "My dear Adolf Hitler, this can't go on much longer; you yourself can't possibly take any more pleasure in all this killing, that you murder evil men instead of making them better." Then he asked me what I thought about conscientious objection to war. I answered, "Yes, my dear Adolf Hitler, we have to hold firmly to conscientious objection, for in every instance killing is against love." Then he made a very angry face.

The nice thing about the dream was that I had a real heart-to-heart talk with him. I was not the least bit afraid; it was as if I were talking to Doris Lester. Perhaps one day this dream will come true. But it must be our concern that our love, including love for our enemies, is expressed in such a way that we reach their hearts, for that is what love is all about. And if we reach a man's heart, we will find there the hidden spark from God, even if he is the greatest criminal.[10]

Local Hostility Toward the Alm Bruderhof

In September, neighbors of the Alm Bruderhof went from door to door to collect signatures for a petition against the community. An article appeared in the daily newspaper of St. Gall, Switzerland:

> Currently in the parish of Triesenberg a matter is being eagerly discussed, which not only arouses general interest in Triesenberg and Liechtenstein as a whole but merits attention far and wide beyond the boundaries of that country; it concerns the Alm Bruderhof at Silum ... Eighty-five people already live there—a cause of certain misgivings in the parish of Triesenberg. They fear—rightly or wrongly—that the Alm Bruderhof might provide an asylum for stateless persons, conscientious objectors, etc., which could lead to political difficulties between Liechtenstein and other countries. In the same way it is feared that the Alm Bruderhof might gradually purchase large areas of land, which would be harmful to the cattle raising and the Alpine economy supporting the inhabitants of Triesenberg. Finally, it is feared in Triesenberg that in the event of war there could be a great food shortage due to the occupants of the Alm Bruderhof. Ninety-five citizens of the parish of Triesenberg made a petition to the parish council requesting it to conclude an agreement with the Alm Bruderhof at Silum that would take these misgivings into account.

Eberhard visited the prime minister of Liechtenstein, Josef Hoop. He advised Eberhard to speak in the church in Triesenberg. Eberhard preferred to speak outdoors. So, on Sunday, September 29, all members of the Alm Bruderhof went down to Triesenberg and waited outside the church. When the service was over, the churchgoers gathered to hear what Eberhard had to say. Heiner recalled:

> He stood with his broken leg, leaning on two sticks, and started to speak. There were some rough young fellows in the back, and they shouted and whistled loudly and threw stones. Again and again he tried to speak. Finally, he said, "Why are you standing in the back? Come up here in front if you are against me." Then the peasants said to the young people, "Shut up, we want to listen." It took quite a while till he won the audience. Somehow the peasants were impressed. He spoke then really to the hearts of these peasants. From that moment on the petition was dropped.
>
> We brought him down and then up again on a two-wheeled cart. Going down it was dangerously fast; one had to be very

careful. It was very painful because it shook him. And then we pulled him up again. It was very steep.

When he returned to Germany, he was not sure if we would have to leave Liechtenstein—we did not know then that this petition was stopped, and we did not know where we would go.[11]

17

The Revelation of John

THE 1935 ANNUAL NAZI Party rally began on September 9 in Nuremberg. At this occasion, Hitler declared the swastika as the German flag and introduced the Nuremberg Laws, stripping Jews of citizenship. In October, Eberhard held a series of meetings on the Revelation of John. He felt it was essential that all members of the community sense the urgency of the moment of history in which they were living.

> The Book of Revelation is a book concerning the kingdom of God. It is a book which proceeds from the throne of God, a book of the fight to conquer the whole earth for God. One may not regard this book as though it constituted a mathematical table or chronicle of future events, but we are to understand it thus: that here is revealed to us in circles, as in the stellar world in wonderful circular movements, how the kingdom of God comes near to the earth and how it ultimately not only encircles the whole earth, but takes complete possession of it by means of shattering it in fire, and, through fire, bringing about the rebirth of a new star, which will belong utterly and completely to God.
>
> Before we go into the letters to the churches and the beginning of the book of Revelation, we must understand the whole purpose and scope of this prophetic writing. Revelation is concerned with God's rulership over all worlds and over the earth. Therefore, we are set before the throne of God; for there is no rulership of God if there is no throne of God. In order for this rulership of God to spread over the earth, however, the earth must be conquered for God. This great future of God, in which he will assume authority over the earth, is a mystery. It is like a sealed scroll, into which we cannot take a look; yet to the prophetic spirit of the church this book shall already be opened now.
>
> But who can open this scroll? Who can open this book in such a way that the church can quite clearly understand the book

today? And who can open this scroll in such a way that the happenings of this scroll become reality when the kingdom of God comes? No prophet is able, of himself, to open this scroll. No angelic prince of God can open this scroll. Only the sacrificed Christ is able to open the seals of this scroll, only the Lamb that is upon the throne. But if the seals are to be opened, that means martyrdom. It means a great, deep distress, even community with the sacrificed Lamb that was slain. And if the understanding of this scroll is to be opened, not only in the future, but rather if the events written down in this scroll are to become reality, then that means a very heavy sorrow, the opening of a time of judgment.

This time of judgment is necessary to introduce the reign of God over the earth, for without such a time of judgment the earth could not be won for God. As the spirit of God in the church can only lead to the experience of perfect unity through deepest judgment, even so at the end of all things the experience of the unity of the kingdom of God can only be won when judgment has preceded it. With the opening of each of the six seals is revealed a time of God's judgment.

So first of all in Revelation we see the throne of God and the seven letters to the churches. Second we see the scroll with its seven seals and how it is opened. And third we see the seven trumpets of the angels of judgment. Fourth, however, we see the mighty struggle between the dragon, or Satan, and his minions on the one side, and Christ, the Son of Man, and his angels on the other side. The dragon, or serpent, the mighty power of Satan, stands against the church. The dragon is the most powerful beast. The church however is compared to a weak and enfeebled woman. This woman brings forth Christ. The dragon tries to devour Christ, and the church flees to the desert.

Meanwhile, there appears on the side of the dragon a seven-headed beast. State power, with its most terrible rulership, appears among humankind. At the same time another beast appears, the degenerate church, which receives honor from the state, the power of the beast. In the midst of these unearthly struggles and terrifying judgment appears once more the Lamb of God with his church. This is the fourth picture we see. The dragon, the woman, and the woman's child; the beast of the state and the beast of the degenerate church; and then once again in the midst of these frightful struggles, the true church.

Now begins the last judgment from the throne of God, passed on the Antichrist and on his followers. Everything breaks open that had held the graves closed, and the first resurrection comes, and God enters upon his rule over the earth. God takes possession of his throne in that the earth is ruled by the kingdom of peace of Jesus Christ. The last judgment on Satan closes this series of judgment pictures, and then the general resurrection and the last judgment out of the book of life take place. The heavens and the earth are renewed. The whole earth is born again and arises new, because it is completely ruled by God. The character of this earth in the eternal kingdom of this new earth is the city of God, the new Jerusalem, the holy city-church.

If we try to summarize this truth, we have the following: the rulership of God over the earth can only be achieved through very heavy judgments, for the power of Satan, the power of evil, must be broken. This power of evil is an impure power. It is a murderous power and a power of physical force. It is a power of money and of luxury. It is a power of lying and deceit. In order to break this power, alarming things have to happen. In order that this fight may give no one cause to forget that it is love itself which is to win the power over all these evil things, the church must be there. In the midst of the luster of mammon lives the church, in poverty. In the midst of bloodshed by cruel tyrants lives the peace-bringing church. In the midst of the loathsome excesses of impurity lives the pure church. In the midst of the lies of false prophecy lives the church of love; but she lives as a martyr church. This church, sent on ahead, makes clear what will appear as God's future, at the end. That is, a city of peace will be revealed over the whole earth; there will be a marriage of joy, the Lord's Supper and the wedding-feast of unity; this will be the kingdom of God. This is the secret of the revelation of Jesus Christ.

One cannot grasp the Revelation unless one constantly holds this complete survey in its different circles before one's eyes, and unless one is in the strongest tension between the judgment of wrath, on the one side, and the revelation of perfect love and perfect peace, on the other side. Only one who has experienced such times in the church, grasps that without such catastrophes of judgment no renewal is possible for the whole history of the earth.

The church is portrayed as the virgin Mary. Jesus is born, and Jesus, as the Child ever newly born in the heart of every believer, in every church upon which the Holy Spirit descends, is about to be swallowed by the dragon and the beast. And just as Mary had to flee, so the church must flee to earth's rocky places, to the wilderness.

And there God shields the escaping church so that poisonous radiations and the lethal force of the beast and the dragon, of the bloodthirsty state and the spirit of Satan, cannot do anything to her. And the struggle breaks out. The church of Jesus Christ becomes newly manifest in her worship of Jesus Christ and of God the almighty. She follows the Lamb wherever he goes; she goes the same way that Jesus went. She proves herself to be true and steadfast, taking no part whatever in bloody violence or imprisoning. She remains free from the symbol of violence and the elevation and worship of mankind, and goes into death by being slain; her members, themselves kept pure from any killing, are killed.

This is the throng of the one hundred and forty-four thousand. It is not the number that matters; rather, this number is again a pointer to the mystery of the greatness of this church and of the symbolic meaning of numbers. None of this must be taken in a statistical sense; it must all be grasped: by the meaning, the spirit, the essence, by its innermost significance.

What we have heard from the prophetic words of the revelation of Jesus Christ—this is the subject of our prayer; this deepest mystery of the kingdom of God, the way it is revealed in the heart of the believer and in the soul of the loving disciple of Jesus in following him, and the way it is revealed in the church in her complete community and in the persecution she has to suffer, and further, the way the whole earth, which more and more falls prey to the sovereignty of Satan, must be conquered by God so that the future of the harvest will come.

These facts—that God rules over all things, first in the hearts of believers and in the church, and then finally over the entire world when his kingdom is completed—this is what we beg for in our prayers and beseech to come to us: that God's kingdom come, that his will be done, now, here on earth as it is done in the heavens; that the name of God be blessed; that this mighty event be made manifest in the forgiveness of sin in the church, by the church praying together daily for this from God and by her beseeching to be protected in the hour of temptation and to be redeemed from evil, from Satan and his might, in the faith that the kingdom and the power and the glory belongs to God.

The purpose of our gathering for prayer is to call upon God to come to us and implore his spirit to come down, to call Christ into our midst, not only for ourselves, but for the great events in the wide world. The reason we live in community is so that we may come before God with the power to pray and so that thereby world history may take a decisive turn, through the return of Christ, right through the end time.

The Bride of the Lamb, who is called to the wedding banquet of the Lamb (meaning the onset of God's kingdom) is the city-church, the city-church that lives in community; it is the city on the hill that Jesus speaks about, an organic unity of communal living, communal faith, communal light, and communal mission that comes from innermost and outermost oneness—it is the city-church. It cannot be constructed by people building it up gradually from the bottom upwards, like the tower of Babel; no, the new Jerusalem can only come downwards to us. In the reality of the Holy Spirit the church comes down to us; and even when people are living together in community as we here are doing, then all the more do they need the Holy Spirit to come down to them each day—to bring down to us the city-church, the actual unity of the new Jerusalem that is the mother of us all.

Faith in the Holy Spirit is faith in this church unity; and it is only when the Holy Spirit comes down that this church, this real manifestation of the invisible church, can become visible on earth as the New Jerusalem. Thus it is not we who are the Bride by virtue of our purification; rather, the Bride in reality is in the Holy Spirit who comes upon us and fills us with the understanding of a bride and the expectation of a bride. Only in this way can God dwell with us and set up true community among us. "Come, I will show you the Bride, the wife of the Lamb." This is the holy city of Jerusalem as it descends from God, from heaven, filled with God's majesty and glory.

Thus we are called to the expectation that at the end of all things Jesus will be revealed. We are passing through the most dangerous times. And in the midst of the world's downfall we look up to him, to the coming one. He is the same as the one who was, who as the historical Jesus spoke his words, lived his life, who was executed by Pontius Pilate and who truly rose again. He is the same as the one who is, who is present in reality in his church. He who was is the same as the one who will come. Jesus Christ, the same yesterday in the person of the past, today in the church of the present, and tomorrow in the time of the future when he comes.[1]

18

November 1935

Two years had passed since Eberhard had broken his leg and it was still not healed. In desperation, Emmy contacted an old friend of theirs, Dr. Paul Zander, a surgeon in Darmstadt. The two couples had been friends since Eberhard and Emmy met in 1907. Emmy's sister Moni had also worked with Dr. Zander during the First World War. Dr. Zander agreed to see him.

Eberhard left for Darmstadt on November 12. Emmy went down to join him the day before the operation, and Moni followed to support her. Emmy describes the last weeks of his life:

> On Wednesday, November 13, we phoned Professor Zander in Darmstadt. He told Moni he had made a thorough examination and considered an operation urgently necessary. I left on November 15 to be there with him.
>
> When I walked into the room, I found Papa looking quite well. He was lying in his bed, and two other, younger men were in the room with him. He was wearing a dark-blue-striped hospital gown. At first he didn't see me; he was leaning on his elbow, busily writing a letter to Hans, on the bedside table.
>
> When he saw me he was very glad, but said, "I would so much have liked to spare you this."
>
> I was invited to the Zanders for supper. Frau Zander received me very cordially. She was glad to see me after so many years. "Sad, though, that it's such a serious occasion," she said right away in the hall. She then told me that her husband had been quite beside himself because Papa had "been running around alone" in Frankfurt with this leg that was so poorly healed. I replied, "He has not only been in Frankfurt like that; he has been in Holland, England, and Switzerland and quite a number of places." She was horrified to hear this.

> About 9:15 Zander himself came, and I spoke with him about the impending surgery. It was to begin at 9:30 the next morning and last until some time around 11:00. He requested me not to go to Papa again before the operation.
>
> The next morning around 10:15, I made my way slowly to the hospital. I sat down in the corridor and waited. I believe it was around 12:30 that the nurse came from the operating room and called me to Professor Zander. Zander was sitting in his white gown in his office next to the operating room. He was exhausted by the operation and told me it had been much more difficult than he had anticipated.[1]

Three days after the surgery, Eberhard developed a fever and suffered increasing discomfort.

> On Wednesday, November 20, I woke up very early in the morning. It was Repentance Day.* I found Papa in the middle of reading a letter from Georg at the Rhön Bruderhof. He asked me, "What is today?"
>
> I said, "Repentance Day!"
>
> Papa: "Did you read the newspaper?"
>
> I: "We had a glance at it."
>
> Papa: "Did you read that Dr. Goebbels has repented?"
>
> I: "No."
>
> Then Papa said, raising his voice loudly, "He will have to give account on the Day of Judgment for every idle word he has spoken."
>
> I: "We must all do that; everyone should do that today."
>
> Papa: "Just let me call a spade a spade. I say it once more: Dr. Goebbels will have to give account before God for every idle word he has spoken."
>
> His leg had become cold again. When I pressed his toes and asked him whether he had any feeling in them, he said groaning, "None at all. It's all dead, all dead!"
>
> Towards evening Frau Zander appeared. She looked quite serious and inquired a good deal about Papa's condition. Then she went out with Moni. I followed them after a while and found them both in the nurses' room crying. They reported that the leg could not be saved; it was completely cold and had no life in it anymore.[2]

---

* *Buss und Bettag,* a Protestant holiday observed in parts of Germany.

The leg would have to be amputated. Emmy and Moni phoned both the Rhön and Alm Bruderhofs with the heavy news and asked Hans and Emy-Margret to come. Emmy's report continues:

> [The next morning] Zander came about 10:30. He told me, "There is no danger to life, and the operation will take only twenty minutes." He looked at the leg and gradually and carefully broke the news to Papa that the leg could not be saved anymore. Papa asked if it could not be postponed another twenty-four hours, treating the leg with warming pads and hot air. Zander replied, "The surgeon must know the right time to operate." He then put his hands on Papa's hands and looked at him for quite a long time. Papa looked up at Zander too and said, "Then I submit to it in trust."
>
> "It should take twenty minutes, and no danger to life," the doctor had said. Moni and I sat in the nurses' room. The minutes crept by. Then a nurse came and called Moni out of the room. That surely meant some bad news! Moni came back. She said that it was worse than the doctors had supposed—a thrombosis, an arterial thrombosis had been discovered, above the knee. I asked right away whether the leg would have to be taken off still higher up. Moni replied that the doctors would try to save as much of it as they possibly could. She also told me she had seen Papa, and he was breathing quietly and sleeping.
>
> After another long wait, Zander came out with the words, "It is terrible, it is terrible." Then he reported about the state of the leg, about the thrombosis, about the destroyed tissues; how he had had to take the leg off quite high up. He was not able to sew it up, but had to leave everything open. "Danger to life, yes—but not without hope, even humanly speaking," so said Zander.
>
> Just then Moni came and asked us to come to Papa. There was no doubt any longer—it was the death agony! Heavily drawn breaths, a great, terrible distress! We sang; we spoke comfort to Papa; we prayed that God might send help. Papa became very still. He breathed more quietly. One felt how the prayer and the intercession helped him.
>
> Oh, how gladly would I have gone with him, my beloved one! How was it possible that he was leaving me alone—but I must not think of that now. In my heart the suffering of Christ became so living for me in this hour—his vicarious suffering and his forsakenness. It was as if an angel came and gave me strength to bear what I could not grasp. I even felt a quiet, solemn joy in the thought of the joy that he was now experiencing, freed from all pain and torment, with his beloved Christ, in the arms of God. How he could now gaze upon his Christ in the great broad worlds

of heaven, Christ, whom he served with his whole life and who was everything to him! How could I mourn at this moment or think of myself, my forsakenness without him? It was as if I too were being lifted up in those hours when the soul of my Eberhard parted from this earthly life.[3]

Eberhard died on November 22, 1935. His body was brought to the Rhön Bruderhof in a closed casket because of the danger of infection. He was buried in the small burial plot on the hill behind the Rhön Bruderhof next to Else von Hollander. Because of the threat of military draft his three sons Hardy, Heiner, and Hans-Hermann were not able to attend his funeral.

19

December 1935 to July 1936

Bereft

THE COMMUNITIES OF BOTH the Alm and Rhön Bruderhofs were stunned by Eberhard's death. In his last year Eberhard had pleaded in many different ways that the members of the community recognize the deep spiritual crisis faced by the world. The previous Christmas he had said:

> Let us ask God fervently that our hearts may be moved and stimulated again by God's good thoughts, by the greatest events, that we may think along big lines—not only in continents, not only in planets, but in the largest constellations; that we may think not only in cycles of years, but in decades, centuries, and millennia, in the dimensions of God's thoughts, in God's great sweeping curves ... Let us not be a small generation met by great things. Let us become worthy of a great time and a great calling.[1]

But again and again small personal concerns and tensions seemed to eclipse this vision and drag down the brotherhood. As Heiner put it in a letter to Annemarie:

> The danger of a dead, sleepy atmosphere has shown me the greatness of the hour God is placing us in. Seldom in our life have we seen the hour of Jesus Christ's death coming so close to us as right now. And what happened in that hardest hour that the earth has ever seen? All the disciples went to sleep. This is horrible, and it shows us how the power of death keeps trying to destroy God's kingdom and anything that manifests God's power.[2]

Some months later Hans-Hermann wrote to his fiancée Gertrud:

> I now understand Papa more and more. He was far, far ahead of us all, so far ahead that he was often very, very lonely. During his last years he was already bound so closely to Christ that everyone else no longer understood him. For him as a man that was humanly difficult, often unbearably difficult; for he was able to see deep into people's hearts and understand them. Lonely, very lonely he was, with his great, infinitely deep love, with his eyes that saw so far into the future. He loved Christ so much that he fought through to the very end against all that opposes Christ, to be completely united with him; no one kept pace with him. And that is what was so hard for him in the last years. I often noticed in him an unexplained sadness, and it came from this. Yet I always saw him happy in our worship meetings and communal mealtimes because there the Spirit was at work in which he lived his whole life.[3]

The brotherhood members of the Rhön especially felt their guilt. They felt that they had not kept pace with him in the spontaneous love and joy they had experienced in the earlier years of their first love. A heavy cloud hung over them that took months to lift. Eberhard had hoped that they would experience a renewal before Christmas. Two days before he died he had said to Emmy:

> We two must travel home before the First of Advent. Then you will ask me and I will ask you whether we both can be accepted into the new brotherhood. And then we shall ask each one individually, Why do you love Christ?[4]

Now each one considered his or her answer to that question.

After the funeral, Eberhard's widow, Emmy, moved to the Alm Bruderhof with her youngest daughter, Monika, so that she could be closer to her three sons in Zurich. Georg and Moni Barth took over responsibility for the Rhön Bruderhof. Hans Zumpe, who had been Eberhard's closest assistant in the last four years, was at the Alm Bruderhof. He was now asked to take on the overall responsibility for both communities.

It was a painful Christmas at the Rhön Bruderhof. Moni described it in a letter to Hardy and Edith:

> In the important Christmas days we were so closely bound to you, particularly in this lively little brotherhood that we experience here. It is and remains an undeserved gift, a great mercy,

that here at the Rhön Bruderhof, where betrayal after betrayal was committed, we feel again how the Spirit has called a band together, to lead once more the life we are called to. Incessant entreaty, striving, and praying to God is the only thing we can do to carry on with utmost activity the cause that was begun here, and now it can be said we do it with joy. How strongly we felt your prayers, as if you were in our midst. The Spirit is not limited to a place. We stood firmly with you and still do, with you and with the upper church. When we sat together in your parents' living room we felt the presence of Papa and Else [von Hollander] and all who are bound to us in spirit. That is our certainty and a joy that we never want to lose.[5]

The entire community worked to build a stone wall with local rocks around the burial ground—a huge project that continued through the year. Moni wrote to her sister Emmy:

> We have all just returned from the burial ground. We all want to work on the wall during our noon break. It was such a fine communal work, and we are making progress, that can be seen. Kaspar Keller and Otto Kaiser are hacking out the bushes on the field behind the burial ground; some women carry the bushes onto the field, so that the rocks are exposed and can be dug out. Then Migg Fischli and Heinz Bolck come with two wagons, and Fritz Kleiner with some men load the rocks. Another crew then stacks a wall at the burial ground.[6]

Leonhard Ragaz published an obituary in his *Neue Wege*:

> The news of the death of Eberhard Arnold came to us as a complete surprise, which moved us deeply, for indeed few knew of his serious illness. In more peaceful times, this news would find a greater response, and we also would find more time and space to describe and appreciate this man's nature and achievement. Eberhard Arnold was among the most important and influential, present-day advocates of "Christian communism." . . .
>
> He is the founder of the Bruderhof in the Rhön, which grew out of the Sannerz settlement. There he also revived one of the most remarkable trends of Christ's cause in the world: that of the Hutterian "Bruderhofs," which in their time presented a unique organism in the powerful Anabaptist movement which is especially active in America today. In accordance with this great movement, he again placed the early Christian understanding of church at the center of faith, hope, and deed, and its center of brotherly love according to the Sermon on the Mount and the Gospels. He

represented all this with self-reliant, spiritual strength. One could raise questions about how he did it theoretically and practically, but no one who has followed his activities can deny that he was an exceptional hero for Christ. With his fellow workers he risked holding out in a victorious struggle with a faith that is seldom found, through the many dangers which threatened this cause and under the most difficult conditions. So in spite of what may appear problematic in his nature and work, he towers high above much that is considered great within the cause of Christ. Let us hold on to what is great in him, after the mortal inadequacy is discarded. The message of discipleship and the church, bound together with that of the kingdom, remains, also if it does not need to take the form which Eberhard Arnold gave it. Indeed, it is that alone which points to the future of Christ.

The Cotswold Bruderhof

Eberhard had written in his last letter to Hans Zumpe: "The Rhön Bruderhof must be kept in Germany to give a powerful witness by its life."[7] But over the next year and a half, this became more and more difficult. Five German brothers returned from Liechtenstein, in spite of the danger, in order to keep the Rhön going. In January Arnold and Gladys Mason traveled to England to try to raise some money.

Hitler was working toward rebuilding Germany's military strength. The land along the Rhine River, the Rhineland bordering France, Belgium, and the Netherlands, had been a demilitarized zone since World War I. On March 7 German troops marched across the river in defiance of international treaty. Nobody made a move to stop them.

About three weeks before that, in mid February, word came that Germans abroad would be mobilized for the military. This affected the young men at the Alm Bruderhof, and the Liechtenstein authorities said they would not be able to protect them. They had until the end of March to report for military service. The European continent was no longer safe, and the young men would have to flee once more. England seemed a natural choice since several people had joined from that country and the community had many pacifist friends there. Arnold and Gladys Mason, already in England, were asked to find property suitable for a third Bruderhof. Arnold later recalled:

We were excited and happy about this decision. It opened up a new future—freedom to live in community away from Nazi oppression—and we began our new task with great joy. As I knew the Cotswold country, we set out in that direction. On the second day of our journey we came to Cirencester, an old, typically Cotswold, country town with an ancient church, market place, and buildings of Cotswold stone. We went to the office of the land agent, who proved to be friendly and helpful. He took us to view Ashton Fields farm, about four and a half miles from Cirencester, and the history of the Bruderhof in England began.

The farm was about two hundred acres and had a large Cotswold-stone farmhouse. There were considerable farm buildings, two cottages, and a bungalow. The owner was a Mr. Dyer, a very friendly man who was selling the farm because he could not afford the necessary repairs. We began negotiations to rent about sixty acres and all the buildings, with a first option to buy the whole property. When this was provisionally accepted, we promptly moved in—we were so eager to take possession of the new place and to provide a refuge for the young brothers who were expected at any time. The next morning, Sunday, Mr. Dyer came in haste to tell us that really such a thing "was not done" in England before proper agreements were made.[8]

The community's young men fled to England by various means, mostly illegally. Kurt Zimmermann wrote:

Hardy Arnold's passport had expired. When he went to the German consulate they would give him a new one only if he would register for military service. Since he refused to do that, he would have to leave for England right away. His expired passport had many English stamps of entry, and so he hoped he could get in. Albert Wohlfahrt too did not have a valid passport. So Albert, with Hardy and Edith and their little Eberhard Klaus, flew to England, to be followed by Bertel. Werner Friedemann, who had been expelled from Switzerland, was given twenty-four hours to travel through Switzerland.

Germany had occupied the demilitarized zone on the Rhine. Everything pointed to war. Then France closed her border to Germany, and no German was allowed to travel through France. All the brothers who were trying to reach England were detained in Zurich because they could not get permission to travel through France. Since Werner had to leave Switzerland within twenty-four hours we quickly decided that he also should fly. But what were the others going to do? Hans Meier spoke French, English, and

Italian. We decided that he should lead these brothers as a group of hikers. Just as they were getting ready for the trip they were informed by telegram of Werner's return. He had not been allowed to enter England and was sent back on the same plane. The stamp in his passport expelling him from Switzerland had been enough to forbid his entry. So Werner joined the group, now five with Hans Meier, and they went on quite an adventurous trip through France and so to England. Heiner Arnold, who was engaged to Annemarie Wächter, was also due for military service. After a quick decision their wedding was held on the Alm Bruderhof. They left the same day for England.[9]

Hans Meier wrote a letter to the Cotswold Bruderhof, giving the plans of his hiking group:

> Shortly before our departure I want to report to you: The brotherhood of the Alm Bruderhof is completely in agreement with our suggestion of the traveling group, codename "Spain." It will be accompanied by me as "Guide." We carry identification papers for a youth group with a guide from the Swiss Youth Hostel Association (international photo ID). Pennant: Blue flower in a green wood. Travel over the Gotthard Pass—Milan—Genoa. Then, according to circumstances, ship to Barcelona or train and on foot and car—Ventimiglia—Monaco—Nice—Marseilles. Then by boat or other option (like the Pyrenees)—Andorra—Bilbao or Bordeaux—to Bristol—or a different port. Taking along a letter of introduction from a Zurich international transport firm to shipping agents in Genoa, Marseilles, Barcelona, Oporto, Bilbao, and Bordeaux. We will be collecting picture postcards and [official] stamps, souvenirs, etc.[10]

So the Cotswold Bruderhof was begun. Many young people in England were interested in community and the new Bruderhof was flooded with guests. Edna Percival wrote from the Alm:

> Every week we get thrilling reports of the burning desire in England for true brotherhood. It is simply marvelous how God has worked through all this and led us clearly and forcefully to our new land, and to an enormous task there. It's like the leading of the Israelites from Egypt—no less a miracle and revelation of the love of God than that was. It's simply a joy to be in such a life with such a calling and so much to do.[11]

Although this news from England was encouraging, the Bruderhof was now divided into three places, each needing to be fully staffed. There were many guests and few mature members capable of leadership. Each community needed a servant of the Word to lead the community. Several different men tried over the next months to take on this task, but they failed again and again to provide the needed spiritual and practical leadership.

Hans Zumpe wrote to Elias Walter in January and told him about Eberhard's death. He begged him "to continue to take care of our spiritual as well as our temporal need and to stand with us as true brothers with whom we want to remain united forever."[12]

He wrote another long letter in June, addressed to the three senior Hutterite elders.

> Especially now that our Eberhard is no longer among us, I wish I could be with you to consult with you and seek comfort and strengthening. How often have I wished in these weeks that the one or the other of you were with us ... Apart from God, we do not know to whom we should turn other than you, with whom we are fully united in all aspects of faith and life, as with no one else on the whole earth.[13]

He told in detail about what the communities had experienced in the intervening months, particularly the founding of a new place in England. Then he described the hardships of the Rhön Bruderhof:

> They lay heavy taxes on us and we do not know how to pay them as we are no longer allowed to send out brothers to sell our books and turned goods. At the same time our creditors threaten to confiscate our home unless we pay. We believe the government is behind such things, hoping that soon we will no longer be able to pay our debts and will be obliged to give up the Bruderhof in Germany, for they do not want us here. We are in a similar situation to the Jews in Germany. We may buy and spend money, but we must not sell and receive money. May God help our Rhön Bruderhof, that also this place belonging to the church of God may remain ...
>
> Here on the Alm Bruderhof in Liechtenstein we are seriously considering whether more brothers and sisters should move over to the new Bruderhof in England because it becomes increasingly difficult to obtain income from our handicrafts and because

we cannot provide sufficient food for our brothers and sisters. But the greater part of our school is here on the Alm Bruderhof, which must either stay on the Alm or be removed wholly to the Cotswold Bruderhof. We have not enough teaching strength to run two schools on two places, and in any case have not enough children to make it worthwhile. We could send the school over to England at once because we have permission to instruct there, but we must first build a house. For that it would be necessary to buy the farm. For all this we have no money; at the moment we cannot even pay for the journey for so many children which with the teachers would be about fifty people . . .

Hasn't the time now come for some of your brothers to visit us? It should not prove so difficult to travel from Canada to England. We would rejoice with all our heart if, through a visit from some of your brothers, we could come again into the close association that we had with you through Eberhard Arnold's journey to Canada and South Dakota . . . We are in especial need of help not only in temporal matters but also in the spiritual sphere where we often wish for more gifts than we have at this time.[14]

20

August to December 1936

Behind the Scenes

IN THE SUMMER OF 1936, Germany had to put on a good front because the Olympic Games were scheduled to take place in Berlin—a decision that had been made by the International Olympic Committee before the Nazis came to power. This would be an opportunity to influence world opinion. A massive new stadium was erected, and the games were broadcast by radio. Joseph Goebbels, Hitler's minister of propaganda, instructed Berlin: "We must be more charming than the Parisians, more easygoing than the Viennese, more vivacious than the Romans, more cosmopolitan than London, and more practical than New York."[1]

However, the Gestapo was watching all religious groups and organizations. Small sects in particular, who were not affiliated with the two mainline churches, were under relentless attack. This included the Freemasons, Jehovah's Witnesses, and numerous other smaller groups that refused to conform to Nazi ideology. Historian John Conway writes that one third of Germany's Jehovah's Witnesses lost their lives "as a result of their refusal to conform or compromise."[2]

The Rhön Bruderhof was certainly being watched. On June 19, 1936, the local Gestapo reported to the ministry of the interior in Berlin the total number of Bruderhof members on the previous May 22, their nationalities, and the number resident at the Rhön Bruderhof. The total they gave was sixty-eight Germans with thirty-eight children, thirty-eight foreigners with fifteen children. Among the foreigners they listed the exact number of Swiss, English, and Swedish members plus one Latvian, one Italian, one Turkish, and one Czech national. There were fifty members and seventeen children at the Rhön, forty-eight members and thirty-five children at the Alm, and six absent on that day.³ Among other things, the report criticized the Bruderhof for the rundown condition of the farm, a state of affairs brought about by the fact that most young men were now in Liechtenstein. It even voiced a suspicion of the use of drugs and ended with the recommendation that the Bruderhof finally be dissolved:

> It can without question be assumed that those listed [as absent] are propagandists. This applies in a particular way to the Mason couple among the three English nationals. As is known here, they are in England active as itinerant speakers on behalf of the Bruderhof.
>
> The man in charge of the Bruderhof as a whole is the bookseller Hans Zumpe, son-in-law of the deceased Dr. Eberhard Arnold. Zumpe very often stays for a longer time at Silum; in his absence Georg Barth, a builder by training, is in charge of the Bruderhof.
>
> The leader, Zumpe, wants to obtain from English banks considerable amounts of capital, to be used for further building projects. On the other hand it is known that the Bruderhof communities have only partly met the financial obligations incurred by the purchase of their farm. They are faced with considerable demands for payments; the creditors are said to consider taking compulsory measures against the Bruderhof.
>
> When looking at the list of members, it is startling to note the marked increase in the number of English members since the year 1935, all of them young people at that. It should also be pointed out that apart from these members the Bruderhof is almost constantly being visited for shorter or longer periods by English and other guests. A control of this flow is practically impossible, for since the injunction against accommodating guests on the Bruderhof itself, these are now lodged at inns and hotels in the surrounding villages, particularly of the Schlüchtern district and the Bavarian section of the Rhön area, but also of the town of Fulda. The already mentioned Mason couple are said to be particularly active in making propaganda for the Bruderhof in England, but other members as well.
>
> One gets the impression that their way of recruiting people is often very questionable. Several times already parents from Germany and also abroad have approached the district magistrate with requests for assistance in getting their sons and

Chapter 20—August to December 1936

daughters back, who have gone to the Bruderhof against the will of the parents...

In my opinion the kind of propaganda carried out abroad by the Bruderhof is highly detrimental to the interests of Germany. That applies to their attempts to obtain money abroad (money that in the opinion of sensible persons has to be regarded as a lost investment from the beginning) as well as to their methods of misleading and deceiving young people. The constant accession of new members shows that the persons in charge in no way restrict themselves to their previous membership but carry out propaganda for their views also in Germany.

It would be quite wrong to regard the Bruderhof as just another branch of the Protestant Church. The Bruderhof has nothing at all to do with the Protestant Church; it is opposed to every sort of denomination. There are Protestants as well as Catholics among the members, Christians and non-Christians— quite a motley mixture. They decisively reject the will to defend oneself in any form. (The members' list makes clear that the male German members up to about 35 years of age pretty well all reside in Silum; they all made their way there at the end of March.) They also contest the absolute primacy of the national community and the state over against all individual interests; they are against the National Socialist race principles and in that context, of course, also against the law for the prevention of inherently diseased offspring. The world view taught at the Bruderhof and publicized in Germany and abroad is the very opposite of National Socialism. Prior to the National Socialist seizure of power they styled themselves *Edelkommunisten* [idealistic communists] ...

From the point of view of the national economy, too, the existence of the Bruderhof has to be seen as totally undesirable. The lands worked agriculturally and the whole appearance of the place, in particular also the livestock, strike one as so slovenly and neglected that one can only regret that the place is not being worked properly by a German farmer. At present the whole outfit looks more like a Russian collective. The members' laziness, apparently one of their strongest qualities, stares at you from every nook and corner.

Finally, mention should be made of a suspicion for which, however, actual proof so far is lacking. With many of their members one is struck by a strange expression in their eyes. It is at any rate possible that this condition might derive from the use of cocaine or some other drug. That would also explain the otherwise enigmatic fact that young people from educated circles leave their homes and families to go and live at the bleak Rhön

Bruderhof. It would also account for the many trips abroad, to Liechtenstein, Switzerland, and England by the Bruderhof members. Up till now the state police office in Kassel has carried out no investigations in this regard, but in my opinion it would do no harm to have the Bruderhof checked out by special agents of the narcotics department.

So far we have found no link between them and the German Communist Party. It appears necessary, though, to ascertain abroad—especially in England, Switzerland, and Liechtenstein—what connections the Bruderhof people have there.

The state police office in Kassel is of the opinion that it is urgently to be desired to find a way to dissolve the Bruderhof at long last.[4]

A year earlier, in July 1935, Hitler had created a new ministry of church affairs as Reich Bishop Ludwig Müller had failed to bring the churches in line. Hanns Kerrl, a former accountant in Prussian law courts, was placed in charge of this new office. The establishment of this ministry meant that the case of the Bruderhof was transferred from the ministry of the interior to the ministry of church affairs. Therefore the report from the Kassel Gestapo was forwarded to the ministry of church affairs which took up the investigations that would lead to the dissolution of the Rhön Bruderhof. At the request of that office,[5] District Administrator Burkhardt wrote a report on September 1, repeating much of what had been said in the report of June 19, and ending with the statement:

> In my opinion it is no longer to be tolerated that there exists in Germany a community whose aims are the very opposite of National Socialism ... Measures taken against the Bruderhof will have to be in the form of sudden strikes, but only after proper contact has been made with the authorities familiar with local conditions.[6]

The German Mennonite church had also been asked for a statement on the Bruderhof. Dr. Ernst Crous, vice president of the Federation of German Mennonite Churches submitted the following report, taking care to emphasize the differences between the Bruderhof and the Mennonites, addressed to the ministry of church affairs, August 20, 1936:

> The Hutterites, named after Jakob Hutter (d. 1536), are a small branch of the great Anabaptist movement of the sixteenth century. They are distinguished from the German and some of the

> non-German Mennonites by their principle of nonviolence and from all Mennonites by the principle of community of goods. They are the only life community of its kind that has survived through the centuries. Certainly, their number has remained correspondingly small: in the United States and Canada about four thousand souls at about forty Bruderhofs ...
>
> The Bruderhof, Post Neuhof, near Fulda, began as an independent foundation of the late Dr. Eberhard Arnold, but was then acknowledged by the Hutterites in America ... Even though we cannot share the old and new Hutterites' understanding of Acts 4:32 ff. and therefore follow a different path, we are nevertheless convinced that these men and women struggle earnestly and sincerely for a truly Christian walk of life according to their understanding.[7]

The regional governor, von Monbart in Kassel, also reported to the minister of church affairs on October 17, supporting Burkhardt's findings. He repeated the familiar charges of hostility to the state, refusal of military service, and rejection of the race laws. However, he felt, confiscation of the property without recompense would be unwise on account of large investments by foreigners. Moreover it would appear they were being persecuted because they were Christians. A better solution would be to acquire the Bruderhof's land for military purposes.

> To begin with, the district administrator for Fulda is correct in his assessment that the Bruderhof is not a Christian community in the sense of the churches, for its members reject any denominational ties. Moreover, although the Hutterian Brethren claim ties to primitive Christianity, they cannot simply be categorized as a religious organization in the generally accepted sense. A large proportion of their members, especially the foreigners, are communists. That is also proven by the repeated seizure of communist writings. There can be no doubt either that in its whole tendency and activity the Bruderhof is opposed to National Socialism. Their propagation of refusal to do military service, their rejection of the National Socialist laws concerning blood and race, their refusal to hold public office, and their denial of private property likewise show that the Bruderhof pursues communist aims, even though with a Christian camouflage. Since the matters involved in these aims are simply questions of state, and not of church, policy, I would again request that it be determined whether they should not be dealt with by the secret state police

and the minister of the interior, i.e. rather than by the minister for church affairs.

The dissolution of the Bruderhof as an organization hostile to the state, which in and by itself would be desirable for reasons of state policy, accompanied by a confiscation of its assets, would meet with great difficulties because numerous foreigners, particularly British and Swiss, have invested considerable sums in the Bruderhof (over 130,000 marks). Given the Bruderhof's good connections abroad, especially in England and Switzerland, such a measure would stir up considerable excitement and because of the lying propaganda of our enemies abroad could easily create the impression that the National Socialist state proceeds very sharply against Christian communities *because they are Christian* [emphasis in original], with the consequence that the members of the Bruderhof, in spite of their traitorous activity (which would be hushed up), would be presented as martyrs for the sake of their faith. Since in my opinion that would be a highly undesirable effect for reasons of foreign policy, I would at this point not recommend such a measure, also because the expropriation of the assets would cause grave difficulties in view of the heavy load of financial obligations, both of a personal nature and in the form of mortgages.

Recently, however, a better possibility of proceeding against the Bruderhof seems to have opened up, because the army needs a large tract of land in the Rhön for a prospective military training area. I intend to direct the army's attention to the 169 acres of the Bruderhof, which has actually completely mismanaged its agricultural property. If then the army takes over the Bruderhof's land for purely military reasons and with proper compensation as provided in the Land Procurement Law, that might be the best solution, also from the viewpoint of foreign relations. No objections could be raised against such a solution, especially because in the process of obtaining land for the military, frequently even state land and entailed estates have had to be made available for the army, so that the surrender of land by the Bruderhof would not be anything unusual ...[8]

These reports indicate why the Bruderhof had not been dissolved long before: the authorities were afraid of the foreign press.

Persevering

Meanwhile, the men and women at the Rhön Bruderhof were trying desperately to keep things going. It had been difficult enough to maintain two communities; now there were three. And yet they continued with courage, as evidenced by Kathleen Hamiliton's letters to her mother, written from the Rhön Bruderhof in the fall of 1936:

> Mother, darling, what a time we are living in! I read the Sermon on the Mount as in Luke in Moffat's translation this morning and it gave great courage. It is as though Christ were actually saying it to us here—and the wonder of it. Especially Luke 6:22–23. Everyone must die sometime, and we are indeed happy and have cause to rejoice if our death is used by God as a witness to truth and as a glorifying of his name. With the mustering of the powers of evil comes the assurance, "Lo! I am with you always," and the unique joy of the Spirit. What Jesus said to his first disciples, he says to us, and all that was once only words to me, that follows what he says about the destruction of Jerusalem, is living up-to-date fact. My heart aches for the world, Mother. Oh, the coldness and heartless cruelty of men in the grip of the power of evil. And if my human heart feels it so, God must feel heartbroken that those whom he made in his own image, i.e. to live in his very essence—love—should so treat each other. But that his power and love may flow through us to the world in need; the world that crucifies Christ in its blindness, today, in its treatment of his brothers; that his kingdom may come here on earth—for that, in the courage given from above, we are ready to take anything upon ourselves. The wonder of having a share in his work of redemption, Mother! The joy of giving our little mortal life for his cause. The cause goes on. Nothing can kill it, for its very nature is love and is imperishable—but the joy of having a share in his cause![9]

> You say, "Surely you are not working in the fields now?" We are working there with every ounce of energy, for the potatoes must be got in. They are the main food both for ourselves and those who come to us. You must remember, we cannot just go to a shop and buy a few tons of them! They are late this year owing to the terribly long rainy period we had earlier in the year, but every effort is being made to save all we can before the hard frosts come. This week I have not been in the potato fields but in the kitchen. So you see I have a wonderful variety of work. The women have not been able to help with potatoes much this

> week, as we have far too few women to do all the most necessary work—just as we have far too few men. But though life is a fight, a very hard fight, for our very existence, what joy there is in it all! It is positive. Emphatically so! And we have recently had the amazing joy of two little new lives being entrusted to us—a son to Fritz and Sekunda and a daughter to Leo and Trautel. Also we have had grand encouraging and inspiring news from Edna and her friends [i.e. the Cotswold Bruderhof] so one feels what a joy and privilege it is just to live. About sleep. I sleep like a top, little Mother, and I am quite warm in bed. I never, in all the six weeks Edna and I were in Britain, slept once as I do after a day lasting from 5:00 a.m. to 10:00 or 11:00 p.m. or later, hard at work, physical, mental, or spiritual. Yes, we are very grateful to be able to say that we have enough to eat. One realizes clearly Christ's prayer, "Give us this day our daily bread." One just wonders what people think who pray it, knowing the pantry is already full! . . .
>
> Just a few words to add, dear. O Mother, there is a wonderful, clear, refreshing and invigorating power at work here, and what can only be described as wonders take place. Materially viewed, one can understand people seeing no further into our life than our celebrated mud—but what a life it is! We simply glory in it.[10]

> A great joy to me is that the other day I got a pair of wooden shoes. I call them my seven league boots. Even wearing my slitzers, there is at least two inches to spare when I am in them! But what a boon it is to have them. When one has to go from one house to another through our celebrated mud, one can hardly say what a difference it makes—and how I have longed for them, but as I possess boots, I thought it was too much to expect a pair![11]

A few German families had returned from the Alm. The brotherhood was consciously taking a risk in asking that they move back from Liechtenstein to Germany despite the military draft, but without their help it was impossible to maintain the witness in Germany as Eberhard had wished. Leo and Trautel Dreher were one of these couples. Their letters express the same courageous determination:

> Our hearts urge us to greet you in this hour with unity and peace, as encouragement and challenge. We don't know what the next days will bring. But one thing we do know: the witness made by our brothers and forebears from beginning to end. May we witness to the one truth that is demanded of us. Isn't it wonderful that we may—and will—hold to this line! . . . It is a deep joy to know that we are united in our prayer on all our Bruderhofs, be

it in our rooms alone or in the communal intercession of our worship meetings—or wherever we might be, according to God's will. One thing is clear, the awareness that we can bow our knees before God alone. That gives us courage for whatever may be ahead. And if only a few of us are affected at first, all the more strongly will we others jump in to replace them. We know we are united with you all in this firm decision. Just because we see the real danger, we receive real faith. If we didn't see the gravity of this hour so clearly before our eyes, we would become superficial. If we did not grasp that it is ultimately a matter of God's kingdom and his coming to this desperate earth, the strength would be denied us ... Today when I went up on the knoll I thought of what the first Christians expected and fought for in faith in what is to come. That unites us ... We will experience that Christ is victor![12]

In mid September the dreaded moment came—a letter from Mayor Zeiher of Veitsteinbach demanding those eligible to register for the military:

All men of the 1900–1905 age group are to register for military service. I therefore request a list of all the persons who come into question.[13]

Five brothers were liable. Edith Arnold on the Cotswold Bruderhof wrote to her husband Hardy:

This is probably the most serious hour that has yet struck our Bruderhofs. If these five smuggle themselves over the border, their wives for sure, but probably the entire Bruderhof will be accused of high treason. So the mother Bruderhof will stand or fall by this. After all our deliberations it seems the best thing now will be not to send them over the border. They could be shot on the spot. There are only two possibilities: either we obtain a special ruling, or the community will be dissolved.[14]

The members of the community sent the following reply to the mayor:

In reference to your request that we report all males born between 1900 and 1905 so that they can be entered in the muster-roll, we take the liberty to reply as follows. There are in fact five members currently at the Rhön Bruderhof who belong to that age group: Fritz Kleiner, Karl Keiderling, Fritz Kaiser, August Dyroff, and Heinz Bolck. These members declare, however, that in line with our Hutterian Bruderhof's religious conviction they cannot per-

> form any military service and therefore cannot comply with the required formalities either ...
>
> Because of the changed circumstances in Germany our expatriate German brothers in America have felt urged to submit a petition to the Reich government via the North American representation of the German Reich. This petition expresses the wish that because of its unswerving steadfastness for over four hundred years in the question of military service the Hutterian brotherhood be granted an exceptional status or complete exemption—a concession it repeatedly received in the course of its four hundred years of existence, also from Prussian authorities. That expected conclusive decision would be of crucial importance for the future of our Rhön Bruderhof, and the fate of the five brothers that belong to the age group now being called up for registry would also depend on that decision.[15]

There was no response to the letter, and the men were left alone for the moment. The Hutterian elders did, in fact, write to the Reich ministry of the interior—a seven-page letter signed by Joseph Kleinsasser and David Hofer (for Johannes Kleinsasser), dated November 13, 1936. With it they enclosed a copy of their petition for exemption for military service to Woodrow Wilson, 1914, and a similar petition of 1917.[16]

Another Raid

On October 7, another raid of the Rhön Bruderhof took place. Before daylight, the members of the community woke up to find a uniformed man standing outside each door. Was this the end? Their response was calm and courageous, as can be seen from Trautel Dreher's letter:

> We stand here as a small militant church, as a state within the state. And the state that is built upon blood and soil, upon power and force, stands against us ... We are thankful for the fact that our way, our cause, the cause of God's kingdom can be represented face to face with the enemy, with the state that will not and cannot tolerate us. And yet these men have respect for our way. They cannot conceal the fact that our consistent attitude from the beginning has aroused their respect for our cause. Now everything is at stake.
>
> For this fight it is absolutely necessary that we study in depth the opponent's cause, National Socialism, not only knowing about it with our feelings, but that we study their cause quite

systematically. For we also respect the conviction of people who with true idealism go all-out for an idea.

This visit was really strange... In the hazy half-light of dawn I saw many unfamiliar figures, and at first felt afraid as I realized what all these grey uniforms meant for us. But it was strange how we were then able to meet them joyfully, freely, and without fear. After all, they were only people like us. And the words: "Love your enemies" is something sobering. Indeed, we realize we will be led into much more difficult situations when we will be severely tested in this "love to our enemies." But we noticed clearly, just as on November 16 [1933], that the ice had to melt in the sunshine of love. How wonderful it is then to know that we are one united brotherhood! And when two people met on the hof a spark sprang from one to the other: "Unity"—"Peace." Not in words, but it was a strong experience. Now both directions confront each other sharply defined; now, in essentials, we may testify to our cause; for this we are truly thankful.[17]

August Dyroff believed this raid was in response to the men's refusal to obey the military summons. He later recalled:

> One morning when we got up, we saw that our compound was full of military police. I tried to go outside to put the ash from our little stove into the dustbin, and there was a sheriff and a few men in plain clothes. I said to one who was outside our door that I would like to put this in the bin. "No," he said, "No, close the door and stay inside." Now what should I do? Our little Martin was sick in bed. He had high fever, and I tried to make a fire so that it would be a bit warm, but he refused to let me out. So I went down again and asked him if I could go to the nurse, to Marie, and he said, "No, out of the question." I said, "This is ridiculous." I argued with him a bit, and the other officer heard it and came very quickly.
>
> "What is the matter?"
>
> I said, "My little baby is not well, and I ask for the nurse to come look at him." I asked him if I could go and fetch the nurse, and he said, "Yes." He commanded the sheriff to go with me to Marie. But my main point was to see what was happening. Everything was quiet. There was nobody outside. In front of each door was a man in uniform, and I was curious about what had happened, and whether they had been there the whole night or not.
>
> In the room below us where Hannes Boller lived, the police had turned everything upside down—everything. They were

> looking for foreign bills of exchange. When one came up to me, I said, "I have no foreign currency. It is not worthwhile to look." But they even looked in the baby's straw mattress. Under the bed, every corner was looked through, but I had always the feeling that that was not the real thing they were looking for. A few days before I had had a card from the military ordering me to register. I sent the card back saying that they know my attitude, and that I would not go. Now I thought they had come to fetch me, but nobody ever said a single word about this. Nothing happened. They took nobody, and as far as I know, they took nothing away. Why they came nobody has ever known. They took from about seven to twelve o'clock to go into every house and every corner to look for something, but they did not tell us what they were really looking for.[18]

This raid was evidently a result of Dr. Burkhardt's suggestion, made in his report of September 1, 1936, that the Foreign Exchange office check whether the Bruderhof was observing the foreign currency laws.[19] The Gestapo reported to the minister of church affairs in their memo of October 26 that the action was "an unannounced but fruitless investigation on October 7, 1936, by the foreign exchange control office at Frankfurt/Main."[20]

∼

A new crisis came at the end of November 1936. Suddenly payment of a large mortgage of 15,000 marks was demanded. This mortgage had been granted in 1928 by the Weimar government for the building of the children's house. This serious financial blow was surely intended to bankrupt the Bruderhof. The Cotswold Bruderhof was able to raise the money; but the Rhön Bruderhof was not allowed to receive foreign donations. The brothers decided to get the money into Germany by "selling" the printing press and other equipment at the Rhön Bruderhof to the Cotswold Bruderhof. Arnold Mason came from England with the cash in his pocket. He met Hans Zumpe in Frankfurt where they went to the Foreign Exchange Control office to propose the sale. The sale was concluded smoothly. Hans and Arnold Mason went to the Rhön Bruderhof to help pack up the equipment for shipment to England. Margrit Meier reported:

Early on Wednesday the mechanic arrived from Frankfurt, the same man who had set up the machine here four and a half years ago. That was the start of an immense amount of industrious work. All other jobs had to be set aside so that as many of our men as possible could help with the packing up. Since Wednesday, [seven of them] have been at work there. The mechanic gives the directions. Boxes are being made, and three times already additional wood had to be fetched from Veitsteinbach. In the evening two big gasoline lamps provide light, in addition to three or four stable lanterns, even though we can get gasoline only in five-liter containers. The mechanic is really pleased with the way our men are working.

By Wednesday evening our high-speed printing press was there no more! It makes our hearts ache, of course; indeed, the whole situation in this country of ours makes one feel extremely sad. So many things have come to our ears these last days, in particular yesterday (Sunday) and also Saturday evening.

The mechanic told of what he experiences in his work, of the need of people in the cities, and about technological development as both a blessing and a curse. After forty years of painstaking research a certain man had made a discovery—I didn't quite get it, so I can't properly describe it, but it will mean that 30,000 workers will lose their jobs. It is horrible to hear about it, also about the political situation.[21]

Mennonite Help

The Bruderhof in Germany was feeling more and more alone and helpless as slowly and inexorably its life was being strangled. But in America one person was actively working to help them: the Mennonite Harold Bender. Bender (1897–1962) had visited the Rhön Bruderhof in May 1930. He saw in the Bruderhof a return to the "Anabaptist Vision"—one of his favorite themes and the topic of an essay he wrote in 1944. In 1931 he had written an article published in *The Christian Monitor*:

> When we arrived at the "Bruderhof" I was impressed at once by the spirit of simple brotherhood and evident love which existed. They were as one great family, from young to old. And I felt this spirit the longer I was among them. Forms and formality were done away with, "Sie" had disappeared and been replaced by the familiar "Du," even with visitors. First names were used, titles forgotten (although Eberhard Arnold is a university graduate with a

PhD), stiffness and all signs of vanity and pride were gone, and in their place was a simple, hearty, friendly good cheer and a spirit of true Christian charity and regard for one another. The spirit of fellowship (Gemeinschaft) is very strong in the brotherhood, as it must be if such a group is to exist at all. Private property is abolished, and a community of goods set up in its place, where all must live and work together for the good of all. I could not help but wonder whether the possession of money and property is not after all a great enemy of Christian love and fellowship, and was reminded of the word of our Lord, "How hardly shall they that have riches enter into the kingdom." . . .

Here in the "Bruderhof" they really love an unworldly life, separate from the world, a separation in comparison to which we Mennonites who emphasize unworldliness are still quite worldly. The life here was and is so different from the ordinary life, even of Mennonites, that I was forced to reconsider the life which we live, and the spirit which animates our brotherhood . . . Again and again the thought came to me, how many of our modern Mennonites would be willing to sacrifice as these people sacrificed, and do it with joy and unwavering faith in the truth and right of their principles?[22]

Emmy Arnold and Hans Zumpe had met Harold Bender at the Mennonite World Conference in July of that year. At that occasion they had seen that the Mennonites of Europe were not taking a united position against National Socialism or participation in war. But a handful of Dutch and American Mennonites had signed a peace declaration and promised to help each other.[23] Bender must have got to work immediately to try to find help for the German group. The Mennonites decided to approach the German embassy, as a letter from Mennonite historian Ernst Correll to Harold Bender and his father-in-law John Horsch shows:

Dear Friends:

The Hutterian inquiry touches me deeply. I entered at once into preliminary negotiations with the proper USA and German offices . . . Opinions voiced to me (very unofficially of course) as to the possible outcome of petitions are rather pessimistic. My feeling, however, is that you and all of those directly concerned should go forward. I am at your service 100% and ready to submit matters personally to [German ambassador to the USA] Dr. Hans Luther who, on the other hand, can merely report but not act.

Yet it seemed pointless to sink a lot of money into the doomed Rhön Bruderhof. Correll ended his letter with a postscript:

> With all respect to the attachment of these "new" Hutterites to the hof and burial place of their founder and relatives it may, under present conditions, be more sensible and beneficial to the cause to put the Rhön Bruderhof under an honest bankruptcy administration and help the Liechtenstein and English Bruderhofs grow by concentrating on the latter two.[24]

Bender also contacted the American Friends Service Committee. Clarence E. Pickett of the AFSC wrote to Paul Sturge, general secretary of the Friends Council in London:

> Harold S. Bender, a Mennonite who has spent a great deal of time in Germany, has been deeply concerned with regard to the little Hutterian group of German pacifists, which is likely, he feels, to be sent to a concentration camp in Germany. Already, some of them have gone to Lichtenstein [sic] for safety, but have now been required by the government of Lichtenstein to return to Germany or to go elsewhere. Thirty-one have emigrated to England.
>
> Our Committee will probably send a letter of information and urgent request for leniency to the German government through Ambassador Luther. The Mennonites and the Church of the Brethren will probably take similar action. It was the judgment of Rufus Jones, William Eves and myself, in conference with Harold Bender and a representative of the Church of the Brethren recently, that it might be well if this matter were laid before the Meeting for Sufferings so that it might consider whether English Friends also might wish to make an appeal to the German government for leniency.[25]

Rufus M. Jones, AFSC chairman, wrote to Dr. Luther at the German Embassy in Washington. He introduced the Bruderhof community and then said:

> They are a quiet, inoffensive sect, who wish to be law-abiding so far as possible, and yet they will find themselves unable to respond to the military demands of the government.
>
> I realize that, from the political point of view, we have no right to interfere with matters that have to do with internal relations in Germany. But representing a group of American Quakers, who have long-established and deep attachments to the German people, we have felt free to express ourselves to you, requesting

leniency and consideration for the Hutterite community. We feel confident that if an exception can be made and this community undisturbed, there would be no serious repercussions; and we believe as a humanitarian step it would once again exhibit the desire of Germany to respect the spirit and life of religious sects whose convictions are deeply and personally held by practically, if not wholly, every member of the community.

 I hope that you will feel that it is right for you to transmit this letter to your government.[26]

Thus closed the year 1936. Forces were gaining momentum against the struggling community. Quietly some of the brotherhood members were beginning to ask themselves how long they should try to hold out in Germany. Should they give up the struggle and all move to England, where doors were clearly opening? Edith Arnold, living at the Cotswold, voiced these doubts in a letter to Emmy:

> The Christmas days were wonderful. On the evening of the second day Heiner, Annemarie, Hans-Hermann, Gertrud, Hardy and I still spent a long time together talking about these last years. Last year was infinitely difficult, and the situation with the three Bruderhofs is actually unbearable. It will be extremely hard if we give up the Rhön Bruderhof; it goes very much against the grain. Not one person in yesterday's brotherhood meeting wanted to use the words, "give up the Rhön Bruderhof"; yet it had to be expressed! Papa said so often there is no sense in letting our men be imprisoned. They will have to suffer, but it is so secret and hidden that it will not be a witness to the world. It is better for them to go where they can represent the witness more powerfully. That is what is also happening with our mother Bruderhof: Secretly, and seemingly without any force being used, it is gradually diminishing more and more, until nothing will be left of the true picture of a Bruderhof. And even if people in Germany are dissatisfied, still there is no real movement there that would justify exposing our brothers to constant danger and leaving them under heavy pressure, which will do harm to their souls. I do not believe Papa would have left the three communities as they are in this situation![27]

21

January to April 1937

Responding to Harold Bender's concern for the poverty-stricken, threatened Rhön Bruderhof, John Horsch of Scottdale, Pennsylvania, contacted his brother Michael, a Mennonite farmer in southern Germany. Michael Horsch immediately sent the community 300 marks "so that they at least have bread," and visited at the beginning of January 1937. He was sympathetic, and wrote to his brother that the reports of dire poverty were not exaggerated. He recommended that the American Mennonites help financially to get the farm back on its feet with seed and fertilizer. The South German Mennonite Conference, of which he was a leading member, would help with a weekly bread supply and heating costs for the winter. On January 25, he wrote again to his brother John to say that he felt "a deep sense of affinity" with the Bruderhof people "who take the discipleship of Christ, his words and promises seriously, just as they are stated, and seek to live in accord with them. It felt good to be there; I felt at home among them."[1]

By now it was clear that their days at the Rhön Bruderhof were numbered. The members remaining in Germany did what they could to salvage what was left. Furniture and books were packed and shipped to England. Livestock was sold. They would try to sell the property to the Reich Resettlement Corporation for peasants whose land had been taken for a military training ground. Karl Keiderling recalled:

> Strangers now began to appear and walked around our property as if they were the masters. Cattle dealers, boys from villages, persons came whom we had never seen before. They brazenly opened the door of the barn or went into the stable to look at the horses. They offered ridiculously low prices for our wagons, plows, machinery, or cattle. When we were not there, they smeared the walls with dirt and drew swastikas on the walls and doors of our

> stables. Building material left on the hill near the burial ground was stolen. Someone tried to set fire to the nursery of pines.
>
> We hadn't a single friend anymore. Friends and acquaintances of former years had withdrawn from us out of fear of the authorities. Dealers from whom we had bought for years now refused us credit lest they be suspected of supporting the Bruderhof.
>
> As rumors got around that we were leaving, our creditors made urgent demands on us. Not a day went by without two, three, or four of our creditors coming to the office. Each day the mail brought bills, demands for payment, threats of legal proceedings, and notices of recourse to the bailiff.[2]

Some of the German brothers liable for military service tried to get into England and miraculously, they made it. August Dyroff set out with his wife Gertrud and the baby. They were dressed in Hutterian costume—Gertrud in a long skirt and head scarf and August heavily bearded. Their luggage was tied up in bundles, and they got into the very last compartment of the train. At the border, officials went from compartment to compartment demanding to see the passports. Finally their door was ripped open. The family feigned sleep, and they heard one official say to the other, "Let those dirty Poles sleep!" He banged the door shut, and the train continued into Holland.[3]

Hutterian Elders Arrive

The Bruderhof had begged the Hutterites to send someone. Their need was desperate. On February 7, two Hutterian ministers arrived at the Cotswold Bruderhof: David Hofer from James Valley Colony, Manitoba, and Michael Waldner from Bon Homme, South Dakota. Eberhard Arnold had befriended both of them six years earlier. Edith Arnold described their arrival:

> The bell rang, and everybody met and sang. As soon as we caught sight of them we felt that brothers had come. They were quite trusting right away; David said, "Good day. Well, this is wonderful, to see one another face to face now, and God protected us on our trip too." It was moving to see these two dignified, white-bearded men, who undertook such a long journey just out of love. That is the most important and wonderful thing that one can say now after such a short time. A really deep love radiates from them, a love that truly comes from Christ.[4]

David Hofer gave his impressions in a letter he wrote home:

> Thank God for his leading and protection, for it was a difficult and dangerous journey; in the two days of storm they said a ship sank and twenty men were drowned, a small ship.
>
> The brothers are very poor. We have eaten with them several times and find that they eat potatoes, peas, and lettuce without having bread with their meals, and yet they work very hard at stonework. How content they are because they now have a little place in England where the government is favorable to them. For the government in Germany wants to take away and sell their property in Germany, as they have heard, which is very miserable. And Hans Zumpe and the brothers want us to go there with him, though this is not yet decided; but we will probably do it.
>
> It is a wonder and amazement what we find, see, and hear here, dear brothers and sisters. But we will postpone our opinion till later, so as not to be too hasty. The noble virtue of patience is necessary here; but the members of the church are content, united, and loving.[5]

David and Michael spent two months at the Cotswold Bruderhof in England. During that time they baptized several new members and helped establish the community according to Hutterian custom.

On March 5, 1937, the Gestapo in Berlin wrote to the minister of church affairs urging the immediate dissolution of the Bruderhof at Neuhof and the confiscation of its property. Kerrl's consent to this action was requested.[6]

Over the next weeks Nazi harassment increased. Several mortgages were called in, and the planned sale of the property to the Resettlement Corporation met a roadblock. The brothers and sisters sensed that a change had taken place at higher levels of government. Civil authorities were now being overruled.

At the beginning of April 1937, the Rhön Bruderhof household consisted of about forty people, including ten to twelve young children. Karl Keiderling remembers:

> On Sunday April 4, 1937, a week after Easter, we held the Lord's Supper. It was a very serious occasion, but there was such a joy of the Spirit among us that we sang many songs expressing faith and

joy. When at the end Trautel Dreher called out, spontaneously, "Now let them come!" she expressed what we all felt. We looked into the future with new confidence and felt ready for anything.

But we were a flock of sheep without a shepherd. We had no servant of the Word with us and no appointed steward. Hans Meier looked after the money but was only called "business manager." We met every evening, but we hoped that the two Hutterian brothers, experienced servants of the Word, might come soon and that we could put ourselves completely under their leadership.[7]

David Hofer and Michael Waldner arrived at the Rhön Bruderhof on April 9. They were awaited eagerly, welcomed with twelve blazing torches, and escorted through the woods and down the hill to the main buildings. David Hofer said, "Now at last we are where Eberhard lived and worked."[8] Every evening for the next week one of the Hutterian ministers led the community in prayer for protection and guidance.

Unknown to all, the Gestapo had issued its order for the dissolution on the very day that the Hutterites arrived, April 9.[9] They had barely four days with the brothers and sisters. They looked round all the buildings and rooms, the meadows and fields, the wagons and implements and livestock. It was a relief and satisfaction for the Rhön circle that the two Hutterites, experienced farmers, considered the Bruderhof "a big, well-built community," that "all cattle, pigs, and horses are of the best," that the seventeen milk cows were "well-looked after," that there was an "exceptionally good breed of pigs." "It is a shame to have to lose it and leave it," Michael Waldner wrote in his diary. David Vetter, in his diary summed up, "Everything was clean and in good order."

The Bruderhof Dissolved

The morning of April 14, 1937, dawned misty and rainy. The men and women of the Rhön Bruderhof went about their usual work: washing and cooking, caring for sick children, packing items to be shipped to England, or doing farm chores. Around 10:00 a.m. Hans Meier caught sight of fifteen or twenty police emerging from the woods and others arriving on bicycles and by car. He hurried to inform everyone in sight, including the two American brothers who were in Eberhard's old study. Now the armed men were appearing from all sides. Numbers vary in the accounts—no one could take it all in—but there must have been about fifty SS besides Gestapo and local constables in their green uniforms.

Local police with revolvers positioned themselves at every door; from earlier raids they knew their way about. The dinner bell was ringing, calling everyone to the dining room. Hans Meier remembered:

> The Gestapo commissar announced first to me as the Bruderhof's steward, and then to the whole gathered community, that as of today the Bruderhof was dissolved on the basis of the Reich president's decree for the protection of the people and state against violent communist attacks, that all Bruderhof residents were to return to where they had come from, and that all German nationals of military age were to register for military service. We declared unanimously that we would not return to our former homes, for we had left them in order to live in community; we also refused to register for military service. Our request for a written copy of the decree of dissolution was refused. The Executive Committee was relieved of its responsibility. All the money was confiscated; and from that moment on no belongings could be kept without the agreement of the district administrator. We were asked to hand over all the account books and all keys; within twenty-four hours all were to be gone.[10]

With the exception of the Executive Committee (Hans Meier, Hannes Boller, and Karl Keiderling) everyone was herded into the dining room. There they were guarded by two officers and no one was allowed either out or in. The office upstairs where the Gestapo commissar summoned the Executive Committee was packed with officials. Commissar Koslowski, a tall, broad man, stood at the desk. A secretary sat there with a typewriter, an official stood in front of the big bookcase; another opened and read the incoming mail. There was a constant coming and going. Karl described it:

> The commissar read again the decree of dissolution, and dictated to his secretary to record that it had been read out to us. After the commissar had dictated for the record, we three were asked to sign it. We said we were not in agreement with it and wanted to have it in writing, but this was refused.[11]

While the three brothers were being questioned in the office, officials went through the offices and bedrooms. The brothers and sisters watched from the dining room windows as the soldiers carried books, writings, and papers in armfuls from Eberhard's study down to the yard to pack them into a car. Nearly all the books from the library had been carried down one flight of steps and thrown in a pile on the floor by the door to the veranda. There was chaos everywhere.

One of the officers exclaimed excitedly that there were still men there of military age who must not leave Germany; the commissar replied that this would have to be discussed with the military command in Fulda. By the end of the day, Constable Weigand served each of the few brothers of military age a summons for a medical examination on May 8.

When the two Americans saw that their room was about to be searched, they received permission to go there:

> It wasn't long before the searchers came to our room. "What are you doing here?" they asked us. "Why aren't you in the dining room?" We pointed out to them that we were foreigners of German descent and did not want our things searched. They asked us what business we had with the people here, where we came from and why. We told them, "These people are our brothers and sisters, to whom we have sent a lot of help from America to build up this Bruderhof; so we are very much interested in what is going to happen here and how things will turn out for them." We saw at once that our presence displeased them and that we were in their way. We asked them to let us stay here for a few days.[12]

In the dining room each person was questioned. A large proportion were foreigners, and they were asked if they wished to go to their national consulate. All gave the same reply. Winifred Bridgwater answered, "We wish to stay together whatever happens; and if one of us is taken into custody, we will all stay together."

An officer came into the dining room, carrying the passports and papers under his arm. He spread them out on the table, looked through all the passports and most important papers, then pushed everything into his briefcase.

By three o'clock all the papers were signed and everyone was allowed to have lunch. No one had much appetite. Charlie Jory came in with three or four eggs from the farm. As nothing had been prepared, Kathleen put water and oatmeal in a big pot and threw in the eggs. After the meal all were ordered out into the yard for an announcement. Karl Keiderling recalls:

They barked at us in Prussian military fashion, "Attention! Get into line! Look sharp!" While we were still getting into line, we realized they were taking pictures of us. Officials with cameras stood opposite us near the children's house steps; and we were photographed from all sides. Some turned their faces away. One of the officers announced, "That's the end of this outfit; the Bruderhof is dissolved and the publishing house—which was folding up anyway. You can all go back to work. You can move freely. No one may take anything connected with the farm, the communal property, household goods, or valuables when you go. Anyone who wants to leave has to get permission from Officer Weigand; he will stay here for now." With that, the officers left in their cars. Besides Weigand, the commissar and another Gestapo officer remained up in the office.[13]

The brothers and sisters gathered again in the dining room to consider the overall picture. The Gestapo had made a complete house search and carried off a lot of things, including personal belongings.

Their first concern was to get word to the Alm and Cotswold Bruderhofs. The phone was watched, but fortunately Arno and Ruth Martin still had their passports. It was decided they should go to Liechtenstein that same evening. Karl wrote:

> How ugly it looked everywhere! Everything in disorder—beds pulled apart, cupboards, and drawers emptied, piles of things on the floor. Julia lay bedridden in the upper story of the children's house. The small children who were down with flu were in that building too, in one room to simplify the nursing; several had high fevers. After all that the grown-ups had experienced that day, it was wonderfully comforting to go to these little children.[14]

Before Arno and Ruth left, David Hofer said a prayer to take leave of them and their infant daughter. Since the community had no money, the American brothers dipped into their pockets for travel expenses. They left in a car with David and Hans Meier for Schlüchtern, to catch the train for Liechtenstein.

Supper was ready in the dining room. The brothers and sisters asked Michael to tell about his community in South Dakota, and he spoke until nearly eleven o'clock. Bit by bit everything became quiet. Hans Meier and David Hofer came back. One light after another was put out in the rooms, and all was dark. The end of a historic day.

The next morning, everything looked strange, disorderly, and forlorn. At 8:30 a car arrived. A policeman got out and ordered the three brothers of the Executive Committee to come at once to the police office in Fulda, to arrange for the travel to Liechtenstein and England. It would be a short and simple matter, and they would be back in the afternoon.

Hannes Boller, Hans Meier, and Karl Keiderling took leave of their wives and children. Everyone watched until the car was out of sight. David said, "They will not return so quickly." Karl's report continues:

> At the District Office in Fulda we were taken up a flight of stairs and down a hall. After a short wait we were ordered inside. It was a big room with high windows, cupboards along the wall and a large brown desk in the middle, covered with papers and portfolios. An armchair and a few other chairs were in the room.
>
> In front of the desk stood an officer, bolt upright with a large folio in his hand. Two or three local government officials were there, among them a man named Larass, whom we knew, who was smoking a fat cigar. There were also four or five higher police officers in uniform. They all looked at us disdainfully but none said a word. It was a sinister atmosphere. We three had to sit down in front of the desk.

The brothers were told that the community members would be allowed to stay together and leave for either Liechtenstein or England. The Germans of military age, except for Karl Keiderling, had also been released from the military. Such leniency was surely a result of the intercession from England and America. However, there were still some financial questions to be resolved; in the meantime the three men of the Executive Committee would be taken into protective custody. They were driven over to the jail, and the heavy iron door banged shut behind them.

~

The community was waiting for the return of the brothers. Two o'clock came, four o'clock; David and Michael walked up the hill to the wood where they were to arrive. Then the car came that had taken them away.

"Where are the brothers?"

"They are not here," was the only answer. The officer ordered the whole community together. He announced that all must leave within twenty-four hours; that the men due for military service could go with them; that all common property was confiscated and must not be touched.

Just at that moment Michael Horsch arrived to deliver the $117.00 from the Mennonite Service Committee in America as aid to the stricken Bruderhof. Seeing that the Gestapo had taken over, Michael was quick to disassociate himself from the Bruderhof. He used the "Heil Hitler" salute, and when he talked with the officers, he believed their allegations of poor management and failure to pay debts; he returned home with the $117.00 still in his pocket.

More detrimental than the loss of his financial contribution was the account of the dissolution of the Bruderhof that Michael wrote to his brother John Horsch and that circulated for years among reputable Mennonite scholars. The June 15/July 1 issue of the Mennonite *Gemeindeblatt* printed Horsch's account. He asserted that neither Mennonites nor Hutterites had been expelled from Germany; community members had simply been told to return home and look for work there. He also maintained that the government officials had dealt with Bruderhof members in a "protective and benevolent manner." The whole action had been undertaken by the German government "*not* because of the members' religious position but for economic and practical reasons," specifically, the need to compensate the Rhön Bruderhof's creditors.

At 6:00 in the evening of April 16, three buses arrived. Because of the bad roads they could not come nearer than three-quarters of a mile from the community grounds. It had been raining almost all day, but just then the sun came out—a small encouragement. The little group set out, carrying the babies and invalid Julia and whatever else they could. They were taken under guard to the train station.

David Hofer, Michael Waldner, and Hella Römer, the bookkeeper, returned to the forsaken compound. Emmy Arnold expressed in a letter the deep gratitude all felt for the presence of these two men:

> It is a divine blessing to have the two Hutterian brothers with us at just this hour. I often have to think of how shortly before his death Papa said to me, "You will see: if an hour of direst need should come upon you in the community, the Hutterian brothers will come to the rescue—that is what I achieved by my one-year stay in America!"[15]

22

May to July 1937

THANKS TO THE GRACE and protection of God, all members of the Bruderhof found their way to safety. A small group arrived at the Alm Bruderhof without incident on April 17. The larger group, which included the wives and children of the three men held in prison, headed for England. However, it would take some weeks to obtain the papers and financial guarantee required by the English Home Office. The refugees went first to Holland where their good friend Jacob ter Meulen at The Hague arranged for their accommodation at the Brotherhood House in Bilthoven. Food and clothing were provided; no expense was spared.[1] Two months later, in mid June, they were finally able to travel to the Cotswold Bruderhof.

The two American Hutterites had stayed on in Germany to support Hans Meier, Karl Keiderling, and Hannes Boller in jail and Hella Römer, in effect under house arrest on the Rhön Bruderhof as the community's bookkeeper. In the Fulda jail a new criminal charge was brought against the three men. They were accused of valuating the property too high and of deceiving and swindling their creditors.[2] This would clear the Nazis of being accused of persecuting Christians. Unfortunately, this charge of fraud was believed and repeated by many.

Hella was released on May 12 and went to the Alm Bruderhof. Meanwhile, several people, including Quakers, relatives of Hans Meier in Switzerland, and the Bruderhof's lawyer, Dr. Eisenberg, were working to free the three men.

In Holland, the Bruderhof made the acquaintance of a remarkable man, Frank Gheel van Gildemeester, who agreed to help. He was a Dutch fish merchant who had worked with the Quakers feeding hungry children in Germany. Later he began on his own to free prisoners held for political or conscientious reasons. After World War I he freed German nationals from French prisons. He was known by people in prominent places.

Gildemeester appeared in the jail in Fulda. He showed the brothers a large silver medal that he had received from the Gestapo chief Himmler personally which authorized him to visit any German prison at any time. He was working at the time to get three Nazis out of a Spanish prison; in return he would free the three Bruderhof men.

Gildemeester and Dr. Eisenberg went to see the grocer, who wrote a statement that he did not feel defrauded by the Bruderhof; he had actually done a profitable business with them. Then Gildemeester showed his medal to the district administrator and threatened to go to Himmler if the prisoners were not released.

The court annulled its previous decision. It declared the Bruderhof innocent of fraud and cancelled the arrest warrant for the three members of the Executive Committee.

On Saturday, June 26, an SS man opened the cell door and bellowed, "Meier, Boller, Keiderling—out!" They were told to get into a black car outside. Had they been acquitted by the civil court only to be taken to concentration camp? The driver gave Hans Meier a note from Dr. Eisenberg telling them to get into this car, take a train to the town of Königstein, and go to a certain hotel. Arriving at the hotel, they heard English being spoken, and then instructions to go to a certain room. There they met four members of the Society of Friends, two German and two English, who operated a rest house for people needing respite from conflicts with the regime.[3]

They were not yet out of danger, but eventually they made it across the border into Holland. They were met by Adolf and Martha Braun in Rotterdam and took the ferry to England. They arrived at the Cotswold Bruderhof on July 2. At the celebration that night they told of their escape. Hannes described what all three of them felt:

> During the eleven weeks we were separated from the community, it became clear to us again and again that love, complete love, casts out all fear. We often exchanged thoughts concerning the possibilities. However strong our longing was to live, witnessing to the outside world together with our brothers and sisters, we felt just as strongly that the other possibility [that of dying a martyr's death], even though much harder, meant at least as much or would be an even greater grace of God. We felt that God

really sees the need of mankind and that his love wishes to help us; this was shown to us very clearly in what happened. It moved us deeply to think how many hundreds or thousands of people are in prison for similar reasons as we were! And we felt that we need to have an even stronger urge than ever to search out and visit these people.[4]

The Cotswold Bruderhof published a newsletter that they sent to their friends and supporters:

> When the Rhön Bruderhof was taken from us we experienced death—a cold and cruel death, but how can we describe the wonderful experience which followed? The gathering of so many people at the Cotswold Bruderhof, in spite of the many practical difficulties it involved, has been a blessing which cannot be overestimated...
>
> Our greatest joy is that the catastrophe of the Rhön Bruderhof has enlarged our contact with mankind. Apart from England, we have found a deep response to the witness in Holland; also in Belgium, Sweden, and Switzerland the interest is growing. We realize clearly that death and resurrection belong together; new life has come to us now that our witness in Germany has come to an end.

∼

The Rhön Bruderhof was auctioned on September 29, 1937. After the war, the Bruderhof filed a claim for restitution with the German government. The proceedings dragged on for several years, but the community was eventually able to collect compensation for the land, inventory, and many individual personal claims. The following court decision of November 6, 1951, makes plain the nature of the National Socialist persecution of the community and thus provides a fitting conclusion to this text:

> This court has no reservation in recognizing that the Rhön Bruderhof was persecuted by National Socialism because of its world view [*Weltanschauung*]. This came about not only because of the attitude of the Bruderhof in regards to military service, but because their Christian and humanitarian principles stood in irreconcilable opposition to National Socialism. That the government agencies of the Third Reich should have tried to undermine the Bruderhof wherever they could is consistent with their

approach to eradicate opponents. The dissolution of the Rhön Bruderhof under the Reich president's order for the Protection of the Nation and State permits no doubt that this was active persecution in its full meaning as defined in the Persecution Act. This court also holds no reservation that the Bruderhof would have overcome its heavy burden of debt if National Socialism had not curtailed its activities.[5]

∼

Seventy-five years have past since Eberhard Arnold died. Many of the community's admirers doubted that the Bruderhof would survive his death. His friend, the Anabaptist historian Robert Friedmann, wrote: "Now it will be shown whether the strength that lay in what he did was so powerful and impersonal that his work will continue. I hope so, and I believe it."[6] Although the years brought physical difficulties and spiritual struggles, again and again his followers found renewal by returning to the solid foundation Eberhard Arnold had built on the rock of Jesus Christ. Emmy lived as a widow for forty-five years and to the end of her life brought her husband's witness alive. In his farewell letter to her, Eberhard had written words that continue to give inspiration and purpose to the members of the Bruderhof communities:

> How small in itself is the life of an individual; how small is the family life of husband and wife with their children; how small also the circle of friends who feel drawn to each other on a personal level; how small are the individual departments like the kitchen or the sewing room or the office; and finally, how small is the whole Sparhof with all its little souls!
>
> But how great are God and His Kingdom! How great is the historical hour of world crisis, of world suffering, and world catastrophe; and yet how much greater is God's hour of world judgment and Christ's hour of coming redemption! How burning should be our longing to learn more and more about all these things, to grasp them ever more deeply. And how ardently we should expect and long for the day itself, the coming day, the liberating and uniting day![7]

Notes

Prologue

1. Courtesy Berlin, Bundesarchiv, Abteilung Deutsches Reich (BArch R 5101/23410 [fol. 237]).

Notes to chapter 1

1. Eberhard Arnold and Emmy von Hollander, *Love Letters*, 4.
2. Karl Kupisch, *Studenten entdecken die Bibel*, 91.
3. Eberhard Arnold, quoted by Emmy Arnold in *Joyful Pilgrimage*, 150–51.
4. Kutter, *They Must*, 78–79.
5. Kutter, 80–81.
6. Eberhard Arnold, unpublished transcript, 22 September 1935 (EA 481a).
7. Eberhard Arnold, unpublished transcript, November 1917 (EA 17/13).
8. Eberhard Arnold to Fritz Böhm, 13 November 1920.
9. *Sonnenlieder,* 174–75, 208.
10. Eberhard Arnold, unpublished transcript, October 1931 (EA 31/31).
11. Baum, *Against the Wind*, 122.
12. Eberhard Arnold, "Abwehr und Angriff im Wahlkampf," *Das neue Werk,* 1920/21 (EA 21/33).
13. Heinrich Arnold, unpublished transcript, 17 January 1980.
14. Berber, *Zwischen Macht und Gewissen,* 31–32.
15. Emmy Arnold, unpublished memoirs, "Memories of My Early Years."
16. Vollmer, *Die Neuwerkbewegung 1919–1935,* 54.
17. Boeckh, "Sehnsucht und Erfüllung in der Jugendbewegung," in *Junge Saat.*
18. Körber, "Zur Frage des Bundes" in Antje Vollmer, *Die Neuwerkbewegung 1919–1935,* 112.
19. Emmy Arnold, *Joyful Pilgrimage,* 38.
20. Arnold and von Hollander, *Love Letters,* 132–33.

21. Arnold and von Hollander, *Love Letters*, 145–46.
22. Eberhard Arnold to Friedrich Kleemann, 27 September 1920.
23. Eberhard Arnold to Frau Wally Classen, 21 October 1920.
24. Georg Barth, diary entry, October 1977.
25. Eberhard Arnold, unpublished transcript, December 1934 (EA 34/31).
26. Eberhard Arnold, "Der Prophet der neuen jüdischen Bewegung. Martin Buber und seine Religiösität," *Die Furche*, November 1917, 46–48 (EA 17/11).
27. Hans Hartmann, book review in *Die Christliche Welt*, Marburg, 19 June 1922.
28. Max Wolf to Dr. Mainzer, 20 June 1921.
29. Unpublished transcript, 28 August 1932 (EA 17).
30. Eberhard Arnold, *God's Revolution*, 113–14.
31. Eberhard Arnold to Lotte Wilmers, 27 September 1923.
32. Eberhard Arnold, unpublished transcript, 18 June 1933 (EA 106).
33. Eberhard Arnold, unpublished transcript, 26 December 1934 (EA 316).
34. Hutterian Brethren, ed., *Brothers Unite*, 186.
35. Eberhard Arnold, in Johann Christoph Arnold, *Eberhard Arnold: Selected Writings*, 152–54.

Notes to chapter 2

1. Eberhard Arnold to Brother Lutz, 30 January 1923.
2. Hans-Hermann Arnold to Hardy Arnold, 24 June 1932.
3. Eberhard Arnold, unpublished transcript, 31 December 1932 (EA 53).
4. Annemarie Arnold, unpublished transcript, March 27, 1977.
5. Emmy Arnold to Hardy Arnold, 30 January 1933.
6. Heinrich Arnold, unpublished transcript, August 18, 1973.
7. Eberhard Arnold, unpublished transcript, 26 March 1933 (EA 85).
8. "Eine Lebensgemeinschaft 'Christlicher Kommunisten': Ein Besuch auf dem Bruderhof," *Frankfurter Zeitung und Handelsblatt*, 10 February 1933.
9. Hardy Arnold, unpublished transcript, 10 January 1985.
10. Klaus Scholder, *The Churches and the Third Reich, Volume 1*, 452–53.
11. Edith Arnold, unpublished memoirs, "My Way."
12. Edith Boeker, diary entry for 9 July 1932, quoted by Hardy Arnold in unpublished memoirs, "Edith Arnold: Wir sind wie Sterne."
13. Hardy Arnold, unpublished memoirs, "Eberhard Claus Arnold," 1935.

14. Edith Boeker, quoted by Hardy Arnold in "Edith Arnold: Wir sind wie Sterne."
15. The entire report of this trip comes from Eberhard's report at home, unpublished transcript, February 1933 (EA 68).
16. Eberhard Arnold, unpublished transcript, 26 March 1933 (EA 86).

Notes to chapter 3

1. Eberhard Arnold, "Leo Tolstoy and Leonhard Ragaz: Commemorating Tolstoy's 100th and Ragaz's 60th Birthdays," *Die Wegwarte*, 4. Jahrgang, 9./12. Heft; Juni/September 1928, 151–53 (EA 28/8).
2. Hans Meier, *Solange das Licht brennt*.
3. Unpublished transcript, 16 October 1932 (EA 23).
4. Eberhard Arnold, unpublished transcript, 16 March 1933 (EA 77).
5. Eberhard Arnold, unpublished transcript, 16 March 1933 (EA 77).
6. Leonhard Ragaz to the Bruderhof, 22 February 1933.
7. Eberhard Arnold to Leonhard Ragaz, 9 March 1933.
8. Eberhard Arnold, unpublished transcript, 2 March 1933 (EA 71a).
9. Richard J. Evans, *The Coming of the Third Reich*, 321.
10. "Die Regierungserklärung," *Frankfurter Zeitung und Handelsblatt*, 24 March 1933.
11. Max Domarus, *Hitler: Speeches and Proclamations*, 275–85.
12. Evans, *The Coming of the Third Reich*, 353.
13. Unpublished transcript, 25 March 1933 (EA 33/100). (Original transcription is incomplete.)
14. Eberhard Arnold, unpublished transcript, 26 March 1933 (EA 85).
15. Trudi Hüssy, unpublished memoirs, "Children in Bruderhof Life."
16. Eberhard Arnold, unpublished transcript, 28 March 1933 (EA 33/116).
17. *Eberhard Arnold: A Testimony*, 90–91.
18. Kurt Zimmermann, unpublished memoirs.
19. Eberhard Arnold, *Innerland*, 247.
20. Eberhard Anold, *Innerland*, 286–87.
21. Eberhard Arnold, *Innerland*, 266–67.
22. Eberhard Arnold, *Innerland*, 276.
23. Eberhard Arnold, unpublished transcript, 1933 (EA 33/33).
24. Eberhard Arnold, unpublished transcript, 19 April 1933 (EA 33/104).
25. Hardy Arnold to Elias Walter, 27 April 1933.

Notes to chapter 4

1. Eberhard Arnold, unpublished transcript, 1 May 1933 (EA 33/106).
2. Emmy Arnold to Hardy Arnold, 2 May 1933.
3. Edith Boeker to Hardy Arnold, 3 May 1933.
4. Eberhard Arnold, unpublished transcript, June 1933 (EA 101).
5. Heinrich Arnold, unpublished transcript, 26 July 1973.
6. Evans, *The Third Reich in Power*, 16.
7. Eberhard Arnold, unpublished transcript, 7 May 1933 (EA 33/107 and 33/109).
8. Leonhard Ragaz, "Zur Weltlage," 5 April 1933, *Neue Wege: Blätter für Religiöse Arbeit*, Jahrgang 1933, 174–96.
9. Ragaz, "Zur Weltlage," 10 May 1933, *Neue Wege: Blätter für Religiöse Arbeit*, Jahrgang 1933, 252.
10. Eberhard Arnold to Robert Friedmann, 13 February 1934.
11. Unpublished transcript, 15 May 1933 (EA 33/6).
12. Eberhard Arnold, unpublished transcript, 13 May 1933 (EA 33/7).
13. Unpublished transcript, 28 May 1933 (EA 33/67).
14. Eberhard Arnold, unpublished transcript, 28 May 1933 (EA 33/67).
15. Trudi Hüssy, unpublished memoirs, "Children in Bruderhof Life."
16. Eberhard Arnold, unpublished transcript, 1933 (EA 33/78).
17. Unpublished transcript, 11 June 1933 (EA 33/54).
18. Eberhard Arnold, *Love and Marriage in the Spirit*, 55–56.

Notes to chapter 5

1. Rabbi David G. Dalin, *The Myth of Hitler's Pope*, 59.
2. Klaus Scholder, *The Churches and the Third Reich, Volume 1*, 326–27.
3. Scholder, *The Churches and the Third Reich, Volume 1*, 332.
4. Götz Aly and Karl Heinz Roth, *The Nazi Census*, 56.
5. Eberhard Arnold, unpublished transcript, 16 June 1933 (EA 104).
6. Eberhard Arnold, unpublished transcript, 30 June 1933 (EA 33/101).
7. Edith Boeker to Hardy Arnold, 11 July 1933.
8. Eberhard Arnold, unpublished transcript, 13 July 1933 (EA 119a).
9. Eberhard Arnold, unpublished transcript, 17 July 1933 (EA 33/23).
10. Susi Fros, unpublished memoirs.
11. Eberhard Arnold, unpublished transcript, 26 July 1933 (EA 125).
12. Emmy Arnold to Hardy Arnold, 9 May 1933.

13. Emmy Arnold to Heinrich Arnold, 26 September 1933.
14. Eberhard Arnold, unpublished transcript, 3 June 1933 (EA 33/40).
15. Eberhard Arnold, unpublished transcript, 20 August 1933 (EA 146).
16. Elias Walter to Hans Zumpe, 12 August 1933.
17. Eberhard Arnold, unpublished transcript, 16 August 1933 (EA 144).
18. Eberhard Arnold, unpublished transcript, 3 September 1933 (EA 33/18).
19. Eberhard Arnold, unpublished transcript, 3 October 1933 (EA 162).
20. Eberhard Arnold, unpublished transcript, 23 September 1933 (EA 157).
21. Edith Boeker to Hardy Arnold, Sunday [17 September] 1933.
22. Eberhard Arnold, unpublished transcript (EA 33/59).
23. Emmy Arnold to Eberhard Arnold, 28 September 1933.
24. Edith Boeker to Hardy Arnold, 2 October 1933.
25. Rufus M. Jones, *George Fox: An Autobiography*, 212–13.
26. Jones, 276.
27. Eberhard Arnold, unpublished transcript, 4 September 1933 (EA 33/34).
28. Hardy Arnold to Edith Boeker, 16 October 1933.
29. Hardy Arnold to Edith Boeker, 10 November 1933.
30. Edith Boeker to Hardy Arnold, [1933].

Notes to chapter 6

1. Richard J. Evans, *The Third Reich in Power*, 618.
2. Eberhard Arnold, unpublished transcript, 21 October 1933 (EA 170).
3. Eberhard Arnold, unpublished transcript, 22 October 1933 (EA 172).
4. Alfred Gneiting, letter, 17 August 1984.
5. Heinrich Arnold, unpublished transcript, 22 November 1978.
6. Jonathan Zimmerman, MD, "An Account of Eberhard Arnold's Last Two Years," 1995 (unpublished).
7. Hans Meier, unpublished transcript, 15 October 1990.
8. Edith Boeker to Hardy Arnold, 12 November 1933.
9. Unpublished transcript, 11 November 1933 (EA 180a).
10. Hans Meier, unpublished transcript, 26 April 1988.

Notes to chapter 7

1. Edith Boeker to Hardy Arnold, 13 November 1933.
2. Eberhard Arnold, unpublished transcript, 12 November 1933 (EA 181).

3. *Fuldaer Zeitung*, 14 November 1933.
4. The following accounts are compiled from various unpublished archival documents.
5. Hans-Hermann Arnold to Hardy Arnold, 18 December 1933.
6. Hans Zumpe, unpublished memoirs, "Our Confrontation with the National Socialist State."

Notes to chapter 8

1. Trudi Hüssy, unpublished memoirs, "Children in Bruderhof Life."
2. Hans-Hermann Arnold to Hardy Arnold, 29 November 1933.
3. Trudi Hüssy, unpublished memoirs, "Children in Bruderhof Life."
4. Hans Meier, unpublished report of trip to Switzerland and Czechoslovakia in November 1933.
5. Hans Meier, letter to friends, 9 December 1933.
6. Leonhard Ragaz to Thomas Masaryk, President of Czechoslovakia, 22 November 1933.
7. Hans Zumpe, unpublished memoirs, "Our Confrontation with the National Socialist State."
8. Jonathan Zimmerman, MD, "An Account of Eberhard Arnold's Last Two Years," 1995 (unpublished).
9. Hans Meier, transcription of shorthand notes, 18 December 1933.
10. Hans Meier, unpublished memoirs.
11. Hans Meier, unpublished memoirs.
12. Hans Zumpe, unpublished memoirs, "Our Confrontation with the National Socialist State."
13. Emmy Arnold to Betty Schmidt, 15 December 1933.
14. Eberhard Arnold to Hans-Hermann Arnold, 10 December 1933.
15. Eberhard Arnold, unpublished transcript, 11 January 1934 (EA 201).

Notes to chapter 9

1. Dr. J. W. Hauer to Hardy Arnold, 2 January 1934.
2. Anna Schmidt to Hans Meier, 3 January 1934.
3. Eberhard Arnold to Lene Schulz, 15 January 1934.
4. Hardy Arnold, unpublished transcript, 10 January 1985.
5. Wolfgang Loewenthal to Hardy Arnold, 10 February 1934.
6. Lene Schulz to Hardy Arnold, 28 January 1934.

7. Eberhard Arnold to Dr. Selig, 29 December 1933.
8. Emmy Arnold to Eberhard Arnold, 9 September 1930; 21 January 1931.
9. Eberhard Arnold, unpublished transcript, [26 July 1932] (EA 32/17).
10. Eberhard Arnold, unpublished transcript, 28 August 1932 (EA 16).
11. *Der Wahrheitszeuge*, A Baptist periodical for church and home, Kassel, 16 October 1932.
12. Eberhard Arnold to Dr. Darré, Reich minister of agriculture, 14 December 1933.
13. Eberhard Arnold to Dr. Selig, 29 December 1933.
14. Dr. Saure, Reich ministry for food and agriculture, to Eberhard Arnold, 2 January 1934.
15. Eberhard Arnold to Hardy Arnold, 27 January 1934.
16. Eberhard Arnold to Hardy Arnold, 27 January 1934.
17. Hans Zumpe, unpublished memoirs, "Our Confrontation with the National Socialist State."
18. Hans Zumpe, unpublished memoirs, "Our Confrontation with the National Socialist State."
19. Courtesy Berlin, Bundesarchiv, Abteilung Deutsches Reich (BArch R 5101/23410 [fol. 140]).
20. Courtesy Berlin, Bundesarchiv, Abteilung Deutsches Reich (BArch R 5101/23410 [fol. 198]).
21. Dr. Burkhardt to Eberhard Arnold, 5 January 1934.
22. Eberhard Arnold to Baron von Mombart, 9 January 1934.
23. Eberhard Arnold to the mayors (undated draft, *an den Bürgermeister*, evidently sent to the mayors of several towns).
24. Emmy Arnold to Hans-Hermann Arnold, 22 January 1934.
25. Emmy Arnold to Hans-Hermann Arnold, 3 February 1934.
26. Karl Keiderling to Lene Schulz, 20 January 1934.
27. Edith Boeker to Hardy Arnold, 26 January 1934.
28. Edith Boeker to Hardy Arnold, 30 January 1934.
29. Hannes Boller to Hardy Arnold, 14 February 1934.

Notes to chapter 10

1. Eberhard Arnold to Hardy Arnold, 27 February 1934.
2. Emmy Arnold to Hardy Arnold, 5 March 1934.
3. Eberhard and Emmy Arnold to Walter and Trudi Hüssy, 21 March 1934.
4. Hans-Hermann Arnold to Hardy Arnold, 9 March 1934.

5. Eberhard Arnold to all brothers and sisters, 23 October 1934.
6. Edith Boeker, diary entry for 28 March 1934.
7. Eberhard Arnold to all at the Rhön Bruderhof, Easter 1934.
8. Emmy Arnold to Trudi Hüssy, 5 April 1934.
9. Eberhard Arnold, unpublished transcript, 8 April 1934 (EA 211).
10. Eberhard Arnold to Jerg Waldner, 12 April 1934.
11. Emmy Arnold to Elisabeth Arnold, 25 May 1934.
12. Eberhard Arnold, unpublished transcript, 31 May 1934 (EA 230).

Notes to chapter 11

1. Klaus Scholder, *The Churches and the Third Reich*, Volume II, 140.
2. Hardy Arnold, unpublished memoirs.
3. J. S. Conway, *Nazi Persecution of the Churches*, 85.
4. Hardy Arnold, unpublished memoirs.
5. Hardy Arnold to Eberhard Arnold, 14 June 1934.
6. Eberhard Bethge, *Dietrich Bonhoeffer*, 332.
7. Eberhard Arnold to Hardy Arnold, 26 June 1934.
8. Hardy Arnold to Eberhard Arnold, 3 July 1934.
9. Bethge, *Dietrich Bonhoeffer*, 336.
10. Bethge, *Dietrich Bonhoeffer*, 559.
11. Evans, *The Coming of the Third Reich*, 334.
12. Evans, *The Third Reich in Power*, 37–38.
13. Hans Meier, unpublished transcript, 3 May 1988.
14. Eberhard Arnold, unpublished transcript, 6 July 1934 (EA 234).
15. http://www.celle-im-nationalsozialismus.de/Stationen/Landeserbhofgericht.html
16. Eberhard Arnold, unpublished document, "Stammbaumerklärung und Geschichte der Familien Arnold/Hollander," 1934.
17. Eberhard Arnold to Elisabeth Arnold, 18 June 1934.
18. Dr. Blanke, 2 August 1934.
19. Eberhard Arnold, unpublished transcript, 24 June 1934 (EA 34/20).
20. Eberhard Arnold, unpublished transcript, 1 July 1934 (EA 34/22).

Notes to chapter 12

1. Eberhard Arnold, "Christians and the State," *The Plough*, Spring 1940. Bible citations changed to RSV translation.

Notes to chapter 13

1. Hermann Arnold, unpublished memoirs.
2. Hermann Arnold, diary excerpts, 1934.
3. Hermann Arnold, unpublished memoirs.
4. *When the Time Was Fulfilled*, 180–87.
5. Eberhard Arnold, letter to the Rhön Bruderhof, 25–26 July 1934 (EA 34/64).
6. Eberhard Arnold, *Vom Leben der Bruderhöfer* (Fulda: Eberhard Arnold-Verlag G.m.b.H., 1934) (EA 34/11).
7. Eberhard Arnold, unpublished transcript, 9 August 1934 (EA 262).
8. Eberhard Arnold, unpublished transcript, 17 August 1934 (EA 267).
9. Unpublished transcript, 19 August 1934 (EA 270).
10. Evans, *The Third Reich in Power*, 43.
11. Eberhard Arnold to Hans Zumpe and Hannes Boller, 9 August 1934.
12. Eberhard Arnold, unpublished transcript, 9 August 1934 (EA 262).
13. Hans Zumpe, unpublished memoirs, "Our Confrontation with the National Socialist State."
14. Trudi Hüssy, unpublished memoirs, "Hochzeiten in der Zeit Eberhard Arnolds."
15. Kathleen Hamilton to her mother, fall 1934.
16. Eberhard Arnold, unpublished transcript, 24 September 1934 (EA 296).
17. Eberhard Arnold, unpublished transcript, 24 September 1934 (EA 294).

Notes to chapter 14

1. Eberhard Arnold to Hans Zumpe, 7 November 1934.
2. Eberhard Arnold, unpublished transcript, 20 October 1934 (EA 305).
3. Eberhard Arnold, unpublished transcript, 11 October 1934 (EA 34/88).
4. August and Gertrud Dyroff to Hans Zumpe and all at the Alm Bruderhof, 11 October 1934.
5. Eberhard Arnold to Hans Zumpe, 7 November 1934.
6. Eberhard Arnold, fragmentary notes of meeting, 1 November 1934 (EA 34/39).
7. Eberhard Arnold, unpublished transcript, early November (EA 34/92).
8. Eberhard Arnold to Hardy Arnold, 24 November 1934.
9. Eberhard Arnold, unpublished transcript, 21 November 1934 (EA 311) (condensed).

10. Eberhard Arnold, unpublished transcript, 12 December 1934 (EA 34/70).
11. Emmy Arnold to Elisabeth Arnold, 28 December 1934.
12. Eberhard Arnold, *Vom Leben der Bruderhöfer*.

Notes to chapter 15

1. Unpublished transcript, 5 January 1935 (EA 325).
2. Siegfried Miers to Martha Miers, 23 January 1935.
3. Eberhard Arnold, unpublished transcript, 9 January 1934 (EA 329b).
4. Hans Zumpe, unpublished memoirs, "Our Confrontation with the National Socialist State."
5. Unpublished transcript, 1 March 1935 (EA 334).
6. Annemarie Wächter to Heinrich Arnold, 3 March 1935.
7. Annemarie Wächter to Heinrich Arnold, 3 March 1935.
8. Annemarie Wächter to Heinrich Arnold, 4 March 1935.
9. Unpublished transcript, 7 March 1935 (EA 342).
10. Unpublished transcript, 8 March 1935 (EA 344).
11. Annemarie Wächter to Heinrich Arnold, 8 March 1935.
12. Eberhard Arnold, unpublished transcript, 8 March 1935 (EA 343).
13. Unpublished transcript, 11 March 1935 (EA 345).
14. Kurt Zimmermann, unpublished journal, 1934-1938.
15. Unpublished interview, September 1984.
16. Annemarie Wächter to Heinrich Arnold, 17 March 1935.
17. Emy-Margret Zumpe, diary entry for 16 March 1935.
18. Josef Stängl, unpublished memoirs.
19. Eberhard Arnold, unpublished transcript, 17 March 1935 (EA 35/70).
20. Winifred Dyroff, unpublished memoirs.
21. Kathleen Hamilton to her mother, 17 March 1934.
22. Kathleen Hamilton to her mother, 23 March 1934.
23. Eberhard Arnold, unpublished transcript, 24 March 1935 (EA 346a).
24. Marianne Zimmermann, unpublished memoirs.
25. Edith Arnold to Hardy Arnold, 3 April 1935.

Notes to chapter 16

1. Eberhard Arnold, unpublished transcript, 23 February 1935 (EA 35/63).
2. Eberhard Arnold, unpublished transcript, 24 March 1935 (EA 347).

Notes to pages 229–51   293

3. Hardy Arnold, unpublished memoirs, "Journey to Holland, England, and Scotland."
4. Eberhard Arnold to Hans Zumpe, 5 May 1935.
5. Eberhard Arnold to Hans Zumpe, 18 April 1935.
6. Eberhard Arnold, unpublished transcript, 26 May 1935 (EA 365).
7. Kathleen Hamilton to her mother, 7 June 1935.
8. Eberhard Arnold, unpublished transcript, 22 July 1935 (EA 415).
9. Eberhard Arnold, unpublished transcript, 24 July 1935 (EA 416).
10. Eberhard Arnold, unpublished transcript, 19 July 1935 (EA 409).
11. Heinrich Arnold, unpublished transcript, 26 July 1973.

Notes to chapter 17

1. Eberhard Arnold, from a series of unpublished transcripts, October 1935 (EA 486, EA 491, EA 491a, EA 491b, EA 491c, EA 508, EA 509).

Notes to chapter 18

1. Emmy Arnold, unpublished document, "Darmstadt Report."
2. Emmy Arnold, unpublished document, "Darmstadt Report."
3. Emmy Arnold, unpublished document, "Darmstadt Report."

Notes to chapter 19

1. Eberhard Arnold, unpublished transcript, 23 December 1934 (EA 312).
2. Heinrich Arnold to Annemarie Wächter, 26 March 1935.
3. Hans-Hermann Arnold to Gertrud Löffler, 25 March 1936.
4. Emmy Arnold, unpublished document, "Darmstadt Report."
5. Moni Barth to Hardy and Edith Arnold, 27 December 1935.
6. Moni Barth to Emmy Arnold, 7 January 1936.
7. Eberhard Arnold to Hans and Emy-Margret Zumpe, 14 November 1935.
8. Arnold Mason, unpublished memoirs.
9. Kurt Zimmermann, unpublished document, "Survey and Diary Notes 1933–1938."
10. Hans Meier to the Cotswold Bruderhof, 24 March 1936.
11. Edna Percival to Nancy Watkins, 5 May 1936.
12. Hans Zumpe to Elias Walter, 15 January 1936.
13. Hans Zumpe to Hutterian elders, 27 June 1936.

14. Hans Zumpe to Hutterian elders, 27 June 1936.

Notes to chapter 20

1. Evans, *The Third Reich in Power*, 571.
2. Conway, 196.
3. Courtesy Berlin, Bundesarchiv, Abteilung Deutsches Reich (BArch R 5101/23410 [fol. 131–32]).
4. Courtesy Berlin, Bundesarchiv, Abteilung Deutsches Reich (BArch R 5101/23410 [fol. 133–38]).
5. Courtesy Berlin, Bundesarchiv, Abteilung Deutsches Reich (BArch R 5101/23410 [fol. 140–41]).
6. Courtesy Berlin, Bundesarchiv, Abteilung Deutsches Reich (BArch R 5101/23410 [fol. 204–12]).
7. Courtesy Berlin, Bundesarchiv, Abteilung Deutsches Reich (BArch R 5101/23410 [fol. 173]).
8. Courtesy Berlin, Bundesarchiv, Abteilung Deutsches Reich (BArch R 5101/23410 [fol. 200–203]).
9. Kathleen Hamilton to her mother, 16 September 1936.
10. Kathleen Hamilton to her mother, 21 October 1936.
11. Kathleen Hamilton to her mother, 13 November 1936.
12. Leo Dreher to Emmy Arnold, 20 September 1936.
13. Burgomaster Zeiher, 11 September 1936.
14. Edith Arnold to Hardy Arnold, 15 September 1536.
15. The board of the Neuwerk Bruderhof to Burgomaster Zeiher.
16. Courtesy Berlin, Bundesarchiv, Abteilung Deutsches Reich (BArch R 5101/23410 [fol. 188–96]).
17. Trautel Dreher to Emy-Margret Zumpe, 11 October 1936.
18. August Dyroff, as reported by his wife Winifred, unpublished memoirs.
19. Courtesy Berlin, Bundesarchiv, Abteilung Deutsches Reich (BArch R 5101/23410 [fol. 204–12]).
20. Courtesy Berlin, Bundesarchiv, Abteilung Deutsches Reich (BArch R 5101/23410 [fol. 149–50]).
21. Margrit Meier to all brothers and sisters, 7 December 1936.
22. Harold Bender, "The New Hutterite Bruderhof in Germany," *The Christian Monitor*, 1931.
23. Emmy Barth, *No Lasting Home*, 195–98.

24. Courtesy Mennonite Church USA Archives, Goshen, IN. Ernst Correll to John Horsch and Harold Bender, 10 October 1936 (Hist. Mss. 1–278 H. S. Bender General Corr. 1931–38, Horsch, John: 1935–38, 8/2).
25. Courtesy Mennonite Church USA Archives, Goshen, IN. Clarence E. Pickett to Paul D. Sturge, 12 November 1936 (Hist. Mss. 1–278 H. S. Bender General Corr. 1931–38, Society of Brothers, 12/9).
26. Courtesy Mennonite Church USA Archives, Goshen, IN. Rufus M. Jones to Honorable Hans Luther, 30 November 1936 (Hist. Mss. 1–278 H. S. Bender General Corr. 1931–38, Society of Brothers, 12/9).
27. Edith Arnold to Emmy Arnold, 31 December 1936.

Notes to chapter 21

1. James I. Lichti, "Linking Bread and Sweat' to 'Blut und Boden': The Role of Stewardship Norms in the German Mennonite Response to the Dissolution of the Rhön Bruderhof," a paper presented at the Conrad Grebel College, Waterloo, Ontario, May 1990.
2. Karl Keiderling, unpublished memoirs.
3. August Dyroff, as reported by his wife Winifred, unpublished memoirs.
4. Edith Arnold to Emmy Arnold, 9 February 1937.
5. David Hofer to the church at home, 11 February 1937.
6. Courtesy Berlin, Bundesarchiv, Abteilung Deutsches Reich (BArch R 5101/23410 [fol. 221–22]).
7. Karl Keiderling, unpublished memoirs.
8. Karl Keiderling, unpublished memoirs.
9. See "Order of the Gestapo," in "Prologue" above. Courtesy Berlin, Bundesarchiv, Abteilung Deutsches Reich (BArch R 5101/23410 [fol. 237]).
10. Meier, *Solange das Licht brennt*.
11. Karl Keiderling, unpublished memoirs.
12. David Hofer, unpublished diary.
13. Karl Keiderling, unpublished memoirs.
14. Karl Keiderling, unpublished memoirs.
15. Emmy Arnold to Hans Zumpe, 2 May 1937.

Notes to chapter 22

1. Adolf Braun to the Alm and Cotswold Bruderhofs, 21 April 1937.
2. Karl Keiderling, unpublished memoirs.
3. Hans Meier, unpublished memoirs.

4. Hannes Boller, unpublished transcript, 2 July 1937.
5. Landgericht Kassel, WiK 1333 [6 Nov 1951], 13–14.
6. Robert Friedmann to Leonhard Ragaz, 27 December 1935.
7. Eberhard Arnold to Emmy Arnold, 13–14 November 1935.

Bibliography

ALL UNPUBLISHED DOCUMENTS CITED in the text are from Church Communities International Archives and Record Center, unless otherwise stated. For historical background extensive use was made of Richard J. Evans's three-volume history of the Third Reich. The author takes responsibility for all translations from the German.

Aly, Götz, and Karl Heinz Roth. *The Nazi Census: Identification and Control in the Third Reich*. Translated by Edwin Black. Philadelphia: Temple University Press, 2004.
Arnold, Eberhard, editor. *The Early Christians in Their Own Words*. Farmington, PA: Plough, 1997.
———. *Eberhard Arnold: A Testimony of Church Community from His Life and Writings*. Rifton, NY: Plough, 1973.
———. *God's Revolution: Justice, Community, and the Coming Kingdom*. Farmington, PA: Plough, 1997.
———. *Innerland: A Guide into the Heart of the Gospel*. Farmington, PA: Plough, 1999.
———. *Love and Marriage in the Spirit*. Rifton, NY: Plough, 1965.
Arnold, Eberhard, and Emmy von Hollander. *Love Letters*. Rifton, NY: Plough, 2007.
Arnold, Eberhard, et al. *When the Time Was Fulfilled: On Advent and Christmas*. Rifton, NY: Plough, 1965.
Arnold, Emmy. *A Joyful Pilgrimage: My Life in Community*. Farmington, PA: Plough, 1999.
———, compiler. *Sonnenlieder: Lieder für Naturfreude, Menschheitsfriede und Gottesgemeinschaft*. Sannerz and Leipzig: Eberhard Arnold, 1924.
Arnold, Johann Christoph, editor. *Eberhard Arnold: Selected Writings*. Maryknoll, NY: Orbis, 2000.
Barth, Emmy. *No Lasting Home: A Year in the Paraguayan Wilderness*. Rifton, NY: Plough, 2009.
Baum, Markus. *Against the Wind: Eberhard Arnold and the Bruderhof*. Farmington, PA: Plough, 1998.
Berber, Friedrich. *Zwischen Macht und Gewissen: Lebenserinnerungen*. Munich: Beck'sche, 1986.
Bethge, Eberhard. *Dietrich Bonhoeffer: Theologian, Christian, Contemporary*. London: Collins, 1970.
Bock, Paul, editor and translator. *Signs of the Kingdom: A Ragaz Reader*. Grand Rapids: Eerdmans, 1984.
Conway, J. S. *The Nazi Persecution of the Churches, 1933–1945*. Vancouver: Regent College Publishing, 2001.

Dalin, Rabbi David G. *The Myth of Hitler's Pope.* Washington, DC: Regnery, 2005.

Domarus, Max. *Hitler: Speeches and Proclamations, 1932–1945: The Chronicle of a Dictatorship,* vol. 1, *The Years 1932 to 1934.* Translated by Mary Fran Gilbert. London: I. B. Tauris, 1990.

Evans, Richard J. *The Coming of the Third Reich.* New York: Penguin, 2003.

———. *The Third Reich in Power.* New York: Penguin, 2005.

Hutterian Brethren, editor. *Brothers Unite: An Account of the Uniting of Eberhard Arnold and the Rhön Bruderhof with the Hutterian Church.* Ulster Park, NY: Plough, 1988.

Jones, Rufus M. *George Fox: An Autobiography.* Philadelphia: Ferris & Leach, 1904.

Kupisch, Karl. *Studenten entdecken die Bibel: Die Geschichte der Deutschen Christlichen Studenten-Vereinigung (DCSV).* Hamburg: Furche, 1964.

Kutter, Hermann. *They Must; or God and the Social Democracy: A Frank Word to Christian Men and Women.* Edited by Rufus W. Weeks. Chicago: Co-operative, 1908.

Meier, Hans. *Solange das Licht brennt: Lebensbericht eines Mitglieds der neuhutterischen Bruderhof-Gemeinschaft.* Switzerland: Brassel, 1990.

Ragaz, Leonhard. *Mein Weg, Band II.* Zurich: Diana, 1952.

———. *Signs of the Kingdom.* Edited and translated by Paul Bock. Grand Rapids: Eerdmans, 1984.

Scholder, Klaus. *The Churches and the Third Reich, Volume I: Preliminary History and the Time of Illusions 1918–1934.* London: SCM., 1987.

———. *The Churches and the Third Reich, Volume II: The Year of Disillusionment: 1934, Barmen and Rome.* Philadelphia: SCM, 1988.

Shirer, William L. *The Rise and Fall of the Third Reich: A History of Nazi Germany.* New York: Simon & Schuster, 1990.

Silverman, Dan P. *Hitler's Economy: Nazi Work Creation Programs, 1933–1936.* Boston: Harvard University Press, 1998.

Zehrer, Karl. *Evangelische Freikirchen und das "Dritte Reich."* Berlin: Evangelische, 1986.

Index

Alm Bruderhof, description, 184–85; draft resisters find refuge, 223–25; founding, 157–64; hostility toward, 234
American Friends Service Committee, 267–68
Anabaptists. *See* Hutterites, Mennonites
anti-Semitism, 23, 24, 48–49, 56; Arnold's attitude toward, 15–17. *See also* "blood and soil"
Arnold genealogy, 173–74
Arnold, Annemarie. *See* Wächter, Annemarie
Arnold, Eberhard (select entries only), 50th birthday, 69–70; leg fracture, 84–85, 121, 142, 162, 163, 184; personal letter, 201–2; death, 241–44
Arnold, Edith, birth of son, 231; letter from, 226, 261, 268; in *Rundrede*, 214–15. *See also* Boeker, Edith
Arnold, Emmy, 100, 102, 139, 229, 246, 277; description of Alm, 158–59; on Eberhard's death, 241–44; on Hitler's appointment, 29; letter from, 71, 77, 126, 161, 164; marriage, 4; at Mennonite World Conference, 266; in *Rundrede*, 43, 93, 209; description of Sannerz, 13; on the Sermon on the Mount, 10–11
Arnold, Hans-Hermann, 25, 244; Eberhard's letter to, 127; letter from, 24, 102–3, 109–10, 246; recuperation in Switzerland, 157
Arnold, Hardy, 25, 131, 244; in Birmingham, 78–80, 133; and Bonhoeffer, 166–70; contacts, 188–89; flight to England, 249; trip to England 1935, 227–29; Eberhard's letter to, 127, 157–58; marriage, 73, 194–95; on Quakers, 79–80; in Tübingen, 32–35; in Zurich, 52
Arnold, Heiner, 25, 63, 99, 100–101, 234, 244; agricultural school, 135; engagement for marriage, 206; flight to England, 250; on Hitler's appointment, 29–30; letter from, 245; in *Rundrede*, 43, 93
Arnold, Hermann (Eberhard's nephew), 183–88
Arnold, Monika, 25, 93, 246
Aryan Paragraph, 166

baptism, 13–14, 142–43
Barmen Confession, 166, 167
Barth, Georg, 25, 59; building design, 73; leadership, 85, 211,

Barth, Georg (cont.) 246; in *Rundrede*, 91, 209; sales trips, 175; description of Sannerz, 15
Barth, Karl, 166
Barth, Moni, 24, 100, 109, 241; letter from, 246–47; in *Rundrede*, 91
Beer-Hall Putsch, 22
Bender, Harold, 265–67
Berber, Fritz, 10
Berlin, 121–24, 200
Bilthoven, Brotherhood House, 127, 278
Birmingham, 78–80, 133
Blanke (lawyer), 174
"blood and soil," 139, 173–74
Bodelschwingh, Friedrich von, 64–65
Boeker, Edith (later Edith Arnold), description of Alm, 159–60; on J. W. Hauer, 33, 34; trip to Holland, 127–28; letter from, 55, 67, 75–76, 77, 90–91, 96; marriage, 73, 194–95; description of ordination, 143; in *Rundrede*, 92; visits Bruderhof, 34. *See also* Arnold, Edith
Bolck, Heinz, 247, 261
Boller, Else, 25
Boller, Hannes, 25, 106, 273; arrest, 1, 276; leadership, 85, 143, 188, 211; and Ragaz, 59; release from jail, 278–79; in *Rundrede*, 91, 209; trip to Berlin, 121–24
Bonhoeffer, Dietrich, 124, 166–70
book burning, 56
Braun, Adolf, 25, 59, 62, 99, 109, 158, 279; agricultural school, 135; in *Rundrede*, 44, 91; sales trips, 134, 174, 175
Braun, Martha, 25, 109, 159, 279

Bridgwater, Winifred, 189, 214, 274
Buber, Martin, 15–16
Burkhardt (district administrator), 61, 264; Arnold's letter to, 90, 114–19; letter forbidding hospitality, 140–41; report to Gestapo, 256

capitalism, 21
Catholic Church, 64, 178
children's home, Rhön Bruderhof, dissolved, 134–35
church (of believers), 14–15; defined by unity, 39–40; as embassy of God's Kingdom, 44, 66, 165, 176, 187–88, 201; prophetic task of, 188; as revelation of God's future, 186–87, 206–7; separate from state, 187
church (established), acquiescence to National Socialism, 73–74; Arnold's break with, 14, 67; as beast of the abyss, 181–82
communism, 32; Arnold's solidarity with, 7, 9; Hitler targets, 41
community, founding of, 13–15
concentration camps, 48, 57
Confessing Church, 178
Conrad, Karl (advisor on church affairs), 122; Arnold's letter to, 86–87, 119–20
Conway, John, 167, 253
Correll, Ernst, 266
Cotswold Bruderhof, 248–49; newsletter, 280
Cromwell, Oliver, 78, 179
Crous, Ernst, 124, 256–57

Dachau, 48
Darré, Richard Walther, 137, 173; Arnold's letter to, 138
Das neue Werk, 7
Die Furche, 4

Dreher, Leo and Trautel, 38, 260
Dreher, Trautel, 272; letter from, 260–61, 262–63
Dyroff, August, flight to England, 270; liable for military service, 261; report of raid, 263–64
Dyroff, August and Gertrud, letter from, 199–200

education, Bruderhof priority, 117; Nazi, 162. *See also* school
Education ministry, Arnold's letter to, 121
Eisenberg (lawyer), 278–79
Eisner, Kurt, 8, 15
embassy. *See* church (of believers), as embassy of God's kingdom
emigration, or martyrdom, 213–14; consideration of, 53, 103, 118, 128, 208, 227
Enabling Act, 35–36, 41–43
enemy, love to, 57–61, 68–69, 76, 90, 97, 116, 217–19
England, 78–80, 133; Arnold's trip to, 227–29; new members from, 189
Entailed Farm Law, 137, 173, 209
Erbhofgesetz. See Entailed Farm Law
Essertines, 111, 128

fascism, Arnold on, 177–78
Fellowship of Reconciliation, 228
Fierz, Olga, 232
First Law of Sannerz, 18
Fischli, Migg, 247
Fletcher, John, 229
flight, of draft-age men, 221–24; readiness for, 47; of school children, 132–33. *See also* emigration, consideration of
Foreign Ministry, Arnold's letter to, 120–21
Fox, George, 78

Frankfurter Zeitung, 31–32
Free German Youth, 9–10, 12
Friedemann, Werner, 222
Friedensburg (governor), 47
Friedmann, Robert, 57, 172, 281
Friends House, 228
Fry, Joan Mary, 228
Fuldaer Zeitung, 98

Gagern, Baron von, 41, 48, 61; wife of, 212
Gandhi, 166, 203, 210
Gemeentetag, 229
German Faith Movement, 33, 131
Gestapo, order to dissolve Rhön Bruderhof, 1; report on Rhön Bruderhof, 253–56, 264, 271
Gildemeester, Frank Gheel von, 278–79
Gleysteen, Jan, 228
Gneiting, Alfred, 99, 231; and Arnold's accident, 84–85; in *Rundrede*, 44, 93, 210; sales trips, 175
Goebbels, Joseph, 242, 253
Goldstein, Julius, 16
government, as beast of the abyss, 35, 59, 180–81; as instrument of God's wrath, 180; respect for, 35, 36, 46, 114, 193, 218
Gravenhorst, Susi, 34, 100
Grimm, Hans, 214

Hamilton, Kathleen, 189, 195, 274; letter from, 223–25, 231, 259–60; in *Rundrede*, 215
Hammacher (school inspector), 110
harvest festival 1933, 77
Hauer, Jakob Wilhelm, 32–33, 131–32
"Heil Hitler" salute, 24, 68, 74, 78, 177, 178, 211; discussion of, 87

Heim, Karl, 4, 32, 117; letter of support from, 106–7
Hildel, Rudi, 109
Hindenburg, death, 192; Arnold's letter to, 90; reelection 1932, 24
Hitler Youth, 24
Hitler, Adolf, 94; acknowledgment of his ideals, 58, 114–15; acknowledgment of his office, 86, 87, 193; appointed Reichskanzler, 28; Arnold's desire to meet, 43, 45, 46, 233; Arnold's letter to, 88–89; assumes title "Führer," 192–93; idolatry of, 24, 177; love to, 90, 210, 219–20; and National Socialist Party, 22; prayer for, 86; speech, 41–43, 172
Hofer, David, 262, 270–77
Holland, Arnold's trip to, 227–28
Hollander, Else von, 24
Hollander, von, coat of arms, 102; genealogy, 174
Hölz, Max, 122
Hoop, Josef (Prime Minister of Liechtenstein), 234
Horsch, John, 269
Horsch, Michael, 269, 277
hospitality curtailed, 140–42
Hoyland, Jack, 232
Hugenberg, Alfred, 29
Hüssy, Trudi, 25, 100; and children, 109; in *Rundrede*, 43, 92; school inspection, 110; description of wedding, 194–95
Hüssy, Walter, 135
Hutterites, Arnold's uniting with, 19–21, 82; arrival at Bruderhof, 270–72; letter to, 111–13, 128–30, 161–63; petition on Bruderhof's behalf, 262, 125–26; in Reformation, 204. *See also* Hofer, David; Waldner, Michael; Walter, Elias
Hütteroth, inspector, 99, 102; Arnold's letter to, 104–6
Hylkema, Teerd Oeds, 228

imperialism (England), 80
Innerland, 74, 86, 119; publication of, 75, 172; quoted, 49–50; signatures buried, 104, 163
isolation of Bruderhof, 83–84, 124

Jacob, Günther, 124
Jehle, Herbert, 168, 169, 170
Jehovah's Witnesses, 253
Jerschke (deputy governor), 140, 212
Jones, Rufus M., 267–68
Judaism, Arnold's appreciation of, 15–18

Kaiser, Fritz, 261
Kaiser, Otto, 247
Kapp Putsch, 8–9
Keiderling, Irmgard, 25
Keiderling, Karl, 25; arrest, 1, 276; description of baptism, 142–43; liable for military service, 261; release from jail, 278–79; last weeks at Rhön, 269–70, 271–72, 275; in *Rundrede*, 91
Keilhau, 56
Keller, Kaspar, 141, 247
Kellner (school superintendent), Arnold's letter to, 114–19
Kerrl, Hanns, 256
kibbutzniks, 17–18
kingdom of God, 19, 36, 175–76, 225–26
Kingsley Hall, 228
Klausener, Erich, 171
Kleine, Ludwig, 99, 210

Kleiner, Fritz, 104, 159, 247, 260; liable for military service, 261; in *Rundrede*, 92
Kleiner, Sekunda, 159, 260; in *Rundrede*, 91, 214
Kleinsasser, Joseph, 262
Klösshof. *See* Möller, Emil property
Körber, Norman, 12–13, 61
Kutter, Hermann, 5–6, 37

labor service, 55
Landauer, Gustav, 7, 15, 75
Lerchy, Julia, 159, 277
Lester, Doris, 190, 228; donation, 134; visit to Alm Bruderhof, 232
Lester, Muriel, 190, 228
Liebknecht, Karl, 7
Löber, Christian, 93
Loewenthal, Wolfgang, 109
London, Eberhard and Hardy in, 228
Lord's Supper at Alm Bruderhof, 161; at Rhön Bruderhof, 271–72; in Sannerz, 14
Loserth, Johann, 172
Luther (German ambassador), 267
Lutheran Church, 66, 178
Luxemburg, Rosa, 7, 15

Martin, Arno, 77, 59, 93, 99, 221, 275; agricultural school, 135; escape from Germany, 222; in *Rundrede*, 44, 92, 209–10
Martin, Ruth, 275
martyrdom, 229, 230; or emigration, 213–14; readiness for, 51, 67–68, 69, 76, 96–97, 199, 211–12, 216
Marxism. *See* communism
Masaryk, Thomas (president of Czechoslovakia), 113
Masereel, Frans, 123
Mason, Arnold, 264
Mason, Arnold and Gladys, 133, 189, 195; purchase of Cotswold, 248–49
Mathis, Anni, 38, 91
Mathis, Peter, 38, 93, 99
May Day 1933, 54–55
Meier, Hans, 55, 63, 90, 94, 101, 273; arrest, 1, 276; trip to Berlin, 121–24; dissolution of Rhön Bruderhof, 273; flight to England, 250; leadership, 85; release from jail, 278–79; report of military conscription, 220; in *Rundrede*, 92, 210; idea for school, 133; trip to Switzerland, 111–13; trip to Zurich, 217–20
Meier, Margrit, 55, 63; in *Rundrede*, 92; letter from, 265
Mennonites, assistance, 265–67, 278; in Holland, 228, 278; statement on Bruderhof, 256–57; World Conference 1936, 266. *See also* Bender, Harold; Crous, Ernst; Horsch, John; Horsch, Michael; Unruh, Benjamin H.
Metz (Farmers' Leader), 139
Meulen, Jacob ter, 278
Michaelis, Georg, 4, 90
militarism, 83, 162
military draft, 220–21, 261; for Germans abroad, 248–50; threatened, 212
military service in Liechtenstein, 162
mission, 211–12, 229; Arnold's desire for, 21, 27, 204–5; despite opposition, 53
Möller, Emil, property, 135, 137–39, 173, 209
Monbart, Baron von, 47, 106; Arnold's letter to, 88, 113–19; report on Bruderhof, 257–58

Morning Light (children's home), 133, 158
Müller, Ludwig, 66, 178, 182, 256; appointed Reich Bishop, 64–65; Arnold's letter to, 81–83; letter from, 81
Mussolini, 26

narcotics, suspicion of, 255
National Socialism, ideals of, 30, 58, 59–60; infiltration in schools, 162; rally, 29–30
nationalism, increase of, 34–35, 54; rejection of, 55, 71; in Student Christian Movement, 4
Nazism. *See* National Socialism
Neurath, Baron von (minister of foreign affairs), Arnold's letter to, 120–21
Neuwerk Movement, 7, 11–13
Niemöller, Martin, 124, 167
Night of the Long Knives, 171
nonviolence. *See* pacifism; military draft
Nuremberg Laws, 236

Olympic Games 1936, 253

pacifism, 34–35, 232; Arnold convinced of, 7; among Quakers, 79–80; vs. peacemaking, 190–192
Papen, Franz von, 29
Pastors' Emergency League, 124, 166, 204
Payne, Godfrey, 190–92
peace of God, 206
Pentecost 1934, 165
Percival, Edna, letter from, 250
persecution. *See* martyrdom
Pharaoh, instrument of God's wrath, 35, 180, 210
Philip of Hesse, 90
Pickett, Clarence E., 267

Piper, Otto, 119
Pitter, Premysl, 232
plebiscite, November 1933, 84, 86, 95–96, 98, 112, 217–18; August 1934, 192–94
Probst, Adalbert, 171
Protestant Church, 66, 178

Quakers, 230, 279; in Berlin post World War I, 7; English, 78–80, 229. *See also* Fox, George; Stephens, John

Ragaz, Leonhard, disagreement with, 39–40, 217–20; discussion of his ideas, 57–59; on the Kingdom of God, 37; letter to Thomas Masaryk, 113; obituary of Arnold, 247–48
raid (Gestapo) of Rhön Bruderhof, April 1933, 48, 52–53; November 1933, 98–103; October 1936, 262–64
Reichstag fire, 35
Religious Socialists, 217–20. *See also* Kutter, Hermann; Ragaz, Leonhard
Revelation of John, 180–82, 236–40
revolutionaries, 7–8, 9
Rhön Bruderhof, activities curtailed, 157–58, 162–63; after Arnold's death, 246–47; celebration of May Day 1933, 54–55; description of, 31–32, 265–66; development of, 73, 136–37, 209; difficulty to maintain, 198, 251, 259, 264; dissolved, 1–2, 272–77; final weeks, 269–70, 272–77; flight of young men from, 221–24; Gestapo report on, 253–56, 257–58; hospitality forbidden, 140–42; hostility toward, 59, 77–78, 103, 113;

Rhön Bruderhof (cont.)
  inspection of, 41, 48, 140;
  purchase of, 19, 135 (see also
  Möller, Emil, property); raid
  98–103, 262–64; restitution,
  280; school (see school, Rhön
  Bruderhof); visit of Zionists,
  17–18
Röhm, Ernst, 22, 171
Romans chapter 13, 36, 46, 177–82
Römer, Hella, 2, 277, 278
Rust, Bernhard, Arnold's letter to,
  121

Sannerz community, 13–15; First
  Law of, 18
Schäfer, Valentin and Maria, 103,
  135
Schirach, Baldur von, 24
school authorities, Arnold's letter
  to, 108
school (Rhön Bruderhof), recognized by government, 47;
  under threat, 53, 108–10;
  permission revoked, 132;
  flight of children, 132–33
schools, Nazi control, 56
Schulz, Lene, 110, 132–33, 158
Selig, P (lawyer), 137, 138, 139
Sermon on the Mount, 10–11, 32
Silum. See Alm Bruderhof
socialism, 7–8
Social Democratic Party, 8, 58
Sondheimer, Friedel, 99
Sonnenlieder, 8, 69
Sparhof, property purchased, 135
  See also Rhön Bruderhof
Spartacus Revolt, 8
Stängl, Josef, 93, 99, 222–23
Steenken, Erna, 215
Stephens, John, 7, 78, 80, 83, 133
Student Christian Movement, 4, 7
Sturge, Paul, 267

swastika, 23, 91, 112, 182; Arnold's
  discussion of, 45, 50; in
  churches, 66
Trogen, 133, 158
Tübingen, 32–35

unity, 18–19, 39–40
Unruh, Benjamin H, 124, 129
Upper Klösshof. See Möller, Emil,
  property

Völkischer Beobachter, 220–21
Vollmer, Antje, 11

Wächter, Annemarie, 56, 99–100,
  139, 158; engagement for
  marriage, 206; letter from, 67,
  213–14, 216, 221; at Morning
  Light, 134; in *Rundrede*, 44,
  92, 214
Waldner, Michael, 270–77
Walter, Elias, letter from, 72; letter
  to, 52–53, 251
Wegner, Liesel, 43, 214
Weigand (officer), 100, 133, 142, 274
Wels, Otto, 43
Werkhof, 37–40. See also Ragaz,
  Leonhard
Wingard, Nils and Dora, 25
Wittig (Assessor), 122
Wolf, Max, 16–17, 56
Woodbrooke, 229
Work camp 1932, 136–37
World War I, effect on Germany,
  4, 6

Youth Movement. See Free German
  Youth

Zander, Paul, 4, 241–43
Zeiher (mayor of Veitsteinbach),
  85, 261
Zimmermann, Kurt, 63, 99, 220,
  249–50

Zimmermann, Marianne, 63, 226
Zionists, 17–18
Zumpe, Ben, 127
Zumpe, Elizabeth, 225–26
Zumpe, Emy-Margret, 63, 127, 222
Zumpe, Hans, 62, 68, 77, 106, 139, 264; joins the Bruderhof, 25; leadership, 85, 143, 196, 246; letter to Hutterites, 251–52; at Mennonite World Conference, 266; in *Rundrede*, 93
Zurich, 195

www.ingramcontent.com/pod-product-compliance
Lightning Source LLC
Chambersburg PA
CBHW021648230426
43668CB00008B/552